Briefings

Also available, as a William Heinemann paperback
Learning to Succeed: Report of the National Commission on
Education.

BRIEFINGS FOR THE
PAUL HAMLYN FOUNDATION
NATIONAL COMMISSION ON EDUCATION

Heinemann : London

First published as separate papers by the
National Commission on Education in 1992/3

This collected edition published in 1993
by William Heinemann Ltd
an imprint of Reed Consumer Books Ltd
Michelin House, 81 Fulham Road, London SW3 6R0B

A CIP catalogue record for this title
is available from the British Library
ISBN 0434 00107 4

Printed and bound in Great Britain
by Clays Ltd, St Ives plc

Contents

Introduction

This book brings together the *Briefing* papers published by the National Commission on Education between January 1992 and October 1993. It is published simultaneously with the report of the Commission, *Learning to Succeed*.

The Commission was set up in July 1991, following my presidential address to the annual meeting of the British Association for the Advancement of Science. In that speech I identified shortcomings in the provision of education and training in this country and the need for a review of the future of education and training. The Government was not willing to set up a Royal Commission. Instead, the British Association itself set up an independent inquiry, generously funded by the Paul Hamlyn Foundation and chaired by Lord Walton of Detchant.

The remit of the Commission was wide:

> 'to consider all phases of education and training throughout the whole of the United Kingdom and to identify and examine key issues arising over the next 25 years.'

As part of its work, a Research Committee was established to ensure that the work of the Commission was underpinned by research evidence of high quality. As well as myself as its Chairman, the Commissioners on this Committee were Sir John Cassels (Director of the Commission), Mr Christopher Johnson (formerly Economic Adviser for Lloyds Bank) and Professor Jeff Thompson (Professor of

Education at the University of Bath). The three Associate Commissioners whom we were very fortunate in having on the Committee were Professor A H Halsey (Nuffield College, Oxford), Professor Peter Mortimore (Deputy Director, Institute of Education, University of London) and Professor Andrew McPherson (Co-Director, Centre for Educational Sociology, University of Edinburgh).

The Research Committee, as part of its work, decided to produce a series of short publications in which outside experts would deal with particular issues of importance for the Commission's work. These *Briefings* thus had a dual purpose. One was to to give the Commission expert insights into key issues, especially those of a controversial nature. But they were also intended to stimulate and help in public debate. With this in mind, we sent them to a wide range of organisations and individuals interested in education and training. The distribution, of course, varied from subject to subject. Thus *Briefing No. 1* was sent to every secondary school in the United Kingdom, and *Briefing No. 3* to every Further Education College, Tertiary College and Sixth Form college.

Each *Briefing* draws together and analyses relevant facts, practices and ideas and suggests ways forward. We used a standard format and encouraged simple and clear presentation. Drafts were approved by myself, the Director, the Chairman and the Deputy Chairman of the Commission. They were edited by Josh Hillman, a member of the Commission staff, to whom we owe the splendid quality and success of the series.

We have indeed been pleased by the reception of the *Briefings*, not only within the Commission for its work, but also from the public. There has been wide media coverage and they received enthusiastic comment in the worlds of both education and industry, in policy circles and in parliamentary debate. We have also been gratified to see their wide use in research literature, in conferences and teaching materials. There has also been interest abroad.

All this has encouraged us to bring the *Briefings* together in this volume, which accompanies the Commission's main report. We hope that they will continue to inform, clarify and influence.

Claus Moser.

Sir Claus Moser
Chairman of the National Commission's
Research Committee

1 Measuring Added Value in Schools

Andrew McPherson

Professor and Co-Director, Centre for Educational Sociology, Department of Sociology, The University of Edinburgh and member of the NCE's Research Committee

Summary

1 Schools' test and examination results are informative, but 'raw' results are misleading indicators of the added value of a school if they are not also adjusted for intake differences.

2 'Raw' results should therefore be accompanied by an assessment of the contribution a school makes to its pupils' progress. The assessment should take account of each pupil's prior level of attainment and of other factors inside and outside of the school that may have influenced progress.

3 The basis of the assessment must be made clear, including any assumptions about the responsibility of teachers or others for the factors affecting progress; and the assessment must have solid theoretical backing.

4 A single statistic may not adequately summarise progress. Different types of pupils may progress at different rates. Parents and teachers may legitimately wish to know about different things. What is needed is a good indicator system.

5 A bad indicator system will hinder progress towards better schools and carry hidden costs.

6 A good indicator system will:
 • take account of different needs and uses
 • be as simple as possible, while recognising the individuality of pupils, families and schools
 • prefer measures of stability and change in performance to single 'snapshots'
 • have built into it the means of monitoring and improving its own validity.

Introduction

The publication of examination and test results, resulting in 'league tables' and calls for calculations of the contribution schools make to pupils' progress – the 'added value' they offer – raise a number of difficult questions. This first NCE Briefing describes the complex factors, values, and interests that should be taken into account when attempting to measure schools' performance.

The Briefing draws on developments in research on school effectiveness to address questions about the value of information on schools' examination and test results. It identifies pitfalls and advocates certain methods. It argues that there is no single solution that can be recommended on technical grounds alone: even the best techniques have limitations. Value judgements will always be involved as well as issues of accountability and cost.

British schools have been required to publish their public examination results for over a decade. The current Education (Schools) Bill says that the government's purpose is to 'assist parents in choosing schools for their children' and to 'increase public awareness of the quality of the education provided by the schools concerned and the educational standards achieved in those schools'. Schools in Northern Ireland are likely to have to publish their results soon, and in addition English and Welsh schools must soon begin to publish the results of national curriculum attainment tests.

Many people are affected by these requirements: parents, pupils and teachers; school governors, school boards and education authorities; indirectly the employers, colleges and universities who select school leavers; and central government itself in Belfast, Cardiff, Edinburgh and London.

But does such information enable us to say with reasonable assurance that one school is better than another, or better or worse than it used to be? How can the information be used, and not abused? And how can we ensure that it will meet the needs of the wide range of interested parties? This Briefing focuses on test and examination results at the secondary stage, but the main arguments can be generalised to other stages of education, and other measurable outcomes.

1. **By themselves, examination results do not show a school's added value.** Test and examination results differ from one school to the next. This is undisputed, and is one of the main reasons given by government for its concern with standards.

   But schools also differ from each other in their pupil intakes. This, too, is undisputed. The type of school influences the gender and denominational composition of the pupil intake. The location of the school influences the ethnic and social mix. Type and location both affect pupils' levels of attainment on entry, as do many other factors.

   A school's 'added value' is the boost that it gives to a child's previous level of attainment. 'Raw' outcome scores do not measure this boost. Test and examination results provide misleading indicators of added value if they are not adjusted for differences between schools in the attainment of their pupils on entry.

2. **Nevertheless, unadjusted results are informative.** Raw outcome measures are informative because they reflect actual attainment and activity. They tell one, for example, that a particular syllabus is being studied to a

certain standard. But they convey information only
when properly presented. They should be based on
entire year groups of pupils and should identify any
special cases or exclusions from the year-group base,
such as pupils with special educational needs and trans-
ferred pupils.

Information about attainment on a subject-by-subject
basis is often useful. But when one is looking at an
individual pupil's attainment, whether overall or in
specified areas of the curriculum, it must be aggregat-
ed, and this will entail value judgements. For example,
it must be decided whether each grade level, or subject
or type of examination, should be equally weighted or
not.

Single outcome measures may not serve all users
equally well and may thereby give one set of users priority over another. For example, summary measures of
attainment may be too general to meet class teachers'
or parents' diagnostic requirements for individual
pupils. Similarly, judgements of value and priority are
also implicit in the choice of a statistic to summarise
outcomes: in the use of a mean or median, for example, rather than a distribution.

3. **Unadjusted outcome information should be accompanied by information on the school's contribution
   to pupil progress.** Parents need information on the
   value added by a school. School managers need information on the quality of the teaching input in a school.
   To meet such needs, one must take account both of the
   level of a pupil's 'prior attainment' before entry to the
   school or stage in question, and of other factors that
   might influence progress.

This cannot be done infallibly because there is no
information available at present about methods

through which schools boost attainment that can safely be assumed to apply to all schools in the future.

For example, studies typically find that about half of the variation among pupils in attainment in public examinations can be predicted from, or statistically 'explained' by, pupils' attainment on entry to secondary school. But such correlations do not necessarily tell us what caused the variations, or whether and how the pupils' prior attainment contributed to their later attainment.

If the cause lay solely with the pupil, then the school's boost, or added value, is the difference between the earlier and the later attainment. This is because the school was not responsible for the earlier level of attainment and its influence on later attainment.

On the other hand, the cause of the correlation between earlier and later attainment might lie partly with teachers. For example, teachers might wrongly expect from their pupils only levels of later attainment commensurate with their earlier attainment; and these teacher expectations might themselves then influence later attainment. If so, not all of a pupil's prior attainment should be subtracted when estimating a school's success in adding value.

The point is that the adjustment of outcome scores must always have a proper theoretical justification. Even the most 'commonsense' of adjustments is based on theory. Theories are not infallible, and therefore the particulars of any adjustment *may* be open to improvement and *must* be open to inspection and argument.

What is not open to argument, however, is that it should always be possible to adjust outcome scores for prior attainment. This is logically entailed in the idea of a pupil's 'progress'. Progress *is*, so to speak, an adjusted outcome score, the *difference* between an earlier and a later attainment. Schools are there to help pupils to make progress, so there can be no argument against the principle of adjustment if one wishes to know the added value of a school.

Nor can one dismiss the practice of adjusting outcome scores solely on the grounds that parents could never understand such adjustments. This would imply that parents could not understand the concept of pupil progress. Were this true, all attempts to inform parents would fail. A similar argument applies to adjustments for factors other than prior attainment, for example family background.

4. **Pupil progress is correlated with various non-teacher factors.** Pupil progress may be correlated with *factors within the school for which teachers are not responsible.* An example is given in section 8. The history and religious denomination, if any, of the school may be associated with pupil progress as well.

   Also correlated with progress are the characteristics of a pupil's *household.* These include: household size and adult composition; the educational level of the parent or parents; and the parents' occupations. Other factors associated with progress include the level of material and social (dis)advantage in the immediate *neighbourhood* of the home, and aspects of the wider *opportunity structure,* including the level and character of local employment opportunities, and the opportunities for further progress in education and training.

5. **The assessment of the effects on pupil progress of schools and other agents should be based on an explicit theory of good standing.** There is substantial agreement amongst researchers, based on solid evi-

dence, about a number of desirable features of any such theory. The first is that schooling is *longitudinal*. It takes place over time as pupils make progress and as schools maintain their effectiveness, improve or deteriorate. Any pupil can have a bad day, any school a bad year. Sensible judgements will therefore be based, not on snapshots, but on repeated measures of pupils and schools.

A second feature is that schooling is *multilevel*: pupils are grouped within classes, classes within schools, and schools within larger administrative and other types of grouping.

Both features are self-evident and should inform the way in which outcome scores are adjusted and used. Where they do not, adjusted scores will fail to inform the full range of users of the information; they may misinform them (see 7 and 8 below); and the statistical robustness of effects will be wrongly estimated.

A third requirement of a good theory is that it must be *multivariate* and *comprehensive* taking account of all factors involved. It is not sufficient to adjust outcome scores only for pupils' prior attainment. Outcome scores must be open to adjustment for other non-school factors that boost or retard progress.

The case for adjusting for non-school factors is not self-evident. But it cannot be dismissed by anyone who believes that a pupil's progress will benefit from the informed involvement of parents, or by anyone who believes that successful education is the product of a partnership between teachers and others. Adjustments are required if we are to avoid misinforming all parties to the partnership about the effectiveness of their several contributions.

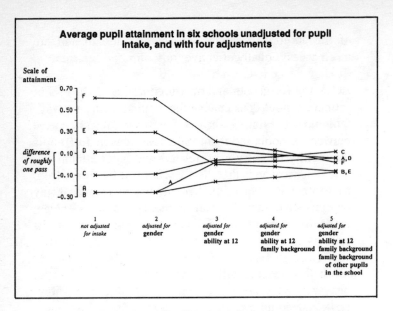

The chart shows the effects of four statistical adjustments for pupil intake on estimates of the quality of six secondary schools (schools A to F). The six schools are chosen from an education authority in which all schools are all-through comprehensives (showing more schools would clutter the illustration). Individual attainment is measured here by the number of passes in public examinations taken at sixteen, seventeen or eighteen years by pupils who were in their final compulsory year in 1983-84. The scaling of attainment is such that a difference of 0.2 corresponds roughly to one pass. Further information can be found in Lindsay Paterson's article (details below) from which this illustration is derived.

- With no adjustments for intake, schools A and B (coincident points) have the lowest average attainment scores, and school F the highest (column 1).

- Although females score higher than males on average, adjusting for the gender composition of the school does not change the estimates (column 2). This is because all of the authority's schools are co-educational and are more or less equally effective for males and females.

- Adjusting for gender and measured ability at the end of primary school does change the estimates, in two ways (column 3). First, it shrinks the range of differences between schools by about half. One reason for this is that ability on entry is correlated with later attainment. The other reason is that the six schools differ more from each other in respect of their pupils' measured ability on entry, than they differ in respect of the progress then made by their pupils. Second, the rank order of the schools is changed. School E, for example, now lies very close to A and C, though its unadjusted attainment score was substantially higher (column 1). (The close proximity of schools A, C and E in column 3 shows how misleading rank orders can be.)

- Adjusting additionally for the family background of individual pupils (various measures of parental and household characteristics) further shrinks the differences between schools (column 4).

- Finally, in column 5, an adjustment is made for the family-background characteristics of the school-leaver body as a whole in each school. This adjustment shrinks the differences between schools yet further and results in further changes in rank order. This is because, in this particular example, the attainment of a pupil having a particular set of characteristics (of gender, verbal-reasoning ability and family background), is also influenced statistically by the family-background characteristics of other pupils in the school (see section 8).

One way of interpreting column 5 is to say that the teachers in the school with the highest added value (school C) boosted the attainment level of their pupils by roughly one examination pass more than in the schools with the lowest added value (schools B and E). Such a conclusion, and the conclusions that can be drawn similarly from columns 3 and 4, are very different from any conclusions about a school's quality or added value that could be inferred from column 1.

Acknowledgement to, and further details in, Lindsay Paterson, *Socio-economic status and educational attainment: a multi-dimensional and multi-level study,* Evaluation and Research in Education, 5:3, 1991 pp.97-121.

6. **A single statistic may not be an adequate summary of a school's effect on pupil progress.** There are two reasons for this. The first is that theories are always capable of improvement. Different theories entail different adjustments to outcome scores. This is already argued in section 3 in relation to adjustments for prior attainment. A similar argument applies to other adjustments, for example for family background. Whether or not an adjustment for family background, or any other factor, is invidious, depends on the theory underlying the adjustment.

    The second reason is that, even when the theory or account of schooling is agreed, different users of the information may reasonably require different adjustments to be made. Two illustrations are given, one in each of the following two sections.

7. **A school may boost the progress of different types of pupil at different rates.** One school may give a special boost to pupils who are already doing well or, alternatively, to pupils who previously have struggled. Another may succeed in spreading learning gains more evenly over all its pupils. A third may succeed in boosting the science attainments of girls in particular, whilst a fourth may give a particular boost to the language-related

attainments of pupils from homes where the first language is not English.

All four schools could, nevertheless, achieve the same average attainment level and the same average amount of added value. In these cases, the averages would obscure as much about the school as they revealed. They would be little help to a parent who wanted to make an informed choice for a particular son or daughter having a particular level of attainment and with a particular language capability.

In other words, a school may add different aspects and levels of value for different types of pupils. A method which can produce only one summary statistic for a school always runs the risk of misrepresenting that school's successes and failures and of misleading parents.

One advantage of a multilevel approach is that, subject to data availability, it allows one to test whether a single-statistic summary is adequate, or whether separate summaries are required for separate types of pupils. Multiple summaries may seem complex. But any complexity is simply a reflection of the respect that good statistics must have for the individuality of the pupils and schools involved.

8. **The interests of parents and the interests of teachers may dictate mutually conflicting but equally valid adjustments to outcome scores.** A pupil's attendance at a particular school may confer advantages which have little or nothing to do with the action of teachers. Some studies have found that the characteristics of the pupil body as a whole are correlated with individual pupils' progress. In such studies, a pupil of, let us say, average prior attainment has tended to make more progress in a school where the prior attainment of all pupils was above average, than in a school where the

prior attainment of all pupils was below average. Similar effects are sometimes observed for measures of family background.

Let us suppose that such correlations are wholly owing to peer-group effects outside the classroom: that is, to pupils learning from each other or preventing each other from learning in ways that a teacher could not reasonably be expected to influence. In summarising the effectiveness or added value attributable to teachers in a school, we would want to discount that part of a pupil's progress that was owing to such peer-group effects. This gives us a first added-value statistic for the school.

Parents, by contrast, will be interested in all of the advantages that will accrue to their child by virtue of their attendance at the school, whether these advantages arise from classroom teaching, from peer-group effects, or from anything else. It is not in parents' interest to discount peer-group effects when assessing the value of a school for their child. This gives us a second added-value statistic for the school.

Thus, a single-statistic summary cannot be presumed in advance to serve teachers and parents alike or, by extension, to serve education authorities and other interested parties. What is required is a multilevel capability – in this example a representation of pupils having certain individual characteristics, themselves grouped within schools so as to have certain collective or 'school-level' characteristics, namely the overall composition of the pupil body.

Again, there is a seeming complexity. We have two estimates of added value for the one school. But the complexity is simply an honest reflection of the different interests of two of the parties to the partnership of schooling. It is not a gratuitous imposition of the method.

9. **Features of a good indicator system.** A good indicator system must allow for the differences that characterise individual pupils and schools, for different explanations of these differences, and for the different interests of the range of parties to whom schools are accountable.

It is the job of statistics to produce the simplest and most economical summary of a school's value that is consistent with this variety and with the purpose or purposes of the indicator. The resultant summary might be simple or it might be complex. But complexity is not in itself an argument against aiming for the best possible indicator system.

Any attempt to improve schooling by means of informing choice presupposes that parents are capable of understanding at least the complexity of an adjusted outcome score. To reject that possibility is to reject the possibility of informing parents.

Nor is the cost of a good indicator system a decisive objection. We do not know the cost of the mistaken judgements, needless anxieties and fruitless 'further investigations' that are triggered by false signals from poor indicator systems. Misplaced complacency is costly too. In industry poor systems of quality control result in poor products and contribute to the very economic difficulties that better schools are expected to address.

A good indicator system will therefore aim to improve its own validity. It will not be content merely to 'indicate'. It will endeavour to describe outcomes and processes directly, to be valid in itself.

Whilst it is unrealistic to expect to build research enquiry into each and every application of an indicator system, the capability for testing its assumptions and improving its procedures should exist somewhere and should be available to everyone with an interest in better schooling. It will take quality to recognise quality.

February 1992

Acknowledgement

The CES is a Research Centre of the Economic and Social Research Council. The ESRC has supported many of the UK developments in school-effectiveness research on which this Briefing draws.

Further Reading

Aitkin, M. and Longford, N. (1986) *Statistical modelling issues in school effectiveness,* Journal of the Royal Statistical Society, A, 149, 1-42.

Drew, D. and Gray, J. (1991) *The black-white gap in examination results: A statistical critique of a decade's research,* New Community, 17, 159-172.

Garner, C.L. and Raudenbush, S.W. (1991) *Neighbourhood effects on educational attainment: A multilevel analysis,* Sociology of Education, 64, 251-262.

Gray, J., Jesson, D. and Sime, N. (1990) *Estimating differences in the examination performances of secondary schools in six LEAs: A multi-level approach to school effectiveness,* Oxford Review of Education, 16, 137-158.

Goldstein, H. (1987) *Multilevel Models in Educational and Social Research,* London: Griffin.

Livingstone, J. (1990) *Performance indicators for Northern Ireland schools,* Summary Series No. 9, Belfast: The Northern Ireland Council for Educational Research.

Mortimore, P., Sammons, P., Stoll, L., Lewis, D. and Ecob, R. (1988) *School Matters: The Junior Years,* London: Open Books.

Nuttall, D.L., Goldstein, H., Prosser, R. and Rasbash, J. (1990) *Differential school effectiveness,* International Journal of Educational Research, 13, 769-776.

Raudenbush, S.W. and Willms, J.D. (1991) *Schools, Classrooms and Pupils:* International Studies of Schooling from a Multilevel Perspective, New York: Academic Press. Especially chapter 1 (Raudenbush and Willms), chapter 2 (Paterson), chapter 5 (Plewis), chapter 6 (Fitz-Gibbon) and chapter 7 (Paterson).

Smith, D.J. and Tomlinson, S. (1989) *The School Effect: A Study of*

Multi-Racial Comprehensives, London: Policy Studies Institute.

Willms, J.D. (1992) *Monitoring School Performance: A Non-Technical Guide for Educational Administrators,* Lewes: Falmer Press, forthcoming.

Willms, J.D. and Raudenbush, S.W. (1989) *A longitudinal hierarchical linear model for estimating school effects and their stability,* Journal of Educational Measurement, 26, 1-24.

Woodhouse, G. and Goldstein, H. (1988) *Educational performance indicators and LEA league tables,* Oxford Review of Education, 14.

2 The Need for a Revised Management System for the Teaching Profession

Ewart Keep
Research Fellow, Industrial Relations Research Unit,
Warwick Business School, University of Warwick

Summary

1 School-teachers form a very large and highly qualified workforce. Managing this workforce raises complex human resource problems. A robust and coherent national personnel system is required for success. Piecemeal action is no substitute.

2 The current structure is fragmented. It is designed to undertake personnel administration, not management.

3 As a result, the implications for teachers may not be properly assessed and allowed for when major changes in education are planned. Chance therefore enters into implementation and success is to a greater or lesser extent put at risk.

4 Successful employers in other sectors see the connection between the different strands of personnel policy and design their organisational system accordingly.

5 There is confusion about the organisational model which education is supposed to be following. Some models – particularly that of the small business model - are inappropriate.

6 The abolition of LEAs would highlight the current weakness of human resource management in the education service.

7 A new, coherent, approach is needed. A well designed strategic national model could provide a framework of policies within which schools could operate more effectively. This would make possible clearer lines of responsibility and better linkages between control of resources and accountability. It would require an intermediary between government and individual schools.

Introduction

Teachers are the most important resource within the education service and represent the largest single cost in educational provision. It is widely accepted that, without a quality workforce, the school system will not deliver high quality education. Human resource management, linking recruitment, staff development, reward systems and career structures, is an integral part of successful management in large-scale modern enterprises. But in education, at the national level, personnel matters have been administered piecemeal, while recent changes have removed the powers of local education authorities to manage their teaching force. A high quality education system needs to include coherent and accountable management of those major personnel issues which are beyond the control of individual schools.

This Briefing examines two questions that need to be addressed urgently:

How much importance should be attached to human resource management within the state school system?

Where within the administrative structure should responsibility for this function rest?

Under present policies, the answers to these questions are not immediately obvious. Yet without answers, little lasting progress on developing a teaching workforce capable of meeting the challenges of the 1990s will be possible.

1. The human resource management issues confronting education would appear complex and large scale even

to the most sophisticated private sector employers.
Current concern is focused on topics such as: teacher
training, both initial and in-service; assessment and
appraisal; reward systems; career structures; the use of
ancillary and support staff; and management development for heads and deputies. Looming over all these is
the need to secure lasting improvements in teacher
recruitment, retention and motivation, and to manage a
workforce where three-fifths of the staff are now aged
over 40. The size of the workforce also needs to be
recognised. State schools represent the largest single
employer of graduate manpower in the UK. In England
and Wales there are about 450,000 graduates (or their
near equivalent) scattered across more than 26,000
schools.

In many respects, the single most crucial personnel
problem facing the school education system is the need
to improve the recruitment and retention of teachers.
Eric Bolton, the then senior chief inspector, in his HMI
annual report for 1987/8 *Standards in Education,* pointed out that teacher supply is 'the most important component of an effective education service'. Successive
reports by the Interim Advisory Committee, the House
of Commons Select Committee on Education, Science
and the Arts and the Audit Commission have all underlined the scale and seriousness of the problem, whether
measured in terms of unfilled posts or inappropriately
qualified subject specialist staff. Once the current recession ends, it must be expected that the tighter labour
markets of the 1990s brought on by demographic
change and increased competition for graduates, particularly those qualifying in disciplines where there are the
most acute subject teacher shortages, will lead to the
rapid re-emergence of recruitment difficulties.

2. **How are these questions being tackled?** Many
improvements in human resource management practices

are taking place at the level of the individual school and the Local Education Authority (LEA). However, the overall importance attached to personnel issues at a national, strategic level is less clear. Recent reforms, such as the introduction of the national curriculum, Local Management of Schools (LMS), the General Certificate of Secondary Education (GCSE) and national testing, all depend on the abilities and enthusiasm of the teaching workforce for their successful implementation. Given this dependence, it might have been expected that consideration of the contribution of personnel issues would have figured in the planning of these reforms. Yet in planning the Education Reform Act, it seems to have been taken as given that teachers would cope successfully with whatever changes were demanded of them, and that the staff required to deliver the initiatives would be found and retained with relative ease. In the case of LMS, the consequences of formula funding for staffing were never properly addressed.

Only with the legislation in place, and unexpected practical problems starting to emerge, have personnel issues started to impinge on national strategy. Delays in introducing teacher appraisal, and the progressive scaling down of national testing, are examples of a growing awareness of the need to avoid over-burdening teachers. This tendency to act first and count the cost later in terms of confusion wastes time and energy. Lowered morale is not conducive to making teaching an attractive career, either for prospective candidates or for serving teachers.

Given the tendency to look to the private sector as the source of models of good managerial practice that need to be adopted within the public sector, the low priority that has been given to the formulation of a strategic personnel management 'vision' appears surprising. It is possible that this reflects an administrative rather than a managerial approach to personnel issues. The tendency for education policy makers at the national level effectively to downgrade the importance of personnel to the status of a second order issue in the process of policy formulation certainly contrasts sharply with much of the literature on private sector business success. The achievement of business objectives, as well as the successful operation of sophisticated personnel policies (such as staff appraisal systems), require personnel management policies to be integrated into strategic business planning.

Besides being integrated into wider business planning, research within successful organisations suggests that models of 'good practice' in human resource management have in common the fact that personnel issues are treated as forming a single whole. The good employer sees the inter-relationship between the systems within the organisation dealing with recruitment, selection, pay, appraisal, training and development, and the shape of career structures that are available. It is by perceiving these links between the different elements, and managing them in order to produce a synergy between them, that effective organisations are able to provide an employment package that enables them to recruit, retain and motivate a workforce capable of meeting their wider strategic goals.

3. **What do current structures in education provide?** At present, there are three levels at which human resource management issues are dealt with - the individual school, the LEA, and national level.

Individual schools have recently been given much greater control over their staffing policies, including decisions about the number of teachers they employ, hiring and firing, staff grading, and the award of incentive allowances. Whether governing bodies and staff have been adequately trained or resourced to deal with this complex new role is open to question. Nevertheless, many schools have made considerable progress in creating human resource management systems and procedures that reflect their developmental aims and educational objectives, set within national regulations such as the statutory School Teachers' Pay and Conditions document.

By contrast, the ability of the *LEA* to manage its workforce has diminished substantially. Traditionally, LEAs have played an important part in managing the overall number of school places; the reorganisation, merger and closure of schools; redeployment of teachers from one school to another in the wake of reorganisation or as rolls rose or fell; providing in-service training and development; helping to appoint head teachers; and supplying personnel advice and support services. Many of these activities have vanished or are under threat. LEAs are now in the invidious position of retaining the legal responsibilities of an employer, but with little power to manage the deployment of their staff. Despite these difficulties, many LEAs continue to support the growth of school-based personnel systems, career development, and the supply of in-service education and training. Their ability to undertake these roles has however been eroded by uncertainty about their continued existence.

At *national level* the Department for Education (DFE), and advisory bodies such as the Schools Examinations and Assessment Council and the National Curriculum Council, currently control or influence a wide range of strategic issues. By determining the shape and content of the national curriculum and its associated key stage attainment targets, the DFE sets the 'product mix' and 'product quality' that state schools in England and Wales must deliver. These decisions affect staffing requirements both for the system as a whole and for individual schools. The DFE also establishes, with the Treasury, the overall sums of money available to support the system. It determines future national staffing requirements, and from these projections fixes the size and subject mix for intakes to initial teacher training. In conjunction with the Council for the Accreditation of Teacher Education, it sets the entry requirements and content of initial training provision. In addition, the DFE disburses targeted funding for in-service training, sponsors Teaching as a Career (TASC), and runs an 'action programme' on teacher shortages.

The range and importance of these activities arguably serves to disguise a fundamental problem. The DFE has no single personnel management department or unit with overall responsibility for personnel issues affecting the teaching workforce. Instead, control of various strands of the DFE's steward-ship of the teaching workforce (TASC, manpower planning, pensions, pay, management training in schools, initial training) is allocated across different parts of the organisation. Responsibility for some of the more problematic or contentious issues has been sub-contracted to groups of secondees, such as TASC and the School Management Task Group. Moreover, the DFE's structures often appear geared up to undertake routine aspects of personnel *administration* as distinct from personnel *management*.

The education system's lack of any central national focus for strategic personnel management is distinctive within the public sector and is particularly noticeable given the size of the workforce involved. Teachers are almost the only significant group of non civil servants whose national personnel issues are dealt with by departmental civil servants. The Home Office's responsibility for Prison Service employees has been the other major example, but following the Lygo Report this is set to change, with a move to agency status and the creation of a management board for the service. In contrast to the National Health Service, these is no education service board of management, no national director of personnel and no central education service personnel function.

4. **While the education system remained decentralised, the weakness of national management was less important.** With the reduction of the role of LEAs and a large increase in power at the centre, control has sometimes been separated from responsibility, and the capacity of the DFE to manage strategic decisions has become a major issue.

   If LEAs were to vanish, the vacuum created would add to the problems of managing the teaching workforce. Moves to 'de-layer' the education system in this way raise important questions about choice of organisational structure and the ability to manage personnel issues strategically. What happens in organisations depends, to some extent, on how they are structured.

5. **At the risk of over-simplification, examination of organisational models adopted by businesses reveals four basic options.** The old three-tier organisation of state schooling (DFE, LEA, schools) corresponded to the structure adopted by many large businesses and also traditionally used by public sector bodies such as local authorities and the NHS. There is a corporate headquarters (the DFE), and divisional HQs (the LEAs) superintending their subsidiaries (the schools).

   If LEAs were to be removed, there remain only three models from which to choose. The first, known as the "strategic business unit", has become increasingly popular in the UK in the last 15 years. The central HQ adopts a 'hands off' policy, confining itself to setting and monitoring the financial targets through which the performance of each unit is judged. The centre also acts as an investment banker for those units that are successful. Divisional structures are weakened or abolished, and responsibility is pushed down to the individual operating unit. GEC and Hanson are examples of companies that have adopted this model.

A second model is the autonomous small business. This applies in small firms where operations normally cover only a few sites and the development of specialist management functions is limited. The third model covers organisations running many businesses or outlets, operating either in a single or in closely-related areas of activity, such as banks or retail chains. The enterprise maintains a strong central HQ that formulates strategic policies, covering product mix, pricing, quality targets, investment, and personnel systems. In some cases a divisional structure may exist, but responsibility for developing and implementing centrally determined policies rests with the manager of each unit or business.

6. **At present there is confusion about which of these three models is being pursued in school education.** The strategic business unit model is probably inappropriate for public sector services. Even in the private sector, research suggests that it is applicable only in businesses producing simple products in stable markets. Two models might be appropriate, and at the moment it can be argued that the education system is trying to follow both simultaneously. It is not clear whether the education system as a whole, or the individual school, is being seen as the 'business'. Responsibility is being devolved to schools, while control of vital strategic decisions and the overall level of resources is being centralised. In some instances, the DFE acts as a strong central HQ, using the national curriculum to lay down the 'product mix' and service standards. At the same

time, individual schools are expected to operate, not as integral parts of a national service, but as independent and competing small businesses. It is likely that moves to encourage grant maintained status would result in increasing emphasis on the small business model.

The small business model carries a number of dangers as far as personnel policies are concerned. Research in the private sector suggests that small businesses are often bad at strategic planning, have short term horizons, lack specialist skills and have poor records on training and development of their staff. It is questionable whether organising a major public service like education along lines that promote these types of institutional characteristics is wise. Furthermore, little heed appears to have been paid to the diseconomies of scale and transaction costs that moves to a fragmented system would bring. Most schools, particularly primary schools, are, in terms of the numbers they employ, very small businesses indeed. It is hard to see how a grant maintained primary school with five or six staff could manage training, develop reward systems, or be able to afford to buy in the outside expertise necessary to do so.

7. **An even more fundamental objection to a highly devolved system exists.** Many of the personnel management problems facing the education system cannot be solved by individual schools. Within a devolved system, 26,000 schools may compete more effectively for the available human resources, but schools can do little to increase the overall supply of teachers. Decisions about the overall funding and target numbers for teacher training rest at national level. For the foreseeable future, many of the personnel issues facing the teaching profession will remain national, and subject to influence by ministers and civil servants. By the very nature of the service it provides, and the political salience of that service, the school system operates, and

is likely to continue to operate, as an entity which needs to have a central national focus for strategic decision making.

8. **There is a need for better management structures within which individual schools can operate.** Insofar as the education system is based on a strong central HQ and strategic decisions are made at national level, human resource management issues should be integrated into the policy making process. This means surely that a genuine human resource management function is needed. This could for example establish a framework of policies covering recruitment and training numbers, career structures in teaching and the design of national in-service training programmes in support of nationally driven changes. It could also help ensure the active dissemination of examples of good personnel practice throughout the education service. National responsibility for strategic human resource management issues might be based within a reformed DFE or in an education service management board similar to that found in the NHS. Alternatively, it could encompass some other form which included representatives of local and/or regional government. It need not stand in the way of a move towards a General Teaching Council or other professional body for teachers. Such a body could play a major role in helping to formulate and implement national policies for the management, in-service training, performance appraisal and development of the profession.

The work at national level might be enhanced by the existence of second-tier organisations. Given the number and geographical spread of schools, it would make sense to have regional or local bodies to help co-ordinate personnel activities and secure economies of scale in areas such as training. Such second-tier bodies might be based on existing LEAs or on new forms of local government. They could alternatively be developed through consortia of local schools. Within the framework provided by national policies and local structures, individual schools would remain responsible, as now, for a wide range of day-to-day personnel issues. The aim of the new system would be to provide the support and guidance needed to enable all schools to develop human resource management policies and procedures tailor made to their specific needs and objectives.

At present, there are at least two dangers. The first is that governments will continue to make confused choices about models of organisational structures for the education service. The second is that they may fail to recognise that some models, particularly that of the independent small business, are inappropriate to the delivery of a high quality public service.

9. **Without a broader approach to the development of human resource management policies, the result may be confusion and disappointment.** In the absence of clear strategic direction and management, individual personnel initiatives will be planned in isolation from one another, each seeking to address discrete problems. For example, there is little value in designing a reward system that takes little account of the way staff are appraised, and neither can be viewed in isolation from career structures and staff development. Such issues need to be addressed as a whole, both in the individual school and across the system. Without this capacity, many of the personnel problems facing the teaching profession will remain unresolved, with all that this implies for the quality of education in the United Kingdom.

10. **What is being suggested is the development of a genuine, coherent human resource management system within the education service,** one where lines

of responsibility are clear and where there is a better linkage between control of resources and accountability for success and failure. Where the ends are willed centrally, accountability for the provision of the means to secure those ends should also be located at national level.

May 1992

Acknowledgement

The IRRU is a Research Centre of the Economic and Social Research Council. The ESRC has supported much of the UK research into personnel management on which this briefing draws.

Further Reading

Coulson-Thomas, C. (1991) *'What the personnel director can bring to the boardroom table'*, Personnel Management, October, 36-9.

Newsom, P. (1989) *'Life in the fast lane'*, Times Educational Supplement, 29 December.

Riley, C. and Sloman, M. (1991) *'Milestones for the personnel department'*, Personnel Management, August, 34-7.

Sisson, K. (1988) *Personnel Management in Britain*, Oxford, Blackwell. Especially chapters 1 and 2 (Sisson).

Storey, J. (1989) *New Perspectives on Human Resource Management*, London, Routledge. Especially chapter 1 (Storey), and chapter 5 (Purcell).

Wallace, G. (1992) *Local Management of Schools - Research and Experience*, BERA Dialogues No 6, Clevedon, Multi-Lingual Matters. Especially chapter 3 (Maden), chapter 5 (Bowe and Ball), and chapter 9 (Keep).

3 Participation of 16-18 Year Olds in Education and Training

David Raffe
Co-Director, Centre for Educational Sociology,
Department of Sociology, The University of Edinburgh

Summary

1 In international comparisons of participation in education and training of 16-18 year olds the UK fares badly.
   Leaving school at 16 to enter a job has a respectability
   not present in other industrialised countries.
2 Full-time participation rates vary across the countries of
   the UK, local authorities and schools. However, the
   variation in participation is more strongly linked to characteristics of individuals, in particular their attainment at
   16. Young people respond rationally to their opportunities and see full-time education as worth while only if
   they are academically successful.
3 Full-time participation is low *but* is rising and will
   continue to do so:
   • education has low esteem *but* more young people
     have well-educated parents;
   • compulsory education is seen as unrewarding but
     GCSE has improved attitudes;
   • A levels are seen to be a risky option and vocational
     studies lack status but expanding higher education
     increases the incentive to stay on at 16;
   • the labour market attracts early leavers *but* this is
     weakening as fewer employers recruit 16 year olds,
     youth training schemes have low status and benefits
     have been withdrawn from unemployed 16 and 17
     year olds.
4 Most young people who leave full-time education at 16
   or 17 continue with some kind of part-time or work-
   based learning, most often on youth training schemes,
   although many only participate briefly. The quality of

this provision is uneven and has been criticised for being narrow, specific and short-term.

5   The existing 'mixed model' of 16-18 education and training in Britain relies too much on employer-led provision, and lacks coherence.

6   An agenda for change is suggested that will offer broad opportunities to all. This includes:
   - more flexibility between part-time and full-time study;
   - a more unified system of academic and vocational courses;
   - 'traineeships' for all those under 18 who are in employment;
   - effective incentives for further learning for *all* young people.

Introduction

The low participation of 16-18 year olds in education and training is widely seen as evidence of the UK's educational malaise. The UK fares badly in international comparisons; of the 13 OECD countries compared in a recent DES Bulletin, the UK had the lowest full-time participation rate among 16-18 year olds in 1986. The UK rate was 33%, exactly half the average for the other 12 countries (66%). Such evidence as is available suggests that our lower participation is matched by lower attainment, especially in vocational skills. But figures on full-time education do not tell the full story.

Britain has a 'mixed model' of 16-18s education, in which a small full-time sector is complemented by a large but irregular sector of part-time and work-based provision (including training schemes such as Youth Training). If part-time education and training are included in participation rates, the position of the UK looks more respectable. The participation rate, at 64%, is now much closer to the average for the other 12 countries (75%). However, to compare countries on this basis is to assume that a part-time student in the UK is receiving as valuable an education as a full-time student elsewhere or as an apprentice in the German dual system. The terms of the 16-18s debate are ambiguous. Is the 'problem' the low level of participation in full-time education? Or is it the low quality of the part-time and work-based alternative? Or is it the poor co-ordination of the two within the British 'mixed model'?

In the next two sections I review the evidence on participation in full-time and part-time education respectively. In the final section I return to the main strategic issue: the future of the 'mixed model' in the UK.

Full-time education

Participation. Fig. 1 illustrates participation in full-time education, excluding training schemes and private further education, for 16, 17 and 18 year olds separately in Great Britain in January of each year since 1974. For all these ages, participation has risen, if not steadily, since 1974, with a particularly rapid increase since 1987. More recent figures show that this faster rate of increase has continued in the 1990s with annual rises typically around 4-5%.

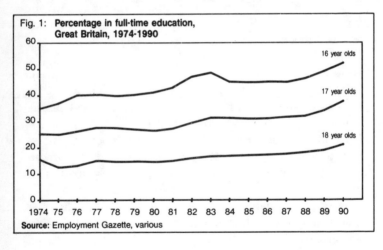

Fig. 1: **Percentage in full-time education, Great Britain, 1974-1990**

Source: Employment Gazette, various

Fig. 2 presents the most recent available data in more detail. Unlike Fig. 1 it covers the whole of the UK. In January 1990, 37% of 16-18 years olds (34% of males, and 40% of females) were in full-time education. This does not mean, as is sometimes stated, that only 37% 'stayed on at 16'. The 37% covers three year groups, and Fig. 2 shows participation significantly higher than this at 16 years, the first year of staying-on.

Fig 2:   Participation in full-time education and youth training, by age: January 1990 (percentages)

	16 year olds	17 year olds	18 year olds	16-18 year olds
Males and Females				
School	35	23	3	19
Other full-time education	17	15	19	17
All full-time education	52	38	22	37
YTS/YTP	23	20	2	15
Others	24	41	77	49
Total	99	99	101	101
Males				
School	33	22	3	19
Other full-time education	14	13	18	15
All full-time education	48	35	21	34
YTS/YTP	28	25	2	18
Others	25	40	76	48
Total	101	100	99	100
Females				
School	37	24	2	20
Other full-time education	21	18	20	19
All full-time education	58	42	22	40
YTS/YTP	18	16	1	11
Others	24	43	77	49
Total	100	101	100	100

Note: Percentages subject to rounding   Sources: Employment Gazette, Northern Ireland Office

Participation rates vary within the UK, being highest in Northern Ireland and lowest (except for 18 year olds) in Scotland. However, school year groups cover a different span of birth dates in Scotland than elsewhere in the UK; Scottish participation is higher than the UK average if based on equivalent school stages, but lower if based on age groups.

Who stays on? Participation rates vary between schools, being highest in the independent sector. They also vary between areas: research has failed to link this conclusively either to local labour-market factors or to differences in LEA policy or provision. Most of the variation in participation is linked to characteristics of individuals, especially attainment at 16. Among 16 year olds with comparable attainments, females and those from ethnic-minority backgrounds are more likely to stay on in full-time education. Young people are not mindless prisoners of culture and circumstance; at 16 they respond more or less rationally to their opportunities. The powerful correlation between participation and prior attainment confirms the obvious conclusion that further full-time education is only seen to be worthwhile for the academically successful.

Why is British full-time participation low? It is useful to think of four types of explanation for low full-time participation in the UK:

*   *national and class cultures*
    Education has low esteem, especially among working-class families, although this may reflect the perceived costs and benefits as much as cultural values;

*   *'push' from experience in compulsory schooling*
    Compulsory education is perceived as unrewarding by many 16 year olds, who feel they have been classed as failures;

*   *'inadequate pull' from post-compulsory education*
    Vocational study lacks status and has limited currency outside the occupation concerned. A levels carry a high risk of failure.

*   *'pull' from the labour market*
    Early leavers do not simply opt out of education; they opt for something else. Britain has high youth wages and a tradition of entry at 16 to a relatively wide range of occupations. 16 year olds who stay on may risk missing job opportunities. The British labour market tends to reward experience more than qualifications.

Why is full-time participation rising? Explanations fall into the same four categories:

- *national and class cultures*
  It is difficult to say if cultures are changing, but there is certainly a compositional change. More young people have middle-class and well-educated parents, the result of social change and of the decreasing number of children in working-class families. Given the strong association between family background and attainment in education, this has encouraged rising attainments at 16 and higher staying-on rates;

- *push from compulsory schooling*
  Staying-on rates are rising among 16 year olds with given qualification levels, especially the less qualified. GCSE and Scottish Standard grade recognise a wider range of attainment than the examinations they replaced; this has encouraged more 16 year olds to stay on to build on the qualifications gained in compulsory schooling. The England and Wales Youth Cohort Study shows a significant improvement in attitudes to schooling coinciding with the introduction of GCSE;

- *pull from post-compulsory schooling*
  Demographic changes have created spare 'capacity' in the education system. Local management of schools, and student-related funding formulae, have encouraged schools and colleges to recruit students more actively. Easier access to higher education has contributed directly to higher participation at 18 years, and indirectly at 16 or 17 by increasing the incentives to stay on;

- *pull from the labour market*
  This may be weakening. Occupations which have traditionally recruited 16 year olds have declined as a proportion of the workforce. Youth Training schemes have not, as once predicted, established themselves as equivalent to A-levels. The withdrawal of benefit entitlements from unemployed 16 and 17 year olds in 1988 appears to have encouraged some young people

to stay on in full-time education instead.

Several of these factors - notably the changing social composition of the age group, the expansion of higher education and labour-market changes - suggest that participation will continue to grow.

Part-time and work-based education and training

Participation: aggregate data. The part-time and work-based sector includes training provided through Youth Training; training supported by Training Credits since 1991; other education and training sponsored and/or provided by employers; and other part-time courses, both during the day and in the evening, usually followed on the student's own initiative.

Most long-duration part-time education and training for 16-18s has been provided through the youth training schemes. Fig. 3 shows participation on the Youth Training Scheme and its predecessor the Youth Opportunities Programme (1978-1983). Only unemployed school leavers were eligible for YOP; the growth in participation in the early 1980s reflects the rising trend in underlying unem-

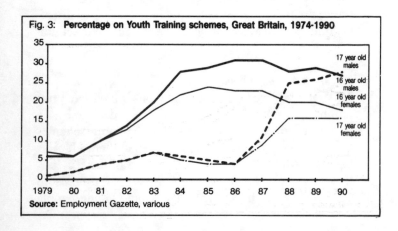

Fig. 3: **Percentage on Youth Training schemes, Great Britain, 1974-1990**

Source: Employment Gazette, various

ployment. The replacement of the (typically) 6-month YOP by one-year YTS in 1983 accounts for the further increase in 16 year olds' participation in 1984; trainees were more likely to be in training at the time of the January count. In 1986 YTS became a two-year scheme, and participation increased among 17 year olds.

Participation by 16 year olds in Great Britain has fallen in the last few years, continuing to do so after YT was introduced in 1990. There were 319,500 young people in training (under YTS) in England and Wales in December 1989; this had fallen to 258,600 in December 1991 (provisional estimates, including 14,000 supported by Training Credits). Participation on the Youth Training Programme in Northern Ireland has continued to grow, from 10,184 to 14,993 since December 1989.

While participation in youth training schemes rose during the early 1980s, participation in other forms of part-time day education fell (Fig. 4). The two trends are related: YTS displaced other part-time education or training among young workers, although its net effect was to increase participation especially in less skilled occupations and among young women. However, the decline in part-time day education was well established before YTS was introduced in

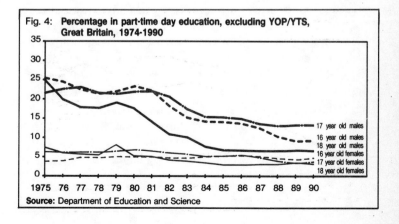

Fig. 4: Percentage in part-time day education, excluding YOP/YTS, Great Britain, 1974-1990

17 year old males
16 year old males
18 year old males
16 year old females
17 year old females
18 year old females

Source: Department of Education and Science

1983, most noticeably amongst males, and reflects other trends, notably the collapse of apprenticeship in the 1970s. Fig. 4 covers Great Britain only; participation rates in Northern Ireland are slightly lower.

Estimates of provision of training by employers can be obtained from the Labour Force Survey. The proportion of economically active 16-19 year olds receiving job-related training rose from 20% in 1984 to 24% in 1988, and to 30% in 1990. These figures include on-the-job training.

Participation: individual data. An alternative perspective is provided by cohort studies which record the participation of individuals over time. For example, in the late 1980s 36% of 19 year olds in England and Wales (45% in Scotland) reported that they had at least started on YTS at some time since leaving school. 94% said they had received some kind of post-compulsory education or work-based training; these include 21% who reported on-the-job training only.

Who participates? Part-time day participation has been higher among males than females (see Figs. 3 & 4). YTS extended opportunities for young women, for the less qualified and for young workers in occupations with little tradition of training. Gross inequalities in participation narrowed during much of the 1980s, but they are now widening again as provision becomes more 'employer-led'. Data on aggregate participation conceal persisting wide inequalities in the duration, type and level of training received, with better-qualified white males, particularly in construction and engineering, among the most advantaged. When part-time participation in education and training is work-based and employer-led, its quantity and nature are strongly influenced by labour-market conditions, which vary locally as well as over time.

Few young people in Britain choose training for its own sake. It is typically a by-product of other decisions or circumstances, a consequence of entering a particular job or of the failure to find a job. The boundary between training and employment is blurred, and most trainees or apprentices consider themselves to be in 'jobs'. The idea of leaving school at 16 to enter a job has a respectability in Britain which it lacks in almost all other industrial countries.

Quality of provision. While most early leavers from full-time education receive some kind of part-time or work-based provision, the duration, type and level of this provision is highly variable. The issue of quantity – of participation in part-time education and training – is inseparable from that of quality.

International comparisons have drawn attention to the low standards and attainments of work-based education and training in Britain. However, it is difficult to generalise. Not only is the quality of provision uneven, but there have been frequent changes in policies and arrangements for provision, partly in response to criticisms of the quality. YTS was widely criticised for the low attainments of its trainees, for its high drop-out rate, for the use of trainees as cheap labour, for the inappropriate occupational balance of skills produced, for the narrowness of much of the training and for its bias towards the specific and short-term needs of sponsoring employers.

The government has acknowledged many of these weaknesses and has sought to remedy them by giving employers greater 'ownership' of YT, by linking funding to the achievement of qualifications, and by basing these on industry-defined occupational standards. The latest initiative - training credits - seeks to make training markets more effective and to give young people themselves more say. Critics complain that the occupational qualifications are narrow and low-level and provide insufficient basis for progression to higher levels of education, that the assessment of the vocational qualifications is inadequate, and that training credits do not remove the sources of market failure.

The succession of policy changes suggests a more fundamental weakness of the British approach. The voluntaristic, employer-led character of work-based education and training in Britain may be at fault. The issue is not whether this approach is intrinsically good or bad, but whether it is appropriate for 16-18 year olds and whether it can be yoked with full-time education into a coherent system for the whole age group.

Beyond the mixed model: the need for a strategy

In its present form, the 'mixed model' dates from the time of the New Training Initiative in 1981, when the government gave the Manpower Services Commission responsibility for raising the skill levels of young people. The education service, at least in England, was deemed too conservative for the radical changes that were necessary. More recently, however, the mixed model has come to reflect divided control, and the absence of a clear strategy. The trend in participation is moving in favour of full-time education. So is the tide of opinion; many commentators are critical of much work-based education and training in Britain and doubt whether the system of National Vocational Qualifications (NVQs), Scottish Vocational Qualifications (SVQs) and industry-defined standards can overcome its limitations. However, some work-based provision is excellent, and there is widespread approval for the flexibility of the NVQ/SVQ system and for the diversity offered by the mixed model.

The way forward may lie in correcting two defects of the current system. First, market- or employer-led provision as it has developed in Britain has failed to meet, and is probably incapable of meeting, the needs of 16-18 year olds. Occupational NVQs/SVQs, based on 'industry-defined' standards, are a good basis for the training of adults, including young adults entering the labour force after a broad-based vocational education; but they are not an adequate alternative to general education for 16-18 year olds. Provision for this age group needs to have more regard to their wider educational needs, to future educational progression, and to the skill needs of a much broader range of occupations. It is not reasonable to ask individual employers to provide this.

The second defect of the present system is its lack of coherence. Full-time and part-time sectors embody differing principles of curriculum, assessment and certification; it is difficult to move between them; the sharp division between academic and vocational routes perpetuates the low status of the latter; and the allocation of young people to different routes reflects gender, geography and (especially) academic status rather than young people's interests and abilities. The incentives to participate have been arbitrarily loaded against full-time education, except for the academic minority. This may be changing, but there is scope for further shifts in the balance of incentives.

Government policy should reinforce the rising trend in full-time participation; but it should also recognise that the problems of participation (quantity) and of quality are inseparable, and that we need a strategy for the system as a whole. The analysis in this paper points to a number of possible measures (see Panel). But such measures should be part of a wider policy, for a more unified, but diverse and flexible system, which offers broad opportunities for learning to all 16-18 year olds.

A suggested agenda for change
A range of policy measures for promoting higher full-time participation and a more coherent system should be considered,
among them the following:

- reforms of courses and credits to make it easier for students
  to move between full-time and part-time routes or to pursue
  the same qualifications via either or both routes;

- a more unified system of courses, possibly modular, to
  erode the academic/vocational divide and enable students to
  keep their options open longer;

- a legal requirement on employers of under-18 year olds to
  provide them with formal 'traineeships', within the unified
  system, entitling them to training on the job plus part-time
  further education funded by the taxpayer leading to recognised qualifications;

- abolition of maximum age restrictions for jobs or training;
  encouragement to employers to regard broad-based vocational and general education to 18 as a 'normal' prerequisite
  for entry to employment;

- encouragement for continuing education and training for 18-
  plus year olds, particularly those outside higher education,
  whose participation rates may be the next major 'problem' to
  confront British education and training; a switch in Training
  Credits to target 18-plus year olds rather than 16-17 year
  olds;
- most importantly, effective incentives for further learning for
  all young people, not just the academically successful.
  Employers should be encouraged to develop their recruitment and personnel practices so as to recognise and reward
  the attainment of relevant qualifications.

May 1992

Acknowledgements
Work on this Briefing was supported by the Economic
and Social Research Council, which also funded much of
the research on which the Briefing draws. I am grateful
for permission to use Crown Copyright material in the
charts, and to draw extensively on unpublished analyses

of the England and Wales Youth Cohort Study. Josh Hillman, members of QQSE group at Sheffield University, and statisticians in the DES, the Employment Department and the Northern Ireland Office were generous with their time.

4 The Problem of Teacher Shortages

Andrew Wilson
Richard Pearson
of the Institute of Manpower Studies

Summary

1 A good education system depends critically on employing a sufficient number of good teachers who are qualified to teach the right subjects in schools in all parts of the country.
2 Teacher shortages in England and Wales were relatively high in 1990 but have been reduced considerably in the past two years. The recession has been a major contributor. The supply of teachers must be maintained in times of economic strength, not only in recessions.
3 Even now, shortages remain. They include vacancies which are hard to fill, mismatch meaning that subjects are taught by teachers not qualified to do so and/or that reduced tuition is given in subjects in which there are too few people available to teach them.
4 Throughout the education service efforts to reduce shortages should be pursued vigorously as current circumstances are particularly favourable to success.
5 The school population will grow over the next decade, partly for demographic reasons and partly because of the trend for more young people to continue in full-time education beyond age 16. The overall demand for teachers will therefore rise.
6 Economic recovery can be expected to make more difficult the tasks of remedying and avoiding the recurrence of teacher shortages, especially in certain subjects and in certain parts of England and Wales.
7   A key priority is to ensure that better information about supply and demand for teachers is available in good time and on a basis that enables potential subject shortages and localised shortages to be identified quickly.

8   In NCE Briefing No. 2, (see p 17), Ewart Keep argued
     the case for 'coherent and accountable management of
     those major personnel issues which are beyond the
     control of individual schools'. Nowhere is this more evi-
     dently necessary than the recruitment and retention of
     teachers.

9   Measures for improving quality have been proposed
     and require serious consideration, for example: the
     introduction of flexible employment patterns; improve-
     ment of in-service training; greater use of support staff
     to enable teachers to spend a higher proportion of their
     time in teaching; and improvement of the physical
     environment in which teaching takes place.

10   There is no room for complacency about the future.
     Hitherto economic expansion and the revival of the
     labour market has led to serious teacher shortages.
     There is a shared duty on government departments, on
     LEAs and on schools to provide the conditions which
     make it possible to ensure that every pupil receives
     teaching of the highest quality at all times.

Introduction

Given the rising public interest in, and concern about the quality of our education system, it is not surprising that reports about teacher shortages regularly hit the headlines. The purpose of this Briefing is to look at the extent of teacher shortages in England and Wales, and what can be done to minimise any future difficulties.

Numbers of Teachers

Teachers are a major professional group in the labour market. In 1991 there were 442,100 teachers (measured as full-time equivalents) employed by Local Education Authorities (LEAs) and grant maintained schools in England and Wales. Just under two thirds were women. The teachers were split almost evenly between the primary and secondary sectors. In addition there were almost as many qualified teachers in the population who were not currently employed in teaching (over 350,000 in 1986 of whom nearly two thirds were women). Further details are given in Figure 1 (overleaf) and Box 2 (p.55).

Teacher Shortages

It is hard to define what constitutes a shortage and difficult to collect relevant data. The most readily available and widely used data on teacher shortages are those on *vacancy rates* produced by the Department for Education (DFE) each January for England. The figures do not, however, take account of 'hidden' or 'suppressed' shortages, where-

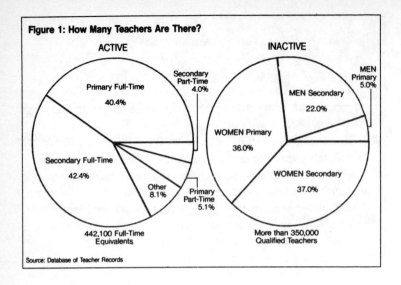

Figure 1: How Many Teachers Are There?

ACTIVE

- Primary Full-Time 40.4%
- Secondary Part-Time 4.0%
- Secondary Full-Time 42.4%
- Other 8.1%
- Primary Part-Time 5.1%

442,100 Full-Time Equivalents

INACTIVE

- MEN Primary 5.0%
- MEN Secondary 22.0%
- WOMEN Primary 36.0%
- WOMEN Secondary 37.0%

More than 350,000 Qualified Teachers

Source: Database of Teacher Records

by staff without relevant qualifications teach specialist subjects and in this respect they tend to underestimate the problem. Conversely, they also include vacancies which are part of 'normal' turnover and in this respect the figures may over estimate the problem (see Box 1).

Box 1
What is a Shortage?
There is no clear, universally agreed measure of what actually constitutes a shortage in relation to a given number of teaching posts.

In practice three potential measures can be considered; these are 'vacancy rates', 'hidden shortages' and 'suppressed shortages'. Issues of teacher shortages also have a quantitative aspect (how many teachers are required?) and a qualitative aspect (are the available teachers appropriate for the posts that exist?).

i) ***Vacancy Rates:*** *The simplest measure is the number of unfilled vacancies for teachers. However, such a measure is not necessarily reliable. Very few vacancies cannot be filled in some way (perhaps by temporary staff, supply teachers or those not fully qualified for the particular post). Quality is therefore an issue (see also 'hidden shortages' below). Second, it is possible that some schools might not create vacancies for staff if they are convinced that a particular post will not be filled by a teacher with the appropriate skills and abilities. Finally, vacancies are a normal part of the process by which any organisation recruits staff and makes appointments. What is of greater interest is the number of 'difficult to fill' vacancies or those which have been 'unfilled' for a significant period of time, but data of this kind are not readily available.*

ii) ***Hidden Shortages (or Mismatch):***
Hidden shortages are said to exist when teaching is carried out by someone who is not qualified to teach the subject. It is often referred to as a 'mismatch' and is usually measured either as the proportion of teachers teaching a subject in which they are not qualified, or as the proportion of tuition provided by such teachers.

iii) ***Suppressed Shortages:*** *Suppressed shortages occur when tuition in certain subjects is reduced, or subjects are simply not taught at all, because the appropriate staff are not available.*

The vacancy rate has fluctuated somewhat in recent years, reaching a peak level of 1.8 per cent in 1990, up from 1.2 per cent in 1988. Since 1990 it has fallen back to 1.5 in 1991 and is believed to have fallen further in 1992 because of the recession. Vacancy rates have traditionally been higher in the primary and nursery sector (2.1 per cent in 1991) than in the secondary sector (1.5 per cent in 1991). There are also marked differences between different parts of the country; Greater London was in the worst position with a vacancy rate of 5.3 per cent in 1990, and within it the Inner London area had an even higher vacancy rate. By contrast the Northern region had a vacancy rate of 0.6 per cent in 1990 and the East Midlands a rate of 0.9 per cent.

Within secondary schools, there are significant variations across subjects, the highest rates being in music, languages and careers teaching. However, languages account for the highest proportion of all vacancies (at 16 per cent), followed by the sciences (14 per cent), English (13 per cent) and mathematics (9 per cent). The lowest rates are in biology and home economics.

In 1988, the latest year for which data are available, 20 per cent of tuition in secondary schools was undertaken by teachers without specialist qualifications in the subject they were required to teach. This is a 'hidden shortage' or 'mismatch'. This 'mismatch' varied widely across subjects, with low levels in chemistry (5 per cent), biology (6 per cent), physics, French, geography and music (all at 8 per cent). Much higher rates of mismatch occurred in computer studies (56 per cent), business studies (37 per cent) and Craft, Design and Technology (35 per cent). However, for virtually all subjects, the degree of mismatch was lower among the older pupil age groups. For example, while mathematics had a mismatch of 15 per cent in years 7 to 9 (11-14 year olds), it fell steadily to only 2 per cent in year 12 (the sixth form). Several other subjects also have had very low levels of mismatch in the sixth form: geography, history, biology, chemistry, physics, English and French (all under 5 per cent).

It can be seen that the available data on shortages show that the problems of unfilled vacancies are focused in certain subjects and locations. There is also a significant proportion of secondary teaching that is being carried out by those lacking the relevant subject qualifications. While these shortages have eased over the last two years, it is not clear how much of this improvement is due to factors beyond the recession and lack of alternative jobs.

Looking ahead, the extent to which shortages become easier or get worse depends on the flows into and out of teaching. These are considered next.

The Flows into Teaching

Teachers can enter the active teaching workforce through three main routes (see Figure 2).

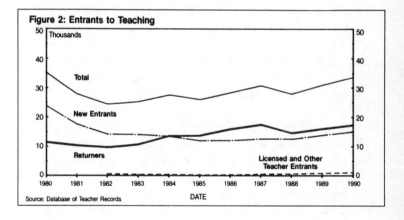

Figure 2: Entrants to Teaching

i) **New Entrants.** Traditionally, new entrants come from teacher training courses at universities, colleges and polytechnics leading to either the degree of Bachelor of Education (or BA/BSc with Qualified Teacher Status) or a one year Postgraduate Certificate of Education (PGCE). These are now being supplemented by the two year, school based PGCE or 'articled teacher' scheme which is targeted at young graduates and received its first intake in 1990. In 1986 bursaries were introduced to attract entrants to training in 'shortage' subjects and, while they had the initial effect of increasing entrant numbers, they do not seem since to have added a further boost to the already rising numbers.

Over the last decade the numbers of newly qualifying teachers have fluctuated between 12-15,000 each year. Numbers are, however, set to grow in the coming years as applications and acceptances for BEd and PGCE courses have shown rapid growth, with a 50 per cent increase in intakes between 1987 and 1991.

Some 13,000 students started BEd courses and 15,000 PGCE courses in 1991. Applications for places on courses starting in 1992 are up by a further 50 per cent, big rises occurring across all the subject areas, including the perceived areas of shortage such as mathematics, the sciences and modern languages. This growth has been fuelled in part by the recession and the sharp downturn in the number of alternative job opportunities open to graduates.

Within these rising totals there is a rising proportion of 'mature' students, who were aged 26 or over when they started their course. Mature students accounted for 35 per cent of the intakes in 1990, up from under 30 per cent in 1987.

These figures tell only part of the story. It is also necessary to take into account wastage from training. In 1991, 13 per cent of PGCE entrants and 22 per cent of BEd entrants did not complete their training. In addition, only around 75 per cent of the students who qualify normally go on to enter some form of teaching within a year of qualifying, with a further 10 per cent entering after a gap of more than one year. Finally it is important to note that not all those qualifying are able to find what they regard as appropriate teaching jobs. Some 3 per cent were still unemployed six months after qualifying in 1990.

ii) **Re-entrants** or qualified returners are the other major source of entrants to the active teaching workforce. The numbers have grown by over 50 per cent in the last decade to total over 17,000 in 1990. Qualified returners accounted for over half the overall intake to teaching in 1990. They include men and women returning after a career break, after ill health, or from other employment. The majority are women returning to primary school teaching.

Among the 350,000 currently inactive teachers, nearly one in five definitely intend to return while another 40 per cent would consider returning, so that there is a large pool of potential returners for the future (see Box 2).

Box 2
The Pool of Inactive Teachers
There are over 350,000 qualified teachers who are not currently working as teachers. A 1991 survey of out-of-service teachers showed that 17 per cent of those not currently teaching definitely intended to return to teaching while 41 per cent would consider returning to teaching. This suggests there is a pool of up to 60,000 people prepared and willing to return to teaching.

The 'definite' returners were more likely to be women in their thirties with young families who intended to return once their children are older. Over half of this group had more than 5 years' teaching experience, this experience being fairly evenly split between the primary and secondary sectors.

This characterisation fits in with the reasons given for leaving teaching, the most common being to 'raise a family' (cited by 28 per cent). Other reasons were 'dissatisfaction with teaching – other than financial reasons' (24 per cent) and 'to take up other employment' (17 per cent). Only 5 per cent of the sample suggested that their main reason for leaving was to do with pay.

When all those who were undecided or definitely against returning to teaching were asked for their reasons for not wanting to return, the most frequently cited reason was 'prefer current employment' (33 per cent) followed by 'dissatisfaction with teaching – other than financial reasons' (27 per cent). Only 8 per cent cited pay as the main factor.

When possible returners were asked what factors would encourage them back into teaching, the most popular measure was the 'availability of part-time work, more flexible hours and jobshares' (25 per cent of respondents) and 'better pay generally' (14 per cent). 'Refresher courses' and 'opportunities to re-acquaint with life in the classroom' were each cited by 10 per cent. The conclusion was that 'pay is a factor influencing decisions on re-entering teaching, but is rarely regarded as the most important factor'.

iii) **Licensed Teachers and Other Entrants.** This is the path to Qualified Teacher Status (QTS) for those who have been trained as teachers in a country other than England or Wales, or who are unqualified but experienced teachers from the independent sector. Licensed teacher status can also be granted to anyone who is over 26 years of age. Licensed teachers have to have completed successfully at least two years' full-time higher education in England or Wales and to have undertaken a period of training in a school accompanied by a programme of teacher education for a period ranging from one term to two years, depending on previous experience. In 1987 such entrants accounted for less than 4 per cent of the total inflow into the profession. However, the recent extension of licensed teacher status to those with no teaching experience might well increase the importance of this entry route.

Overall, then, the supply of new teachers is currently growing fast, although much of the recent growth is probably due to the recession. It is also noticeable that recruits, comprising both new entrants and re-entrants, are increasingly mature students or adults and that there is a large pool of inactive teachers who provide a significant potential resource available to the education system. This contrasts with the traditional image of a profession fed by 'young graduates' only.

Flows Out of Teaching

On the face of it the numbers leaving the profession annually are high. The proportion of qualified teachers leaving rose from 7.8 per cent in 1988 to almost 10 per cent in 1990, although the figure has fallen back again in the last year. The crude figures can however be misleading, as retirement and early retirement accounted for over half (58 per cent) of the teachers leaving the profession in 1990. Only one in six of the leavers left teaching for alternative employment outside education, and about 7 per cent of leavers left to start a family or look after young children. The destinations of the other 18 per cent of leavers were unknown. To put these figures in perspective, only 3,160 teachers were known to have left in 1990 to take up work outside teaching, a total that had risen from 2,560 three years earlier. The number of retirements due to ill health had however doubled over this period to total 3,290 in 1990.

There is little information available about the motivation of teachers and their reasons for staying in or leaving teaching. A recent pilot survey did however show that teachers were motivated by inherent 'job satisfaction', 'good relations with pupils', 'being rewarded fairly' and 'working in a well managed school', and that up to a third had poor experiences of these factors (see also Box 2).

As well as flows out of teaching it is also important to consider the turnover of teachers within the profession (i.e. those teachers who resign to move to other teaching posts), since this also represents a potential disruption in pupils' education. Teacher turnover stood at 13.1 per cent in 1990. There were significant regional variations. The turnover rate amongst teachers in secondary schools in Greater London was 17.4 per cent, and that in the South East (excluding London) was 15.0 per cent. Both these figures represent a slight fall in the turnover rate of 1990, following increases in the previous two years. The turnover rate amongst newly appointed teachers in London was even higher; 24 per cent of newly qualified teachers moved within 2 years, and 42 per cent within 5 years.

Alleviating Shortages

Various initiatives have been undertaken, or proposed, to reduce teacher shortages. These include:

- Nationally widening access through the introduction of more flexible training courses, especially part-time training opportunities and shortened BEd or PGCE courses. The 'licensed' and the 'articled' teacher schemes are currently growing sources of new entrants. Such flexibility is particularly attractive to mature entrants.

- Bursary payments for trainees in shortage subjects. While such payments have had an initial effect on recruitment it seems that such effects may not be long-lasting.

- The promotion of teaching through the Teaching as a Career Unit (TASC), which runs regular national advertising and publicity campaigns competing directly with the efforts of graduate recruiters in other sectors.

- Locally, in some LEAs and individual schools, the introduction of more flexible working arrangements, including part-time jobs, job-sharing, career breaks and crèche facilities. These would particularly benefit women teachers and might not only encourage ex-teachers to return (see Box 2), but could also have benefits in terms of retaining teachers currently in service.

- Re-training which helps reduce the problems of mis-match and hidden shortages.

- Re-examining teacher workloads and the amount of time spent on administrative activities. Recent research shows that on average only about half of teachers' time is devoted to direct teaching and lesson preparation. Administrative and other duties take up the largest part of teachers' time and many of these activities might potentially be delegated to support staff.

- Reviewing pay and reward structures and levels in order to attract teachers in shortage subjects and locations. This is a very controversial area. Opponents of differential pay say that it would be divisive, that shortage subjects change over time and that differentiated salaries could prove to be insensitive to such changes.

- The Department for Education, LEAs and schools need to continue with and develop initiatives of these kinds to minimise future shortages. Some of these policies, initiated by LEAs, may however be much harder to extend or implement when schools are locally managed or grant-maintained. It is also important that the effect of initiatives should be carefully assessed from the point of view both of their overall impact and of the extent of the 'additionality', i.e. the extent whereby additional teaching resources result as distinct from an effect whereby a 'solution' simply redistributes teachers and creates a problem elsewhere. Moreover, it is also essential to monitor effects on quality as well as quantity.

Future Trends

Looking ahead, the school population is projected to grow by over 12 per cent over the next decade, generating a demand for more teachers. At an operational level changes in school management, most notably local management of schools and 'opting out', will also influence the demand for teachers. While subject provision is now largely determined by the National Curriculum, the balance of staffing within subjects will still be determined locally. The key determinant of the demand for teachers will, however, be the level of funding allocated to education.

In 1990 the DES produced an assessment of future supply and demand trends. The department used demographic data together with a 'high demand' scenario based on current class sizes (with average pupil teacher ratios of 17:1), and a 'low demand' scenario based on class sizes 10 per cent larger. The figures suggest that on the supply trends prevailing in 1990 shortages would worsen over the period to 1997 unless class sizes grew, while if there were improvements on the supply side there would be no worsening of existing shortages at current class sizes. The department did not however provide an assessment based on an assumption of smaller class sizes. Such a development would lead to a worsening of the gap between supply and demand. The DES report also provided supplementary data relating to individual subjects.

It is clear that schools will require more teachers in the

coming years. Given that the decade started with shortages, improvements will be required both in making full use of existing and inactive teachers and in the supply of new entrants, if shortages are to be minimised and the education system is to function satisfactorily.

June 1992

5 Breaking Out of the Low-skill Equilibrium

Dr David Finegold
Rand Corporation, California, USA (formerly Senior Research Fellow at the Centre for Education and Industry, University of Warwick)

Summary

1 **Britain has a low-skill equilibrium.** In other words, the supply of skills and the demand for skills are roughly in balance, despite the relative lack of skills in the UK compared with other leading industrial countries.

2 **We should abandon myths which prevent us from breaking out from the low-skill equilibrium.** One myth is that all the fault lies with the education and training system; a second is that 'British attitudes' are to blame; a third is that we have already done enough to solve the problems.

3 **Companies' demand for skills tends to be low because of**
   - short-termism in financial markets and cost-accounting systems
   - traditional arm's-length relationships between buyers and suppliers
   - poor co-operation between companies on matters where they have a common interest
   - industrial relations weaknesses
   - managers who lack sufficient education and training
   - and, in consequence, too much reliance on low-value-added products and services.

4 **The supply of skills tends to be low because**
   - companies' recruitment and promotion structures mean that individuals do not have enough incentive to invest in higher-level skills - the youth labour market encourages 16 and 17 year olds to take well-paid jobs with no training
   - costs are not shared in a way that encourages investment in education and training

- there has been up to now a confused jungle of vocational qualifications
- the structural problems underlying the low-skill equilibrium have not been tackled.

5. **There is a range of policy measures which might be considered to break the deadlock** – see list on page 74.

Introduction

For more than a century researchers and policy-makers have concluded that Britain has failed to provide the majority of its population with the same level of education and training as its main industrial rivals and that this failure has, in turn, been a cause of the decline in British competitiveness. Despite repeated attempts at reforms, concern about the adequacy of the skills base remains and has, if anything, intensified in the last decade. This NCE Briefing identifies the causes of this long-standing problem, shows why a market-driven reform strategy is unlikely to solve it and suggests how Britain might create a high-skill economy.

Myths about the British Skills Problem

The first step is to understand the nature of the British problem. This entails dispelling three current myths:

Myth No. 1: The Education and Training System is Solely to Blame
Both James Callaghan's Ruskin College speech and the Black Papers argued that the British system of education and training is failing to meet the needs of an advanced industrial economy. While there are unquestionably major deficiencies in the British system, the focus on the supply side has obscured the two-way nature of the problem by ignoring the extent to which inadequate demand for skills from employers is at least equally to blame for lack of investment in education and training. This 'disastrous paradox' was recognised by the Balfour Committee as long ago

as 1929 (see Barnett):
'British industry was desperately short of well-educated and skilled personnel of all kinds compared with its rivals; ... and yet, this fraction [of skilled workers] was actually more than British industry wished to employ.'

Myth No. 2: The Problem is British Attitudes

Historians such as Martin Wiener and Correlli Barnett have argued that Britain's relatively poor economic performance can be traced to a distinctive set of English values, such as an 'anti-industrial spirit' and the 'cult of the practical man'.

In reality there is plentiful evidence that seemingly irrational attitudes, such as the decision of many young people to leave education at 16 or managers' reluctance to train the majority of their workforce, are rational responses to the situations in which they are placed.

If incentives are altered, it is possible for attitudes to change, as the example of the Ford Employee Development Assistance Programme has clearly demonstrated. When the company offered workers £200 to spend on an educational course to be taken in their free time, it expected, on the basis of its US experience, that about 5 per cent of employees would participate. In fact, more than half the workforce has taken up this opportunity for further learning.

Myth No. 3: The Problems Have Now Been Solved

Whereas a majority of pupils left full-time education at the first opportunity in 1988, now over 60 per cent of 16 year olds are remaining in full-time education and more than 90 per cent are in some form of education or training. Growth in higher education enrolments has also been impressive.
These development are welcome in themselves but must be interpreted with caution for the following reasons:

(a) *Serious deficiencies in post-16 provision remain.* The figures quoted for participation by 16 year olds hide deficiencies which are discussed in detail by David Raffe in NCE Briefing No. 3 (see p31). It should be noted particularly that participation falls off steeply after age 16 and that the qualifications obtained by trainees, if any, are mostly at low level.

(b) *Optimistic projections* could well prove wrong. While structural changes in the economy have propelled a long-term increase in staying-on rates, there is a danger in extrapolating from the recent surge in participation. The combination of a sharp decline in the number of young people and the prolonged recession has probably inflated the figures. As the economy recovers, many young people may prefer jobs to remaining in education. Nor is it certain that the system can continue to expand at its current rate without major additions to capacity.

(c) *Other countries are staying ahead.* The improvements in UK staying-on rates must also be viewed against the more sustained growth in educational investment by our main competitors. For example, countries such as the USA, Japan and Sweden still have proportionately more than twice as many 16-18 year olds remaining in full-time education as Britain, and newly industrialised countries such as South Korea already have more students continuing into higher education (36%) than our target for AD 2000 (1/3). This is on top of the 'skills deficit' of those already in the British workforce.

(d) *We have a two-tier system.* If we look in more detail at UK education and training statistics (see Table overleaf), they reveal a consistent pattern. The top 15-20% of the age group in terms of academic ability do relatively well. They reach a high level of attainment by the end of schooling, receive a generous subsidy to continue into higher education, and then obtain the vast bulk of the training provided by employers. By contrast, the great majority in the age group gain relatively poor qualifications and have little incentive to remain in education and training. As a consequence, most leave the system with limited opportunities to improve their skills throughout their working lives.

	UK	Germany	Sweden	USA	Japan
Participation rates in full-time education. (% 1987)					
16 years old	50	71	91	95	92
16-18 year-olds	35	49	76	80	77
New entrant rate to higher education (1987)	37	30	40	31	52
Management - % with degree or professional qualification (1987)	20	60	N/A	85	85

Sources: DFE, OECD.

The Low-Skill Equilibrium

To understand the reasons for Britain's relative skills failure I have developed a new framework for analysing the relationship between education and training systems and the economy in the advanced industrial countries. It begins with the distinctive characteristics of investment in higher-level skills (e.g. the long pay-back period, the danger that a company which invests in training may have its skilled workers poached by competitors). For each characteristic, it then identifies the institutional factors, such as the structure of qualifications and employer organisations, that can create incentives or disincentives for the three main investors in skills – individuals, company managers and government policy-makers – to follow the high-skill path.

Applying this framework to the British case it becomes apparent that the economy has been trapped in a low-skill equilibrium in which the majority of enterprises staffed by poorly trained managers and workers produce low-quality goods and services. The term 'equilibrium' is used to suggest the interdependence between the different institutions that make up the skills-creation system and the decisions of the three main factors. For example, it will not pay individuals to remain in education to develop technical skills if companies are not prepared to invest in the research and development, new technologies and training required to make a high-skill strategy work. Likewise, managers will be reluctant to reorganise the work process and make these new investments if they do not have access to a supply of well-educated workers and new recruits.

The following sections outline the institutional components of the skills-creation system that have suppressed the supply and demand for skills in the UK, noting those elements which have improved or deteriorated in the last decade.

Financial Markets and Cost-Accounting Systems

In Japan and Germany, banks have developed long-term relationships with both large and small enterprises enabling managers to focus on building their market share and to invest in higher-level skills. In the UK, as in the USA, the dominance of the stock market and short-term lending practices of banks have led companies to concentrate on meeting quarterly profit targets and maximising immediate return on investment. The pressure toward short-termism in the 1980s has been intensified by the deregulation of financial markets and increase in hostile takeovers.

Relations Between Firms

For small and medium-sized enterprises, it is often the type of links between buyers and suppliers that determines managers' willingness to adopt a high-skill strategy. In the UK relations between firms have – with some important exceptions – commonly been at arm's length, where price rather than quality is the main criterion and contracts may be terminated with little notice, discouraging small firms from investing in the skills of their workforce. Recently, the introduction of Japanese sub-contracting practices which focus on much closer, longer-term relationships and the exchange of information and expertise, have driven some small suppliers to transform their organisations and upgrade their training investment, but these cases are still the exception.

Employers' Organisations and Co-operative Institutions

The UK has no shortage of employers' organisations. The problem is rather the relative weakness and overlap between these bodies – the Confederation of British Industry, chambers of commerce, non-statutory training organisations, local employer networks and, most recently, the Training and Enterprise Councils (TECs) and their Scottish equivalents. They do not represent all firms and lack the power to deter companies from poaching. In his comprehensive study of the competitiveness of nations, Professor Michael Porter (1990) found that co-operative organisations that could encourage firms to share the costs of training, technology diffusion, export marketing etc. were crucial to the development of successful 'clusters' of high-skill, high-value-added companies. He concluded: *'mechanisms that facilitate interchange within clusters are generally strongest in Japan, Sweden and Italy, and generally weakest in the UK and US'*.

Industrial Relations and Wage Bargaining

The most significant improvement in the British skills-creation system in the 1980s has occurred in industrial relations, where employers have been able to overcome restrictions that previously confined training to a select group of workers and made it difficult to realise the full benefits of investments in new technology. This has not however been accompanied by a shift toward a more positive role for organised labour in the training process. With a few exceptions such as the Electricians, British unions have not made training a key priority in collective bargaining, and they have been virtually eliminated from the education and training policy-making process. The danger is that without some safeguard - such as the German Works Councils provide - employers may be tempted to exploit rather than improve the skills of the majority of their workers.

Management Education and Training

Another factor that contributes to Britain's low-skill equilibrium is that the people responsible for making the decisions on firms' product strategies and skill requirements - company managers - are themselves too often poorly educated and trained. Only 20 per cent of senior managers in the UK have degrees, compared with more than 60% in France and Germany and 85% in Japan and the US. Roughly half of all UK firms (and 75% of small companies) provide no formal training to keep the skills of their managers up to date.

The Vicious Circle: Low Supply of Skills

The factors discussed above create incentives for most UK-based companies to focus on low-value-added products and service markets using low-skill forms of work organisation. This sends signals to the majority of individuals that it will not pay them to invest in higher-level skills. The relatively low supply of skills, both among existing workers and in new entrants, creates a further disincentive for companies to pursue a high-skill strategy. The decisions of individuals, managers and policy-makers about skills are also linked by the additional factors discussed below.

The Youth Labour Market

One of the distinctive features of the UK's skills-creation system is the continued existence of a youth labour market that offers 16 and 17 year olds relatively well-paid, adult status jobs with little or no formal training. In its recent White Paper, the Government refused to contemplate any education and training requirement on the 16-18 age group

for fear that 'there would be fewer jobs for young people'.
The question is whether it is in either the individual's or
the country's interest for school leavers to enter jobs which
do not provide training leading to qualifications.

Distribution of Education and Training Costs

The way in which the costs of investing in higher skills are
distributed among the three main investors has restricted
the number of places on offer. At the 16-18 phase, relatively high wages in Britain increase the cost to employers and
make them reluctant to take on trainees who may then be
poached by others. The problem is magnified in the training of technicians and supervisors, where an even greater
portion of the costs falls on individuals and their employers, unlike France and Germany where the state covers all
or most of the off-the-job training costs. The National
Institute of Economic and Social Research has estimated
that the net cost to an employer of training a single technician, who might then leave the firm, is £14,000.
Conversely, in higher education the state bears a far higher
percentage of the costs for each full-time student than in
other countries and provides no assistance to individuals
who are studying for degrees through far more cost-effective routes, such as part-time or distance learning.

Qualifications

A clear structure of qualifications linked to labour market
rewards can provide strong incentives for employers and
individuals jointly to invest in skills, the employer by providing some wages and the necessary education and training and the individual by accepting lower pay during the
training period. This process works well in certain sectors
of the British economy (e.g. accountancy, law, health care).
For most occupations, however, the jungle of qualifications
and low skill differentials have combined to discourage
individuals from investing in higher-level vocational or
technical skills.

The Government is attempting to solve this problem through the creation of a framework of National Vocational Qualifications (NVQs) and, more recently, General NVQs. There is an on-going debate about whether this approach, based on the specification of various 'competences', can capture the general, flexible, transferable skills that are crucial to enable individuals to cope with rapid economic and technological change. There is also a risk that performance indicators expressed in terms of numbers of NVQs obtained may tempt providers to push young people into routes which cost less (as in various service trades or business studies as opposed to engineering).

Reforming the System

The main factor capable of altering the incentive within the skills-creation system is the government. In practice its ability to shift the economy out of low-skill equilibrium has been hindered by a number of structural weaknesses in the policy process. A major constraint has been the lack of co-ordination of education, training and labour market policy either within or between departments. Another has been the rapid rotation of ministers that has led to a short-term policy perspective and reform overload.

Nevertheless the government has taken a number of steps, some already mentioned (e.g. expanding higher education, reforming industrial relations and setting up a national system of qualifications), towards creating a high-skill economy. Other achievements include: the National Curriculum, which sets clearer targets for each young person's school education; a common exam (GCSE) at 16 that has contributed to improved staying-on rates; and the attraction of Japanese inward investment which has had knock-on effects in improving work and training practices.

Unfortunately the government has done less well in many areas. On the supply side, the retention of A-levels in spite of the near universal opposition of business, universities and educationalists, has stifled moves to create post-16 routes that will motivate the majority. At the same time, uncritical commitment to the free market has prevented the resolution of structural problems which deter individuals and employers from investing in training and which therefore tend to perpetuate the low-skill equilibrium.

In NCE Briefing No. 3 David Raffe provides an agenda for action to improve post-16 education and training (see p44). I list in the box opposite a set of complementary proposals to stimulate the supply of, and demand for, skills and so to break out of the low-skill equilibrium.

Skills: Measures to Stimulate Supply and Demand

1   Legislate to remove all 16-18 year olds from the adult labour market. Instead they should either:
    (1) continue in full-time education, or
    (2) enter a formal traineeship with an employer, when they will be released two days a week (or the equivalent in blocks of time) to train for a qualification up to NVQ Level 3. The employer pays an allowance of roughly a third of the adult wage: off-the-job further education is paid for by the state.

2   Abolish the examination at 16-plus. With the National Curriculum, testing at Key Stage 4 and the moves to encourage young people to go on learning until at least 18, age-linked examinations are becoming an anachronism.

3   Reform the financing of higher education to open up opportunities to all adults. Give adults an entitlement - equivalent to £1000 a year for 3 years - to be applied towards the cost of education at any time in their working lives. Those who choose to follow a full-time degree course would repay the additional cost through a graduate tax system.

4   Measure the performance of education and training providers and TECs in terms of value added. The use of single outcomes takes no account of the quality of intakes.

5   Require public companies to report what they spend on education and training in their annual reports. Companies should have to follow common accounting conventions in arriving at their figures.

6   Give TECs a financial incentive to set up company membership schemes covering the main sectors in the local economy. They might have the power to impose a small subscription, say 0.2% of payroll, on local employers to finance high-quality shared services (training, research and development, technology diffusion etc.). Grants to employers could be targeted on the training of trainers, supervisors and qualified assessors, so that in-firm training is of high quality.

7   Encourage TECs to form regional networks on the lines already existing in Wales, London and the North-West. In this way they can address skill and economic development issues transcending local boundaries and also deal more effectively with the EC.

July 1992

Further Reading

Barnett, C. (1990) *The Audit of War*, Macmillan.

Callaghan, J. (1976) Ruskin College speech. In Times Educational Supplement, 11/10/76, p72.

Cox, C.B. and Dyson, A.E. [eds.] (1971), Black Paper 2: *Crisis in Education*. London, The Critical Quarterly Society.

Finegold, D. (1992) *The Low-Skill Equilibrium: An Institutional Analysis of Britain's Education and Training Failure,* DPhil in Politics, Oxford University.

Finegold, D. and Soskice, D. (1988) '*The Failure of Training in Britain: Analysis and Prescription*', Oxford Review of Economic Policy, 2, 2.

Finegold, D. et al (1992) *Higher Education: Expansion and Reform,* London, IPPR.

Institute for Public Policy Research (1990) *A British Baccalaureat,* London, IPPR.

Porter, M. (1990) *The Comparative Advantage of Nations,* London, Macmillan.

Prais, S. (ed.) (1990) *Education, Training and Productivity,* National Institute for Economic and Social Research.

Ryan, P. (ed.) *International Comparisons of Vocational Education and Training for Intermediate Skills,* London, Falmer.

6

Opening Wide the Doors of Higher Education

Professor A. H. Halsey
Fellow of Nuffield College, Oxford, and member of
NCE Research Committee

Summary

1　At the time of Robbins (1963) academics were looking
towards a continuing modest expansion of higher education and envisaging a system not fundamentally different from the past, with access remaining highly
restricted.
2　At that time the stereotype of higher education was a
three-year residential system of high quality learning,
mostly for young men.
3　Between 1963 and 1990 there has been a dramatic
expansion in the student body from 216,000 to
1,086,300 with the age participation rate moving from
7.2% to 20.3%. Its composition has crucially shifted;
women and part-time students now claim a far greater
share.
4　In the same period higher education has, in successive
steps, invaded further education and is now moving
towards the American conception of higher education
as embracing all post-compulsory or post-secondary
schooling.
5　Children of manual working-class families remain, as
before, very much less likely to enter higher education
than those of professional and managerial parents.
6　Entry standards have risen in the last 20 years. The
'pool of ability' has not been exhausted; on the contrary,
it is expanding.
7　For the traditionalist, the pattern of institutional expansion may seem to have diluted the quality of experience
of higher education; for the reformer, expansion is
opening up opportunities appropriate to a modern economy and an increasingly well-educated citizenry.

Background

There is a general social and political will to expand British higher education in the 21st century. The object of this Briefing is to clarify the meaning and significance of this educational ambition by looking at the record of the immediate past. The Robbins Report (1963) confirmed the fact of expansion in the 1950s and heralded further expansion in the 1960s and 1970s. What then about the 1980s and 1990s? The number of students enrolled in degree courses has risen every year since Robbins: but the more interesting questions are: what kinds of students in what kinds of institutions and what proportions of their contemporaries in the population at large do they represent?

Expansion of higher education

From 1963 to 1990 expansion continued in such a way as to obliterate Robbins as a numerical landmark. Absolute numbers of students in the higher education system rose every year. In 1962 the total number of full-time students was 216,000. By 1989/90, including home and overseas students, part-timers in universities, the Open University, the polytechnics and other colleges offering advanced courses, it was 1,086,300.

Apparently therefore Britain has had, and indeed still has, a straightforward record of successful development of its investment in higher education through fluctuating economic fortunes. In fact the story is less simple and more interesting. Less simple because the numbers have risen at varying rates. More interesting because the definition has

widened from the original concept with which Robbins
began. Higher education, in successive steps, has invaded
further education. The stereotyped view of higher education as a three-year residential system of high quality
learning for young men has been overtaken. The definition
moved gradually, and continues to move, towards an
American concept of higher education as all post-compulsory or post-secondary schooling.

The statistics cited begin with full-time or sandwich-course
students and end with all full-time and part-time students
in a wide range of colleges in addition to those in the universities. The White Paper (Higher Education: A New
Framework, Cm 1541, May 1991) described the higher
education system in the United Kingdom as one in which
the polytechnics and colleges (including Scottish central
institutions) took 53 per cent of the student total, with the
Open University taking 4 per cent and the universities 42
per cent. Underlying this description lies the commitment
to mass provision of post-compulsory opportunities
towards which educational reformers have been slowly
moving for at least a century.

At the universities it may be seen from Table A that full-
time student numbers rose from 119,000 in 1962/3 to

TABLE A: Universities in Great Britain - staff and students

Year	Full-time students (thousands)	Staff/ Student Ratios
1962-3	119.0	n/a
1972-3	239.4	8.2
1982-3	295.4	9.5
1986-7	301.3	10.0
1990-1	352.6	11.6

Source: Statistics of Education

352,600 in 1990/91. But the annual rate of increase was by no means steady. It averaged 12 per cent between 1962/3 and 1972/3 during which time the former Colleges of Advanced Technology were incorporated and the new greenfield universities of the 1960s opened their gates. These were direct consequences of the Robbins surge. But advance slowed down in 1972/3 and turned to retreat after 1981 when severe funding cuts were imposed. There was absolute decline for 1982 to 1985 when economic slump gave way to boom, from which point growth accelerated each year to 1990, recapturing the expansion rates of the late 1960s and the early 1970s.

Diversification

At this point we are in a position to see the evolving institutional and opportunity pattern of developments since Robbins. The general pattern of expansion is disaggregated in Table B for the period from 1970 to 1989.

TABLE B: Expansion of higher education in United Kingdom by type of establishment, sex and mode of attendance, 1970-1990

		Universities			Polytechnics & Colleges			Open University		
		1970/ 71 000s	1989/ 90 000s	% rise	1970/ 71 000s	1989/ 90 000s	% rise	1970/ 71 000s	1989/ 90 000s	% rise
Full-	Men	167	200	20	107	170	59	-	-	-
time	Women	68	151	122	114	169	48	-	-	-
Part-	Men	18	31	72	110	159	45	14	47	236
time	Women	6	23	283	12	103	758	5	42	740

Source: Education Statistics for the United Kingdom (HMSO)

It is confirmed that the total enrolment rose but the composition of the student body crucially shifted. The traditional pattern of higher education - the full-time male undergraduate in a university - was the one that rose most slowly, by

20 per cent. The alternative forms expanded more rapidly. For example, the number of part-time female students at polytechnics or colleges of higher education rose by 758 per cent and Open University enrolment of undergraduates rose by 368 per cent, from 19,000 in 1970 to 60,500 in 1981 and 89,000 in 1989. Thus for the traditionalist, the experience of higher education has been one of dilution, presented as expansion. For the reformer, on the contrary, access has widened to offer opportunities appropriate for a modern economy and an increasingly well-educated citizenry. For the traditionalist more looks worse. For the reformer more means different.

Demographic and educational trends

Demographic and educational factors underlie the trend of higher education numbers. The total number of 18 year olds in the UK peaked at over a million in 1965, fell to 800,000 in 1973, rose again to nearly a million in 1981 and then fell to nearly the 1973 level in 1990. These wide, even wild, oscillations were, however, evened out by the rising productivity of the secondary schools. The percentage of the age group in England with two or more A-levels in GCE rose from under 8 per cent in 1962/3 to approaching three times that proportion by the late 1980s (20.9 per cent of boys and 22.2 per cent of girls in 1988/9).

For full-time students in higher education as a whole there has been an increase in the age participation ratio (defined as the proportion of home students under 21 years to the 18 year old population of Great Britain in the year of entry). Before the Second World War it had been less than 3 per cent. Just before Robbins in 1962/63 it was 7.2 per cent. It rose steadily until 1972/73 but then the ratio fell (to 12.7 per cent in 1977/8) and did not climb back to the 1973 level again until 1984 when it rose to 15.2 per cent and further to 20.3 per cent in 1990. According to DES calculations the Age Participation Index (virtually the same as APR, i.e. the number of home initial entrants to full-time higher education as a proportion of the 18-19 year old population) was 13.7 in 1984 and reached 19.3 in 1990. The interesting movements in this index from 1978 to 1989 are displayed in Figure 1 for men and women separately and distinguishing universities from other higher education institutions. The index is projected to increase to 28.1 in 1995 and 32.1 in 2000 (Appendix 2 of Cm 1541). There is, in short, a declared intention of continuing expansion to include more than ten times the post-war proportion of young people by the end of the century. It had already risen by a factor of seven by the beginning of the 1990s.

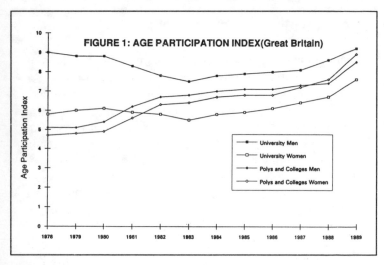

Quality

But does more mean worse? For the universities we can now check Robbins' confidence that student quality had not declined and need not fall, on the Committee's expansions plans, from the record of the A-level qualifications of accepted home candidates over the period from 1971. Standards were distinctly higher in 1991 than they were in

1971. They rose markedly between 1976 and 1984 and then fell back slightly. It cannot, of course, be maintained that the merit or the aptitude of candidates is exactly represented by A-level results, which in any case have a rather low correlation with degree results. But in the terms of the argument before and after Robbins there is no better practical calculus. The 'pool of ability' has yet to be exhausted. On the standards that obtained when Robbins reported there remains ample scope for expansion of higher education if recent trends continue.

For the higher education system as a whole the picture is less clear. Part-time students and older entrants with 'non-traditional' qualifications have to be taken into account along with higher degree candidates and students from overseas. The most direct and simple measure of degree-seeking potential for the nation is the profile of qualifications of successive school leavers. The quality of the young, as judged by examination performance at the end of secondary schooling, had been rising gently since before the period of expansion ushered in by the Robbins Report. In 1965/66, 12.9 per cent of boys and 8.6 per cent of girls obtained two or more A-levels in English and Welsh secondary schools. By 1988/89 the percentages stood at 14.7 and 14.8 for England and Wales. Moreover, using the more stringent criterion of a very high score in three A-level subjects (AAA, AAB, AAC, or ABB) the proportion of high flyers among university entrants rose from 25.3 per cent in 1971 to 35.7 per cent in 1984 but since then has fallen back to 31.2 per cent in 1991 (see Table C overleaf).

The general line of development is clear. At the time of Robbins, the academic world was looking cautiously towards modest expansion and envisaging a system of higher education not fundamentally different from the previous one of highly restricted access. Public discussion, supported by a growing conviction among industrialists

TABLE C: British university entrants: A-level scores of home candidates accepted through UCCA, 1971-1989 (% with various scores)

Scores	3-8	9-12	13-15	
1971	28.0	46.7	25.3	
1976	29.8	43.9	26.2	
1981	24.2	45.7	30.0	
1984	14.8	49.3	35.7	
1988	16.6	48.5	34.9	(61,225)
Scores	6-15	16-25	26-30	
1989	12.6	54.2	33.2	(70,219)
1990	17.1	51.4	31.6	(80,251)
1991	17.7	51.0	31.2	(84,661)

Source: UCCA Statistical Supplements.
Note: Only candidates with three or more A-levels are included and the best three counted with grade A=5, B=4 etc. before 1989. The scoring system was changed in 1989 to include AS qualifications.

and politicians that a much more highly educated younger generation was needed to ensure the wealth of the nation, took a more expansionist view. The experience of larger numbers in the post-Robbins decade encouraged more and more university teachers to believe that larger proportions of each new generation were capable of receiving what they had to offer.

The bulk of the expansion took place in the polytechnics and colleges. A 1989 survey contains judgements of student quality at graduation as well as admission. It suggests that quality on entry has been maintained in universities and has been allowed to fall only slightly in polytechnics (now renamed universities) and that universities and polytechnics have seen themselves as capable of giving considerable added value to the ability of the students they admit (Table D).

TABLE D: Description by academic staff of academic ability of students entering and graduating from universities and polytechnics in 1989 compared with a decade earlier

Percentage of responding academic staff

Change over decade	On Entry		On Graduation	
	University	Polytechnic	University	Polytechnic
Lot worse	4	8	1	2
Little worse	23	30	15	16
About same	40	26	48	32
Little better	23	25	25	32
Lot better	10	11	11	18

Source: Halsey, A.H. (1992) Decline of Donnish Dominion, Appendix 1.

Returning to the characteristics of the universities, it must be noted that staff-student ratios have deteriorated over the post-Robbins period. The ratio is defined in terms of full-time students and full-time staff who are wholly financed from university funds (see Table A). The measure is a crude one, but it unequivocally describes decline, from 8 per cent in 1971/2 to 11.6 per cent in 1990/1. What are the implications?

If we look at international comparisons, British universities emerge as uniquely privileged from the point of view of intensive contact between teachers and learners, not only because of the ratio, which is typically 17 or 18 in comparable foreign institutions, but also because of residential arrangements, student maintenance and an entrenched culture of devotion to tutorial and pastoral relationships. The consequence is that drop-out rates are low and graduate output compares better with other countries than undergraduate input.

Furthermore, modern teaching techniques, especially capital intensive methods of the kind used in the Open University, allow internal differentiation of staff-student contact, adapted to the type of course or subject and the stage of education or training of particular students.

The question of teaching quality must therefore remain open. All we can say is that some departure from the traditional ideal, and some retreat from the universities' defence of the unit of resource, has been a feature of post-Robbins expansion.

Gender and social class

The expansion of opportunity for women may be regarded as a further exemplification of the same general pattern. The proportion of all students who were women was less than a quarter before World War Two, began to rise significantly after the mid sixties, and became 42.8 per cent in 1989. Those who consult the facts will accordingly have mixed emotions. In the polytechnics sexual equality of opportunity is established. And, as is clear from Table B, the growth in full-time university undergraduate places has accommodated more women both absolutely (83,000 extra women compared with 33,000 extra men) and relatively (122 per cent increase for women compared with 20 per cent increase for men). But the evidence of differential relative expansion is also there. Women have gained on men but their advance has been disproportionately in the newer forms of higher education. All part-time categories have risen faster for women than for men over the two decades.

For social classes the general tendency towards inequality of educational attainment persists. General Household Survey data show that, measured in relative terms, the proportions of those entering higher education from manual working families have scarcely shifted by comparison with those from the professional and managerial classes. For degree holders in 1974 whose fathers were professionals or managers, the ratio was 2.75, i.e. they were graduating at nearly 3 times the rate that would obtain if degree-holding were randomly distributed. At the other extreme the children of semi-skilled and unskilled workers had a ratio of 0.28 and the children of skilled manual workers 0.52. By 1985 these ratios had moved to 2.05, 0.36 and 0.50 respectively. The numbers of entrants to higher education from manual social origins had risen absolutely but not relatively to their numbers in the population. This is cold comfort for those who seek the 'classless society'. Moreover, the movement from grants towards loans inaugurated in 1989, and the logic of education as a 'positional good', might well produce greater class inequality in British higher education in the future.

Conclusions

Given the expansion of the 1960s and the declining attraction of higher education in the 1970s, either retrenchment or a sombrely revised programme of educational expansion with very different assumptions about the funding and working conditions of intellectual labour had to follow in the 1980s. Growth faltered in the mid-seventies but the national income rose again, at least for the majority, in the 1980s. Educational expansion went on, partly by enlarging the definition of higher education, locating it in colleges which had been previously allocated and administered under the heading of 'further' education, and in the Open University, as well as in what came to be labelled 'conventional' universities. Part-time attendance and short courses multiplied as continuing education was partly absorbed into what was previously stereotyped as a full-time, three-year, residential degree course.

Why then did this expansion continue and even become the first priority of all political parties? The answers are not complete. Both economic fortunes and political pressure moved in the late 1980s. A restructuring of the economy with movement towards integration with continental Europe had educational consequences. The quest for competitive advantage impelled renewed educational expansion. International comparisons in the preparations for '1992' also stimulated reorganisation of training arrangements and reinforced pressure towards inclusion of vocational education in schooling. From different standpoints and with different assumptions, all political parties began to share the view that a mass system of higher education was inevitable for twenty-first century Britain.

Plans for funding the new expansion remain vague. The government's drive towards increasing reliance on tuition fees will give more freedom to market forces. The government will also encourage universities and colleges to seek funds from private sources, particularly from industry and commerce, benefactors and alumni. Higher education is assured of a continuing share of public expenditure, but the context within which its size will be determined is the drive to reduce public expenditure overall, intense competition between government departments for funds and the calls of other educational priorities. The emphasis on securing increased efficiency will persist. Amid the uncertainties, one thing is sure. The binary line has lost its official status and a post-binary system has begun. What the shape and size of higher education will actually turn out to be in AD 2000 is still unclear.

August 1992

Note: For an up-to-date and detailed analysis of admissions to British universities, see Halsey, A. H. and Heath, A. (ed., 1993) *Access to Higher Education,* Oxford Review of Education (special issue), Vol. 19, No.2.

7 Selection for Secondary Schooling

Dr Geoffrey Walford

Senior Lecturer, Aston Business School, Aston University

Summary

1 The main reason for the introduction of comprehensive schools was to alleviate problems of selection in the tripartite system. But there has never been a true `comprehensive' system in Britain. Comprehensive reform meant that selection for different types of school based on measured abilities was largely replaced by selection according to where children lived.

2 A system of well-funded comprehensive schools provides the best opportunity to ensure that all children receive the highest quality education possible. The claim that comprehensives have led to a decline in overall educational standards is not proved. The most reasonable conclusion is that the more truly comprehensive the system, the more likely it is to have led to a slight overall improvement.

3 Moreover, the differences in social and academic effectiveness between schools nominally of the same type are more important than any possible difference between systems.

4 Research from Scotland, where in 1981 parents were given greater power than their equivalents in England and Wales to select a school, is relevant. It shows a widening of educational inequalities producing a two-tier system benefiting some children to the detriment of children overall.

5 Recent changes in England and Wales pose a number of serious concerns:
   (a) they have broadened and confused even further the range of criteria used for selection and are likely to lead to a diversity of unclear selection criteria which will discriminate against children from families that under-value education;

89

(b) they have rekindled and aggravated problems caused by selection which comprehensive schools attempted to overcome;

(c) most importantly, they are likely to result in the development of a hierarchy of schools which will provide the poorest education for those children most in need and the best for those who already have the most advantages.

6   The following is a recommended solution to address these concerns:

(a) on transfer from primary schools all children should move to similar well-funded comprehensives;

(b) *all* families should be required to select three or four schools in order of preference;

(c) entry to oversubscribed schools should be based on random selection from amongst those who apply.

Introduction

In England about 92% of children in the maintained sector are now in comprehensive schools. The figure is over 98% in Wales and Scotland. Only in Northern Ireland does a selective system dominate. Elsewhere selection of children for different types of school has largely become a thing of the past.

However, recent changes to the education system, such as the introduction in England and Wales of City Technology Colleges and grant maintained schools, and growing pressure for the reintroduction of grammar schools have revived the debate about selection between different types of school. At the same time, open enrolment and increased choice of school have highlighted the question of selection between schools nominally of the same type. This briefing paper reviews the debate on selection, assesses the effects of new forms of selection in these changed circumstances, and makes some radical proposals in the light of this.

Before comprehensives

In England and Wales, free secondary schooling as a separate stage was introduced following the 1944 Education Act. The idea of developing different types of school to suit the differing abilities and aptitudes of various children had grown during the inter-war years. The Norwood Report (1943) enshrined the idea of three groupings of children with different 'types of mind' who were to be educated according to their abilities to profit from either a grammar, technical or 'modern' type of curriculum. The

Act itself did not establish three types of school, but most local education authorities followed a tripartite or bipartite plan. The proportion of children to be offered a place at a grammar school depended on the number of places available in each LEA, and the final selection of children was often influenced by headteachers' reports as well as examination marks. The 1944 Act brought the majority of the denominational schools into the state maintained sector, but a significant private sector was retained where the main selection criterion was the ability and willingness to pay fees.

Why did the comprehensive system develop?

In 1951 less than 1% of secondary age children in the maintained sector were in comprehensive schools. By 1961 the figure had risen to about 5%, in 1971 it was 35%, and in 1981 it was 90%. The movement towards comprehensive education was the result of pressures from an uneasy alliance of groups and individuals with a range of ideologies, interests and visions for the future. They responded to a diversity of problems in the selective system including:

- considerable social class differences between the intakes to the three types of school;
- unsatisfactory reliability and validity of tests used to select children according to either aptitudes or academic potential;
- selection at 11 (12 in Scotland) being to the disadvantage of children who were 'late developers';
- large differences in the proportion of children selected for grammar schools in different LEAs;
- increased demand for a 'grammar school-type' education, due to rising parental expectations and demographic trends;
- real and perceived differences in status, quality of staff and funding of different types of school.

Some advocates of comprehensive schools also believed that putting all children in the same sort of school, where they would have equal physical facilities and equal access to high quality teachers, would raise the aspirations of all children, bring about greater equality of opportunity within the schools and lead to greater equality outside in the world of work.

Research on examination results from different systems

One of the main claims put forward by advocates of selective education is that separate grammar, technical and secondary modern schools are better able to meet the needs of a diverse range of children. They claim that comprehensive schools have led to a lowering of overall academic standards. Can this claim be tested?

Three very different studies which compared overall examination performance of children in selective and non-selective systems were published in 1983[1]. One compared the public examination results of a sample of local education authorities (Marks et al.), the second examined the performances of members of a longitudinal national sample (Steedman), and the third analysed questionnaire responses from a Scottish national sample of school leavers (Gray et al.). Each drew upon data which had not been collected with this comparison in mind and which had significant omissions. There were difficulties in defining different types of school and in methods of taking account of social factors.

The first study by Marks et al. claimed that 'substantially higher O-level, CSE and A-level examination results are to be expected in a fully selective system than in a fully comprehensive system', the second found no clear overall advantage or disadvantage accruing from selective or comprehensive schooling, and the third suggested that 'comprehensive education had a levelling effect on attainment, raising fewer pupils to the highest levels of attainment, but helping more of them to progress beyond the minimum. It appears to have raised average attainment.'

In fact, in all cases, once background factors had been taken into account, the overall differences were small. More significantly, these studies were all conducted at a time when the comprehensives were much newer than the selective schools, and when some parents were moving to the private sector to avoid comprehensives.

More recent follow-up research to the third study shows that once the comprehensives in Scotland had become established, they contributed to a rise in examination attainment and to a decrease in social class differences in attainment[2]. By looking at national representative samples of pupils who left school in 1976, 1980 and 1984, the authors also demonstrated that the decreasing gap in attainment levels between middle-class and working-class children was due to a small but significant levelling-up of working-class attainment and not levelling-down of middle-class attainment.

The need to take account of the time taken for schools to become established is also indicated in a study of a South Wales community[3]. The authors found that there were problems in the comprehensive schools, but argued that the comprehensives were failing some pupils because they had not yet adjusted to their new clientele. They described a range of internal organisational aspects (such as poor management, lack of pupil involvement and inadequate pastoral care provision) which made these schools less effective. Compared with these factors, whether the system was selective or not was unimportant.

Since the time when these earlier studies were reported

there has been increasing sophisticated research on how added value in schooling ought to be measured (see NCE Briefing No. 1, p.1) but the number of selective school systems has declined to a level where further meaningful comparisons between systems are impossible. We are left with a group of studies, unsatisfactory in various ways, which give partially contradictory results.

What can be salvaged from these studies? The most reasonable conclusion is that any differences in the overall examination effectiveness of the two systems are small. However, once comprehensives have become established they appear to reduce social class differences in attainment. A return to selection on measured ability at eleven would initiate a further long period of instability and would probably reduce overall attainment. More significantly, all of the studies found that there were far larger differences between the examination successes of different schools of the same type than between the average examination results of different systems, even after such factors as social class had been taken into account. The most important finding from these studies is that individual schools differ greatly in their effectiveness.

The practice of comprehensive education

As has been made evident in the previous section, selection did not disappear when the so-called comprehensives replaced the tripartite system. It simply became less overt – and potentially more unfair because the criteria for selection became more varied and confused. Even before the creation of new types of school in the late 1980s, selection was evident within various LEA comprehensive systems.

In practice, there was great variation between comprehensive schools. First, some LEAs called the bulk of their schools comprehensives yet retained a few small, highly selective, grammar schools. Second, voluntary aided and controlled denominational schools offered a different type of school even where all schools were comprehensive. Many parents saw these schools as closer to grammar schools than the county comprehensives[4]. Third, there were also differences between individual county comprehensives. Recent school effectiveness research[5] has confirmed what most parents always believed – that schools differ markedly in their academic and social effectiveness. The research has also shown that schools vary in their effectiveness for different children, and that a variety of factors, both internal and external to the schools, are correlated with effectiveness. In most comprehensive systems children were allocated to schools on the basis of catchment areas, and schools served relatively homogeneous social class intakes. Parents who were able and willing to pay simply moved to within the catchment areas of their chosen 'good' schools.

The so-called comprehensive system thus allowed affluent and well motivated parents to ensure the quality of schooling for their children within the maintained sector. Within the former tripartite system, there had always been the risk that such children would not be selected for grammar school. In contrast, the 'comprehensive' system gave security. This explains why there has been so little pressure from parents at the local level to return to selective education once comprehensives have become established. National opinion polls have sometimes shown majorities in favour of more grammar schools, but when the possibility has arisen locally parents have strongly supported comprehensives[6].

New forms of selection

During the 1980s there was a shift away from comprehensive schooling towards the establishment of new types of

school and increased choice between schools. At oversubscribed schools, the fact of selection has now become more
overt but the criteria on which pupils are selected have
become even more varied and confused. The problems of
selection for grammar schools are being reintroduced and
amplified. The City Technology Colleges (CTCs) provide
a good example of this new diversity and confusion of criteria. All of the CTCs are oversubscribed and are forced to
select from amongst those who apply. They are not
allowed to select children on academic ability and so,
instead, the criteria used are largely based on the degree of
motivation of parents and children. Parents are required to
make a special application for admission on behalf of their
child, and to pay any daily transport costs to the college if
the child is accepted. Parents have to be prepared to be
interviewed, to state that they support the college's aims, to
help to ensure that homework is done, and to express the
intention of the child to continue in full-time education
until age 18. Children have to be willing to work at a
school with a longer school day and shorter holidays. As a
result, children and families where there is a low level of
interest in education simply do not apply.

In a study of the first CTC at Kingshurst, Solihull[7], heads
and teachers in the nearby LEA schools claimed that the
CTC was selecting those very parents who have the most
interest in their children's education, and those children
who are most keen and enthusiastic. They argued that the
CTC was selecting children who, while they might not be
particularly academically able, were seen as invigorating
the atmosphere of any school, providing models for other
children, and being most rewarding for teachers to teach.

The 1988 Education Reform Act introduced further ideas
designed to hasten market processes and develop new
forms of selection. Both grant-maintained schools and
open enrolment were designed to increase competition
between schools and to encourage parents to make choices

between schools. Advocates claim that less popular
schools will improve their performance to attract more parents, and the quality of education for all children will thus
rise. There is no evidence to support this view, and it is difficult to see how schools can raise standards when per-
pupil funding under Local Management of Schools (LMS)
means that resources will reduce as numbers fall. Further,
as choice is limited to the number of places available in
each school, once there are more applications than places,
the ability of parents and children to choose a school leads
to schools selecting the pupils they want. While some
grant-maintained schools may become academically selective, most will probably rely on a range of criteria similar
to those of the CTCs. The iniquity of selection through
catchment areas is being replaced by selection on a broad
range of criteria which favour those families with the
greater interest in education. Rather than society giving
extra help to those children most in need, selection on a
diversity of criteria assists those children from families
where education is already highly valued.

In summary, the new forms of selection currently being put
into place will mean that our society is likely to provide
the poorest schooling for those children most in need and
the best for children who already have the most advantages. This is not only a personal tragedy but is also a
waste of individual and national talent.

Evidence from Scotland

The evidence available on choice and selection from
Scotland is relevant, since 1981 Scottish legislation gave
families greater power to select a school than did the corre-
sponding 1980 Act for England and Wales. One study[8]
found that the legislation was leading to a widening of educational inequalities and producing a two-tier system of
schools. Well motivated parents and children were able to

reject local working-class schools because they saw them as undesirable, but by doing so they ensured that their judgement was likely to become a reality for those children who remained. A few pupils from areas of multiple deprivation had been integrated into alternative schools, but this had led to increased social segregation for those remaining in the local school. The authors believe that greater parental choice has benefited some children, but has acted to the detriment of children overall.

This finding is echoed in another national representative Scottish study[9] which found that it was the better educated parents and those of higher social class who were more likely to have exercised their choice. These authors believed that the legislation on parental choice has increased social segregation between schools and that the disproportionate gains in attainment made by children with parents who are manual workers (brought about by comprehensive education) are likely to be retarded or even reversed.

These studies show that, rather than raising standards overall, as hoped and even predicted, greater inequalities and a hierarchy of schools are likely to develop. The children of well motivated, highly educated or wealthy families are more likely to make applications to the popular schools. These oversubscribed schools will select children on a diverse and unclear range of criteria, but in a way likely to be heavily skewed towards children from families already highly valuing education. These popular schools will thus improve further through the financial and cultural support of the parents and children selected. In contrast, children from families which do not value education highly will probably find themselves in schools at the bottom of the hierarchy with low levels of financial and parental support. Any pre-existing differences between schools will widen.

Reforming the system

A fair society will seek to ensure that all children receive the highest quality education possible. This is best done through a system of well funded comprehensive schools. A broad and balanced curriculum for all children up to age 14 overcomes problems of 'late development' and early selection. After this age, children are mature enough to be allowed to choose some degree of specialisation in their education alongside a core curriculum. Each school should offer a range of specialisms in most of the academic, technological and creative areas. The establishment of a diversity of schools, each offering a single specialism (as proposed in the White Paper, *Choice and Diversity*) would automatically lead to greater differences in esteem and widened inequalities between schools. It would actually reduce opportunities for children to make mature choices about their future.

There is no perfect solution to the problem that some schools will be more popular than others, and that there will be insufficient places in some popular schools for all who apply. However, the problem would be reduced if ways could be found to minimise the differences in popularity between schools, and to ensure that some children are not disadvantaged in the choice-making process. The legitimate desires of parents who are concerned about the schooling of their own children need to be harnessed to encourage high quality education for all children. This is best done by clarifying the choice-making process and introducing clear, simple and unbiased selection criteria for oversubscribed schools.

No child should be allocated to a school. Instead, all families should be required to select three or four schools in order of preference. Funding should be made available for travel and other incidental costs to ensure that reasonable choices are not restricted by family income. Independent information centres and advisers should be established to encourage and help all families in this decision-making process.

Where there are fewer applications than places available the first preference would be automatically granted. Schools would have no right to reject a child, and the power to exclude or expel a child would be removed from the schools and given to the local authority. Where schools are oversubscribed, successful applicants should be selected randomly from those who apply[10]. Random selection is essential, for it guarantees that some parents are not able to ensure the success of their own children by purchasing a home near to the school they aspire to use, or by being able to present themselves as more committed and concerned at interview. Exceptions to the principle of random selection should be at an absolute minimum, and might include children with specific physical disabilities being granted preference for a school with special facilities. Random selection introduces uncertainty, and so it becomes necessary for concerned parents to work for high quality schools for *all* children rather than devoting their efforts entirely towards the schooling of their own children.

Requiring all families to make a choice will broaden and deepen concern for education. More uncertainty in selection will ensure that high quality schooling for all children will become a political imperative. Somewhat paradoxically, requiring all families to make a choice, where there is uncertainty of that choice being granted, will reduce the importance of that choice. An extended hierarchy of schools is less likely to develop and schools will be given the chance to ensure that they give the highest possible quality education to all children.

October 1992

References

1 J. Gray, A.F. McPherson and D. Raffe (1983) *Reconstructions of Secondary Education: Theory, myth and practice since the war* (London, Routledge and Kegan Paul); J. Marks, C. Cox and M. Pomian-Srzednicki (1983) *Standards in English Schools: An analysis of examination results of secondary schools in England for 1981* (London, National Council for Educational Standards); J. Steedman (1983) *Examination Results in Selective and Nonselective Schools: Findings of the National Child Development Study* (London, National Children's Bureau).

2 Andrew McPherson and J. Douglas Willms (1987) *'Equalization and improvement: some effects of comprehensive reorganisation in Scotland'* (Sociology, 21, pp. 509–539).

3 David Reynolds and Michael Sullivan with Stephen Murgatroyd (1987) *The Comprehensive Experiment* (Lewes, Falmer).

4 Bernadette O'Keefe (1986) *Faith, Culture and the Dual System* (Lewes, Falmer).

5 See, for example, David Reynolds and Peter Cuttance (1992) (eds.) *School Effectiveness. Research, policy and practice* (London, Cassell), David J. Smith and Sally Tomlinson (1989) *The School Effect* (London, Policy Studies Institute), and Stephen W. Raudenbush and J. Douglas Willms (1991) (eds.) *Schools, Classrooms and Pupils, international studies of schooling from a multilevel perspective* (London, Academic Press).

6 Geoffrey Walford and Sian Jones (1986) *'The Solihull adventure: an attempt to reintroduce selective schooling'* (Journal of Education Policy, 1, 3, p. 251).

7 Geoffrey Walford and Henry Miller (1991) *City Technology College* (Milton Keynes, Open University Press).

8 Michael Adler, Alison Petch and Jack Tweedie (1989) *Parental Choice and Educational Policy* (Edinburgh, Edinburgh University Press).

9 Frank Echols, Andrew McPherson and J. Douglas Willms (1990) *'Parental choice in Scotland'* (Journal of Education Policy 5, 3, pp. 207–222) and J. Douglas Willms and Frank Echols (1992) *'Alert and inert clients: The Scottish experience of parental choice of schools'* (Economics of Education Review 11, 4, pp. 339–350).

10 See Geoffrey Walford (1990) *Privatization and Privilege in Education* (London, Routledge) chapter 6 and Geoffrey Walford (1993) *Choice and Equity in Education* (London, Cassell) chapter 9.

8 Learning Before School

Kathy Sylva
Peter Moss
Institute of Education, University of London

Summary

1 Early childhood is an important time for learning. High quality early childhood care and education services can make an important contribution to young children's learning, leading to improved educational performance and better social behaviour, especially for children from disadvantaged backgrounds. There is also a strong case for these services on social and economic grounds. Cost-benefit studies reveal major benefits for children, parents and society.

2 Early childhood care and education services are unevenly distributed, and receive limited public funding; most provision is in the private market and depends on parents' ability to pay. The UK has one of the lowest levels of publicly-funded services in Europe.

3 There are not enough affordable good quality services, and many services suffer from chronic under-resourcing. There are major and unjustifiable inconsistencies between different types of services.

4 A wide ranging review of this incoherent system is urgently required and should lead to the adoption of a national policy on early childhood and care and education services. The UK needs a comprehensive and coherent system of affordable high-quality services, open to all children and their carers. This review should cover all children, whether or not their parents are employed.

5 Investment in such a system is necessary and cost-effective – everyone gains, no one loses.

Introduction

This Briefing is about early childhood care and education. For young children, 'care' and 'education' are interdependent and inseparable: they need both. Early childhood is an important time for learning. Children develop physical competence, knowledge of how the world works, and skills for getting on with others. They become attuned to sounds that begin and end words, they learn that we read text from top to bottom, they notice that stories 'make sense'. In addition to knowledge and skills, the Rumbold Report (DES, 1990) reminded us that 'attitudes and behaviour patterns established during the first years of life are central to future educational and social development'. In short, the foundations are laid for later learning.

Learning occurs in a variety of environments, and for children under 3 as well as over 3 – given the right conditions. We examine learning outside the home, its impact on later development, its costs and benefits and the way our provision for early learning compares with that of other countries. It will be shown that the nature and quality of early learning outside the home enhances children's development or, sadly, impedes it.

The range of early childhood care and education services in the UK

The UK has a diverse range of early childhood care and education services (see panel overleaf).

Types of pre-school provision
Nursery education:
Maintained nursery schools, and nursery classes which are integral parts of primary schools. Open during the normal school day and during school terms; the great majority of children attend part-time. They take children aged three and four.

Reception classes
A large number of primary schools admit children to reception classes before they are five. The great majority attend full-time.

Day nurseries
Day nurseries look after under fives for the length of the adult working day, and most take children under and over three. Children attend part-time or full-time. Some are run by local authorities, usually by Social Services Departments; the majority are run privately, by voluntary organisations, community groups or employers, or by private companies or individuals as a business.

Playgroups
Playgroups provide for children between two and a half and five. Most are run on a self-help basis by parents or community groups, with a few paid staff. Most are open only part-time (three hours or less per session), and children on average attend two to three sessions a week. Some offer 'extended hours' and may be used by working parents.

Childminders
Childminders look after under fives, and also older children outside school hours, in domestic premises, usually the childminder's own home. They offer this service all the year round for the full working day. In the great majority of cases, the arrangement is private, with parents and childminders negotiating terms. In a few cases, local authorities sponsor children as childminders.

Table 1 shows the number of *places* in most types of early childhood services in 1980 and 1991, for England. During this period, places in publicly funded services (nursery education, reception classes, local authority day nurseries) and playgroups showed relatively slow growth – under 35% – while by contrast, the private sector of registered childminders and private day nurseries grew very rapidly.

Table 1: Number of places in early childhood care and education services[1] England: 1980, 1991

	1980	*1991*	*% change 1980-1991*
Nursery education[2]	130,997	177,863	+36%
Reception class	205,673	272,178	+32%
Local authority day nurseries	28,437	27,039	-5%
Private nurseries	22,017	79,029	+259%
Playgroups	367,868	428,420	+16%
Childminders	98,495[3]	233,258	+137%

Sources: DES (1992); DoH (1992)
[1] Excluding private schools, unregistered childminders, nannies.
[2] Full-time equivalent places calculated on the basis that two part-time pupils occupy one full-time place.
[3] For 1982; no data available for 1980 or 1981.

Table 1 does not show how many *children* used the available places, an important distinction as many places, especially in playgroups and nursery education, are used by more than one child on a 'shift' system. The most recent evidence on usage comes from the 1986 General Household Survey, which covered the UK except for Northern Ireland. At that time, 42% of children attended some form of service, rising from 6% of children under 12 months to 76% of 3 year olds and 89% of 4 year olds. Playgroups were the most widely used type of provision overall and for 3 year olds, schools for 4 year olds. Since 1986, levels of attendance will have increased somewhat, mainly due to growth in private services.

Most children going to playgroup attend for less than 10 hours a week. Most children in nursery education (88% in 1991 in England) attend on a part-time basis of 5 half-day sessions a week. Most playgroups and childminders (which between them provide more than half of all places) are under-resourced; this is reflected in poor pay and conditions and low levels of training for most workers in these services. The provision made for 4 year olds in reception classes is often inappropriate for this young age group, due to inadequate resources for staff and equipment.

Early childhood services may be diverse, but this does not mean that all parents have a wide choice. Due mainly to financial constraints on local authorities, most places are in services in the private market and depend on parents' ability to pay, taking no account of family income or circumstances. Among the services included in Table 1, the proportion of places dependent on parental fees, as opposed to public funding, rose from 56% in 1980 to 60% in 1991; including private schools, unregistered childminders and nannies would increase the private market share still further. Distribution of services is also uneven geographically.

Comparisons with other European Community countries

In most countries in the European Community, children start compulsory schooling later than in the UK, generally around age 6. Before, most countries provide (or are aiming to provide) 2 or 3 years of publicly funded nursery education (or kindergarten). High levels (over 80%) have already been achieved in a number of countries (France, Italy, Belgium, Denmark), while other countries (Spain, Germany) have made such levels of provision a target (see Table 2). In the UK, the government's 1972 commitment to provide nursery education for all 3 and 4 year olds whose parents wanted it was never fulfilled, and has been dropped. In 1991, in England, there were full-time equivalent places for 14% of children aged 3 and 4, although 25% received some nursery schooling due to the use of full-time places by part-time pupils.

Table 2: Places in publicly funded childcare as % of all children in the age group

	Date to which data refer	For children under 3(%)	For children from 3 to compulsory school age(%)
Belgium	1988	20	95+
Denmark	1989	48	85
France	1988	20	95+
Germany	1990	14	77
Greece	1988	4	65-70
Ireland	1988	2	55
Italy	1986	5	85+
Luxembourg	1989	2	55-60
Netherlands	1989	2	50-55
Portugal	1988	6	35
Spain	1988	n/a	65-70
United Kingdom	1988	2	35-40

Source: Moss, P (1990)

The gap in provision in the UK has been filled by playgroups and early admission to primary school, services found in significant numbers in only two other European countries, Ireland and the Netherlands; neither has any nursery schooling. Government statements that British provision for 3 and 4 year olds compares well with the rest of Europe are misleading. Most UK provision is in playgroups (under-resourced and offering most children short hours of attendance) and reception classes (inappropriate in many cases for 4 year olds); most provision elsewhere in Europe is in publicly funded nursery education.

Below 3 years old, all EC countries provide some publicly funded services. In France and Belgium, a substantial proportion of 2 year olds are in nursery education. Otherwise, most publicly funded provision for this age group is made in day nurseries or, in some cases, with childminders. Except for Denmark, France and Belgium, publicly funded provision for this age group is low; services for children under 3 are mainly provided privately, by childminders, nannies, nurseries and, above all, relatives. The UK has one of the lowest levels of publicly funded services for this age group – for less than 2% of children under 3 – and does not include children of employed parents as a priority for this limited provision.

The impact of day care on children's later development

Can attending early childhood care and education make a difference to children's learning and later development? Osborn and Milbank (1987) studied more than 13,000 UK children born in 1970 and compared educational and social outcomes for 'day care' children (for example local authority day nurseries) with those who had gone to half-day 'educational' programmes or remained at home. Towards the end of primary school the day care group had lower maths and reading scores and a higher incidence of behaviour problems. Research from Sweden, however, presents a different picture of day care; Andersson (1992) found day care experience gave children a *better* start in school in his examination of the development of 128 children attending day nurseries run by the local authority in Gothenburg.

The major reason for the differences in 'outcome' for the UK and Swedish studies appears to be different social policies. There is little publicly funded day care in UK, and it is intended for families 'in need', a highly selective intake. Richman and McGuire (1987) found that children attending local authority day nurseries in London had ten times more behaviour and emotional problems than children attending playgroups. The families of day nursery children had multiple problems, with parents needing a great deal of emotional support and help with child-rearing. Moreover, these children, whose educational needs are the greatest, are often cared for by staff with limited knowledge of primary education and how to provide a foundation for it (Sylva, 1992). By contrast, local authority nurseries in Sweden are widely available to 'ordinary' families, and are used by children from all walks of life.

Research from the US also provides evidence of differing developmental outcomes for children attending day care. Howe (1990) studied 80 children from a wide range of social backgrounds, half enrolled in high quality nurseries (with adequate numbers of stable and well-trained staff), and half in low quality nurseries. The former fared well on educational and social assessments later on in school. The picture was different in the low quality nurseries, with children enrolled before their first birthday doing particularly poorly at school. These 'early entry' children were distractible, low in task orientation and had considerable difficulty getting on with peers. The results point clearly to the importance of service quality in determining the impact of day care on children's development: good quality provision can enhance development, poor quality provision does not.

The effects of early education on later development

So far we have examined the effects of children's early attendance in 'day care'. We turn now to the research evidence on learning which takes place in 'early educational' provision, or nursery education, which is usually provided for children between the ages of 3 and 5 or 6. The most rigorous study of the long-term costs and benefits of nursery school has been carried out in the US. Berrueta-Clement (1984) and his colleagues studied 126 children from impoverished families who attended a high quality, intellectually oriented nursery education programme intended to give children a firm foundation for starting school. The design of the study was simple; half the children were randomly assigned to the programme (later called 'High/Scope') and half stayed at home, which they were destined to do anyway since there was no public provision available at the time.

Progress of the two groups of children was followed carefully from the moment they began the special nursery school until the age of 19 when many had jobs and families of their own. The results showed that the children who attended the nursery school were doing better all through the school years than their peers who had not attended the pre-school programme. The most compelling results came from the two groups of children when they were young adults. The group who had attended nursery school were functioning well in society; they were more likely to have jobs, to have completed school or training, and less likely to be sent to 'special education' classes. The children who did not attend the pre-school programme (the control group) were more often detained or arrested by the police, scored lower on tests of 'everyday problem-solving' and the girls experienced more teenage pregnancies (see Table 3 overleaf).

Berrueta-Clement and his colleagues carried out a cost-benefit analysis on the intervention programme. First they calculated the cost of operating the programme, then they estimated the price to the government of children *not* attending the programme, i.e., the cost of criminal proceed-

Table 3: The effects till age 19 of high quality nursery education in the US

	Group who attended pre-school	Group who did not attend pre-school
Percentage employed	59	32
Percentage graduating from high school or equivalent	67	49
Percentage with college or vocational training	38	21
Percentage ever detained or arrested	31	51
Percentage of school years in special education	16	28
Rate of teenage pregnancies per 100 (female only)	64	117
Functional competence score (highest possible score = 40)	24.6	21.8

Source: Berrueta-Clement et al. (1986)

ings, special education, social security benefit to single parents, etc. In the end, they concluded that for every $1,000 invested in the children who attended the pre-school programme, $4,130 was returned to the taxpayer (after controlling for inflation) by way of savings on educational or social problems later in life.

Schweinhart and his colleagues (1986) carried out subsequent research to examine the long-term effects of different kinds of pre-school curricula: the High/Scope curriculum above, which featured adult guided play; a traditional 'free play' programme; and a formal, skills-based nursery curriculum. They selected 68 children from disadvantaged backgrounds in the US and assigned them randomly to the contrasting programmes. By the age of 5 the IQs of all the children had been increased significantly, but by the age of ten the IQ gains had 'washed out'.

However, children were seen again when they were 15 and marked differences between the groups emerged in social behaviour and in practical skills. Children from the two play-oriented programmes (High/Scope and traditional 'free play') were getting along better in their schools, scored higher on tests of functional competence (practical reading, writing and calculation), and were less likely to be involved in criminal activity such as drug abuse. The formal 'skills-based' group engaged in twice as many anti-social acts as the children in the two play-based programmes. The study by Schweinhart suggests that children who are encouraged to be independent, active learners while young will be more community-minded and responsible in adolescence. The results are buttressed by the similar outcomes in Berrueta-Clement's research and in a meta-analysis of 11 American pre-school programmes (Lazar and Darlington, 1982).

The High/Scope researchers claim that a 'virtuous cycle' began when children left the nursery to enter formal school. The children who experienced the pre-school programme based on active learning were 'ready' for school and their teachers quickly learned to expect good academic progress. They were not disappointed and soon parents also began to expect their children to do well. Once the children left their nurseries, the social environment changed in that adults had a more positive view of their talents and future.

A UK study focusing on the effects of early education was carried out by Jowett and Sylva (1986). They studied 90 children over the course of their first year at primary school. Half were 'graduates' of well resourced local authority nursery education, while the other half (matched on age, sex and social background) had attended playgroups, poorly resourced and managed by parents working on shoestring budgets. All the children came from working-class homes and all were studied throughout their first year in school. Did their different pre-school histories make a difference in the way they adjusted to school? Such a result would be predicted by the High/Scope researchers whose theory about the importance of apparent competence at school entry has been outlined above.

There were many differences between the two groups of children as they settled into school. The nursery education 'graduates' were more persevering when they encountered obstacles in their work and more learning-oriented when they approached the teacher. They spent more of their time in 'academic' tasks, so demonstrating higher motivation for school. The researchers were not able to follow the children throughout their school careers but their short-term results make it clear that well-resourced nursery education, staffed by fully qualified teachers, fostered autonomy, perseverance and academic motivation in ways that playgroups operating on parental enthusiasm and a limited budget could not.

A recent study of a large sample of children in a northern metropolitan area (Blackburne, 1992) shows that children who had experienced nursery education had higher SAT scores in year 2 than their peers without nursery experience, especially in maths.

In its 1989 report, the House of Commons Select Committee on Education reviewed a large body of literature on the benefits of pre-school education and said: 'We conclude from the evidence that education for under fives can effectively contribute to the various social, education and compensatory objectives set out in the 1972 White Paper. It can not only enrich the child's life at the time but can also prepare the child for the whole process of schooling.'

The way forward: review, policy, action

Early childhood care and education services, provided that they are of high quality, can make an important contribution to young children's learning and lead to improved educational performance throughout schooling and better social behaviour. The benefits are particularly clear for children from disadvantaged backgrounds and for children over three, although some evidence points to benefits for children younger than three and from a wider range of social backgrounds. These services are important for other reasons. They can provide a range of functions – care, socialisation, support, economic – for a range of different groups – children, parents, families, local communities, employers. Children and parents have many educational and social needs which services can help to meet; but to do this, services need to be 'multi-functional'; the term 'early childhood care and education services' reflects this broad approach.

Early childhood care and education services in the UK are inadequate in many ways. They are unevenly distributed and receive limited public funding; consequently there are insufficient affordable good-quality services and a restricted choice for many parents. Services lack coherence and there are unjustifiable inconsistencies and inequalities between different types of service. There is also compartmentalised thinking about services; the need for 'childcare for working parents' is often discussed in isolation from services for children with non-employed parents; the Children Act concentrates public responsibility for provision on a minority of children 'in need' (defined in terms of disability or problems of health or development); 'preschool education' is often equated with 'nursery education' for three and four year olds.

Yet despite their importance, and their manifest inadequacies, there has never been an overall review of early childhood care and education services in the UK, nor a comprehensive and coherent national policy. The need for a review and a policy is increasingly urgent. More and more mothers of young children go out to work. Recent education reforms have paid little attention to children under five. Within the European Community, the UK government is party to a recently-adopted Council of Ministers Recommendation on Childcare. Implementation of the Recommendation would benefit from a review of current services. With access to services increasingly dependent on the private market and parents' ability to pay, there is a pressing need to consider the respective responsibilities of government and parents for ensuring all children have equal access to good-quality early childhood care and education services.

A review of early childhood services must be wide-ranging. It should be accompanied by two other reviews. The first would look at policies to reconcile employment, caring for children and gender equality. The second would look at the costs of child-rearing and the allocation of these costs; it would include the funding of services and the question of costs and benefits. This review should build on existing cost-benefit studies of early childhood care and education services, which reveal major benefits to offset the costs of provision. American work has quantified educational and social gains for children. UK reports from the Institute of Public Policy Research (Cohen and Fraser, 1991) and the National Children's Bureau (NCB: Holterman, 1992) quantify other benefits, and these show how public investment in services would be offset by increased government revenues due to higher employment among women and a reduction in families dependent on welfare benefits.

These three linked reviews would provide the basis for framing a national policy on early childhood care and education. Then action is required. The UK needs a comprehensive and coherent system of high-quality and affordable early childhood services; these should offer diversity of provision while being flexible enough to provide a variety of functions for all children and their carers. In such a *multi-functional* system of early childhood care and education services, children with employed parents would not be treated in isolation from other children; their need for secure care would be one of a number of educational and social needs to be recognised and met.

Investment in such a system would pay for itself. The recent NCB report costing early childhood care and education services identifies benefits to children, parents, workers in services, employers, the national economy and the government. In short 'everyone gains ... and no one loses'.

November 1992

Further Reading

Andersson, Bengt-Erik (1992) '*Effects of day-care on cognitive and socioemotional competence of thirteen-year-old Swedish schoolchildren.*' In Child Development. 63, 20–36.

Berrueta-Clement, J., Schweinhart, L.J., Barnett, W.S., Epstein, A.S., Wiekart, D.P. (1984) '*Changed lives: the effects of the Perry pre-school programme on youths through age 19.*' Monographs of the High/Scope Educational Research Foundation. No.8

Blackburne, L. (1992) '*Nursery children get head start.*' Times Educational Supplement, July 24.

DES (1990) '*Starting with Quality.*' (Rumbold Report) London: HMSO.

DES (1992) *Statistical Bulletin 5/92.* London: DES.

DoH (1992) '*Children's Day Care Facilities in England 1991.*' London: DoH.

Holterman, S. (1992) '*Investing in young children: costing an education and day care service.*' London: National Children's Bureau.

Howe, Carollee. (1990) '*Can the age of entry into child care and the quality of child care predict adjustment in kindergarten?*' Developmental Psychology 26 No.2, 292–303.

Jowett, Sandra and Sylva, Kathy. (1986). '*Does kind of pre-school matter?*' Educational Research. 28: No.1 p21.

Lazar, I. and Darlington, R. (1982) '*The lasting effects of early education: a report from a consortium of longitudinal studies.*' Monograph of the Society for the Research in Child Development, 47.

McGuire, J., Richman, N. (1986) '*The prevalence of behaviour problems in three types of pre-school group.*' Journal of Child Psychol. Psychiatry. 27:455–472.

Moss, P. (1990) '*Childcare in the European Community 1985–1990.*'

Brussels: European Commission.

Osborn, A.F., Milbank, J.E. (1987) *The effects of early education.* Oxford: Clarendon Press.

Schweinhart, L., Weikart, C. and Larner, M. (1986). '*Consequences of three preschool curriculum models through age 15.*' Early Education Research Quarterly, 15–45.

Sylva, Kathy, Siraj-Blatchford, Iram and Johnson, Serena. (1992) '*The impact of the UK National Curriculum on pre-school practice: some 'top-down' processes at work.*' International Journal of Early Childhood. 24, 40–53.

9 Change and Reform in Initial Teacher Education

Tony Edwards
Professor of Education, University of Newcastle upon Tyne

Summary

1   Initial teacher education (ITE) has been integrated within the wider system of higher education, but is now under centralised supervision implemented by the Council for the Accreditation of Teacher Education (CATE) working to criteria set by the Secretary of State.

2   There is an obvious tension between government control over entry to the profession, and the aspirations for professional self-government represented by the long campaign for a General Teaching Council.

3   Despite the increasing diversity of courses of ITE there is almost no follow-up evidence about the quality of teachers who emerge from different forms of training. There are evident risks in extensive innovation without thorough evaluation of existing practice.

4   For example, current reform of ITE will make it more school-based. Some extreme proposals for transferring responsibility entirely to schools assert without evidence that so-called 'traditional' training has failed, and ignore the diversity which already exists within the two main routes.

5   The government has now changed the role of CATE from accrediting courses by their content to accrediting them by their outcomes. The growing emphasis on teacher competences has important potential benefits. It should challenge the view that initial training is sufficient for an entire career, and make more visible the range and depth of expertise demanded of teachers. It will also enable useful comparisons to be made with ITE in other European countries as mobility of professional labour increases, and with training for other professions.

6 However, the emphasis on competences raises difficult questions about the knowledge and understanding underlying professional practice which are further highlighted by the recent government announcement about the amount of time in ITE courses which must be spent 'on school premises'.

7 Whatever the pattern of delivery, it is much more important that schools should be fully involved in planning and implementing coherent training programmes, and that the complementary and distinctive contributions of schools and higher education institutes should be clearly defined in their new partnership.

Introduction

Until recently, Initial Teacher Education (ITE) was regarded as worthy but unexciting – of concern mainly to those who provided it, and to the DFE because it controlled the numbers to be trained. It has now become a target for radical reform. This is partly because teacher shortages prompted emergency measures to alleviate them, partly because the national curriculum and other changes in schools are making new demands on entrants to teaching. But there have also been strident claims that present patterns of training help to perpetuate a damagingly 'progressive' educational establishment, and so contribute significantly to low standards in the schools.

This paper outlines some of the main changes in ITE which are occurring from within or being proposed from outside. It considers two particular sources of possible improvement in which great confidence is placed – namely, a shift to more 'school-based' training, and an increasing emphasis on the 'competences' of new teachers. Finally, it identifies distinctive contributions which Higher Education Institutions (HEIs) should continue to make to the professional preparation of teachers.

The existing system of ITE

There were in 1991 almost 46,000 students in ITE in 91 universities, polytechnics and colleges in England and Wales. The two main training routes are four-year courses for undergraduates including BEd degrees and BA/BSc degrees incorporating qualified teacher status, and one-

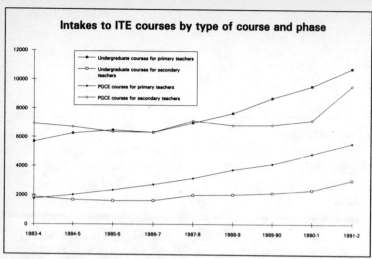

Intakes to ITE courses by type of course and phase

Legend:
- Undergraduate courses for primary teachers
- Undergraduate courses for secondary teachers
- PGCE courses for primary teachers
- PGCE courses for secondary teachers

year courses for graduates called the Postgraduate Certificate of Education (PGCE). The undergraduate route has always been dominated by courses for primary teachers (10,726 entrants in 1991/2 as compared to 3,002 for secondary teachers) and the Figure above shows that courses for primary teachers are now a significant proportion of the PGCE route (5,537 entrants as compared to 9,527 secondary PGCE entrants).

There are growing numbers of entrants on part-time and other non-conventional courses, which have been targeted mainly at subjects where teacher shortages have been both chronic and acute and at potential recruits who are either constrained by family circumstances in the kinds of attendance they can manage or who are thought likely to be put off by the length and supposedly theoretical character of mainstream ITE. In 1991/2 there were 1,113 entrants to two-year BEd courses, 162 entrants to two-year full-time PGCE courses and 224 entrants to two-year part-time PGCE courses. The Articled Teacher Scheme introduced in 1990 was also intended to pilot a new mode of largely school-based training, providing a two-year school-based professional preparation bridging the interface between the one-year PGCE course and an induction year. Its small scale (447 entrants in 1991/2) makes extrapolation difficult because any demonstrable benefits in the quality of training would need to be assessed against the economies of scale obtained in the main system.

Of the new students in 1991/2, 30% went to universities and 70% to polytechnics and colleges (including the few remaining monotechnic colleges, descendants of the erstwhile 'training colleges' to which reference misleadingly continues to be made). The familiar assumption that most have moved from and back to school without any intervening experience of the 'real' world is contradicted by an entry which has become increasingly diversified by age. A recent survey showed that 60% of new ITE students were over 24 and 29% over 31. Ethnic minority groups, however, continue to be strikingly under-represented; one-third of courses reported no such admissions, and the few where numbers were significant tended to be part-time, specialised, and in areas where the local ethnic minority population is substantial[1]. It would be appropriate if the teaching force in a diverse society were itself to become more socially and ethnically heterogeneous.

Professionalism and political control

It was a long process to take the training of teachers for elementary schools beyond mere apprenticeship, and then to recognise that secondary teachers need something more than the subject knowledge demonstrated by a university degree. Since the early 1970s, the expansion in BEd and concurrent degrees and of primary-orientated PGCE courses has done much to bridge the gap between the two previously distinct training traditions and to move towards an all-graduate profession.

What teaching has not achieved, however, is the control over entry and standards that the 'full' professions enjoy. The recently renewed campaign for a General Teaching

Council (GTC) represents a struggle for independence, from both government and quasi-official advisory bodies, which began in the last century and is still unresolved. A GTC now has the support of almost every organisation in the education world, was supported in principle by the House of Commons Select Committee for Education, Science and the Arts and has considerable cross-party backing. Taking the Medical and Engineering Councils as models of professional self-government, the body being proposed would monitor training courses, determine fitness to teach, maintain a register of those so qualified, supervise professional conduct, and maintain professional standards in schools of all kinds (including those which are independent or grant-maintained).

Such a Council would run counter, however, to government intentions of increasing its powers over what remains the largest graduate workforce in the largest public service. Indeed, the previous delegation of training to HEIs trusted to monitor their own standards has been replaced by a system of supervision implemented by the Council for the Accreditation of Teacher Education (CATE). CATE's membership is nominated by and accountable to the Secretary of State, is deliberately not 'representative' of teacher associations or any other relevant bodies and works to his criteria in judging the acceptability of courses. Neither in its composition nor its mode of working has CATE begun to achieve either the professional credibility or the independence which a GTC could provide, and some recent appointments have been overtly partisan. The criteria defined in 1984 were substantially revised in 1989 and again in 1992 without reference to the requirements being discarded. They constitute a large step towards a national curriculum for teacher training, setting limits to permissible differences in course structure, content and (in the 1992 version) the outcomes of training.

ITE and teacher supply

Until recently, the numerically dominant training route (the Teaching Certificate, replaced by the BEd) was a largely self-contained occupational ladder which trapped those taking it in so far as it led nowhere else. The expansion of concurrent degrees and especially the increasing PGCE share of the total output is now integrating recruitment to teaching more closely with the rest of the graduate employment market, making it a sensitive indicator of economic confidence. Thus the current recession has boosted entry to all main forms of teacher training by sharply reducing opportunities elsewhere, and has done so even in the traditional shortage subjects of mathematics, physics, chemistry and modern languages.

The consequent alleviation of supply problems may, however, be only temporary, especially if economic recovery is added to what is already a formidable problem of retaining a high proportion of those who trained for an increasingly hard-pressed and under-appreciated profession. There is no evidence to support claims that existing modes of training deter many potential teachers. It is more likely that recruitment would be damaged if entry to so demanding an occupation became too abrupt or took on too much of the appearance of a craft apprenticeship. In this context, the BEd degree gains some protection from those who criticise its blending of subject knowledge with professional training because its output is too large to be lightly risked. At the same time, the PGCE has the obvious advantage of being open to expansion or contraction with immediate effects on teacher supply.

Modes of training and teacher quality

The dangers of going too hard for extra numbers led the

then Senior Chief HMI to warn in 1989 that there are 'no quick, high quality routes into teaching'. Recent innovations, however, have been presented not as short-cuts in recruitment but as leading to more 'practical', and therefore 'better', training. Argument about them is too often an exchange of assertions because, while relevant research is now under way[1], there is no follow-up evidence about whether different modes of training produce better or worse teachers, or even different kinds of teacher.

The most far-reaching assertion has been that so-called 'traditional' forms of ITE require radical reform. The attribution of pervasive failure – as distinct from that conventional school judgement 'could do better' – is unsupported either by extensive HMI observation of courses or by HMI surveys of their output. In 1989, 95% of a large sample of new teachers were judged by their schools to have been 'adequately prepared for the job they are required to do'. Similar findings are reported in the 1992 survey, with headteachers considering that ITE is responding well to radical changes in the curriculum and in the running of schools[2]. HMI's general judgement on BEd and PGCE courses in 1991 was that they provided 'an appropriate balance of theory and practice', and that of all the work inspected during the previous year '85% was judged satisfactory or better' – a proportion which compares favourably with HMI judgements of other forms of professional training they inspect[3].

ITE's most strident critics wish to exclude 'theory' altogether. Their diagnosis of its failings is part of a much larger campaign against the 'outmoded' progressive and egalitarian ideas which teacher educators are seen uniformly to espouse. This diagnosis relies heavily on an ignorance of current practice which allows convenient travesties of it to be 'demolished'. The perceived remedy is then to shift training entirely to the schools on the grounds that teaching can be learned only by doing it and that all the beginner needs (given the necessary subject knowledge) is supervised practical experience.

The case for transferring responsibility to schools has also arisen from within ITE, but without implying that the task of teaching can be reduced to a simple passing down of knowledge. It is believed that the status and quality of the profession would be greatly enhanced if overall responsibility for ITE were given to a GTC, and local responsibility to specially designated 'training schools'[4]. The case made for this differs from that mounted by ITE's most strident critics, but it too raises fundamental questions about the nature of teaching and so about appropriate preparation for it.

The competence approach to ITE

In the government's recent reform proposals[5], and in the decisions which followed the consultation period[6], the role of CATE is changed from accrediting ITE courses by their content to accrediting them by their outcomes. The professional skills and knowledge which schools can reasonably expect of new teachers is specified so that the quality of individual students, and of the institutions in which they train, can be assessed by how far those targets are achieved.

This approach is becoming prominent in occupational training. Applied to teaching, it has important potential benefits. It challenges any view of *initial* training as sufficient, with accumulating practical experience, for an entire career. By doing so, it could help to remedy the biggest single weakness in the training system. For although there are large differences even between schools in the same authority, new teachers are much more likely to be treated as 'full' members of staff than to be given the help and suitably limited responsibilities which beginners in other professions can reasonably expect. The profiling of strengths and weaknesses at the end of initial training provides a baseline for continuing professional development. In aggregate form, it will make much more visible the range and depth of expertise demanded of teachers; reinforce current efforts to chart teachers' progress from 'novice' to 'competent' to 'expert'; facilitate comparisons between different modes of training; and also enable comparisons to be made with ITE in other countries (especially within the European Community, as mobility of professional labour increases) and with training for other professions. But there are complications to be considered.

ITE raises typically difficult questions about how the knowledge and understanding which 'underpin' effective professional practice are to be acquired and assessed. The difficulty is apparent in the list of 'competences expected of new teachers' included with the DES reform proposals[5]. For example, it is hard to see how 'setting appropriately demanding tasks' or devising 'an appropriate range of teaching strategies' can be separated from a well-informed understanding of how children learn – at different stages in their development, in different curriculum areas, and in different cultural contexts – from which a working definition of what is appropriate should be derived. If that separation is impossible, then good practice cannot simply be observed. An over-specific listing of competences also overemphasises the apparently measurable, overrides differences between subjects and contexts, and is likely to embody a particular model of what constitutes 'good' teaching with which many practitioners may disagree.

The partnership of schools and HEIs in 'school-based' training

There is tension between trainers and practitioners in all professions. Training tends to be attacked as too 'theoretical' and detached from 'reality', and to be defended as a way of promoting innovations and improvements which can then permeate a profession. Attempts to ease that tension often involve insisting that trainers regularly practise their profession, as occurred with the CATE requirement that tutors demonstrate their credibility through having 'recent and relevant' classroom experience. The more radical solution is for practitioners to provide the training.

Early in 1992, mounting political pressure to make ITE more 'practical' brought government proposals that not less than 80% of 36-week secondary PGCE courses should be school-based, that an equivalent requirement would be placed on secondary-oriented undergraduate programmes, and that 'the school and its teachers' should be 'in the lead in the whole of the training process'[5]. Almost all those consulted, schools and HE alike, agreed that the school-based time proposed was excessive and that the role of HE would be unacceptably diminished by it. They also agreed that the proposed pace of implementation was unmanageably fast. The present Secretary of State has slightly altered the timetable, emphasised the 'joint responsibility' of schools and HE, and reduced to (for example) 24 weeks of a 36-week PGCE 'the minimum time students are to spend on the premises of partner schools'[6].

Defined by location, courses are already on average about 50% school-based. However, as recent surveys[1,7] have indicated, that time is not necessarily related either to the quality of training or to the school's role being extended much beyond the traditional provision, supervision, and assessment of practical teaching. It is much more important that schools should be fully involved in the planning and implementing of a coherent training programme and in assessing its outcomes. A more equal and more clearly defined partnership was already being established before the recent government prescriptions, both as a matter of principle and because local management of schools and the pressures on schools to cost their services require the formalising of arrangements previously left to the vagaries of goodwill. The new requirement that schools and HEIs negotiate explicit training contracts extends that process.

As long as HEIs retain responsibility for the final qualification, however, they will have to assess and monitor the suitability of their partnership schools. How those schools are to be selected is among the practical problems which HMI[7] identified as needing to be solved *before* there is 'any general increase in the involvement of schools'. The 'best' schools as judged by pupils' examination results or national curriculum test score may not necessarily be the most suitable for training teachers. In any case it is not easy to generalise when, for example, subject departments within a secondary school might be of variable quality.

There are also practical problems with the selection and training of 'mentor' teachers such as the provision of resources and staff time to support their enhanced role and the protection of schools' prime purpose of teaching pupils against too large a diversion of effort. It would be difficult to apply the current reforms to primary education when many primary schools are too small to provide a broad training base, and when the extent of students' new learning (for example, of child development and of the demands of national curriculum subjects far removed from those in which they have specialised) points more clearly to a concentration of training than to its dispersal.

The critical question about the new pattern of training is about which components gain credibility and relevance from being focused on the circumstances and children of particular schools, and which gain from a wider frame of reference. The government's initial proposals[5] were much clearer about wanting to increase trainees' classroom experience than about what might be progressively learned from it. While the gross error of assigning 'theory' to HEI and 'practice' to schools was avoided, they were still treated as separate activities. This is to misunderstand the nature of theory in professional practice, as was noted in the earlier discussion of teacher competences.

Much of the competence which teachers develop comes from the accumulation of experience, from knowing that certain things work without necessarily being able to offer an explicit justification for doing things that way. There are also routines and rituals, at the 'technician' end of practice, which can be learned from observing experienced practitioners. But important as this 'craft knowledge' is, especially for new teachers, because so much of it relates directly to classroom management it is incomplete.

The wide scope of professional knowledge certainly includes the 'knowledge and love of subject' which some advocates of entirely school-based training have regarded as sufficient. But even for secondary teachers whose degrees appear to be directly relevant to the national curriculum, there is much work to be done before the subject as learned becomes the subject to be taught. This is a matter both of understanding its structure and particular contributions to a balanced curriculum and of considerable new content.

These are challenges for all teachers, though they are more obvious in certain cases: physicists teaching school science; engineering graduates teaching mathematics or technology; literature graduates teaching English or a foreign language to national curriculum targets relating to linguistic knowledge and skill; and the polymathic teachers needed by primary schools. This is why both subject knowledge and its application are at the centre of ITE. Complementing them should be an introduction to the heavy pastoral demands made even on new teachers; to the organisational, cultural and political contexts in which they will work; and to competing ideas about the nature of 'education' and what it is to be 'educated'. Such things will help them to determine the kind of teachers they wish to be.

Even *initial* teacher education needs this scope. HEI's distinctive contribution comes from making reference to and drawing on evidence from a wider range of contexts, curriculum developments and teaching strategies than any one school can provide. It also comes from making the theories and the assumptions about children's learning embedded in classroom practice more explicit than they are for many experienced teachers, and so more open to reflection and investigation. The encouragement in new teachers of a questioning, self-critical approach to their own practice should be reinforced by some experience during their training of the research and the curriculum development work in which HEI staff should be actively involved. Of course the practical problems which teachers face are too varied, unpredictable and complicated to be solved simply by the direct application of 'expert' knowledge to particular cases. Within the now dominant rhetoric of the 'reflective practitioner'[1] is the notion of teachers resolving dilemmas and choosing between alternative strategies. They do this by exercising professional judgement informed both by familiarity with the particular circumstances in which they work and by conscious reference to that more general understanding of the complex processes of teaching and learning which the study of pedagogy should provide.

Among the strongest arguments for substantial HE involvement in teacher education are the independence of universities and colleges, and their commitment to inquiry and the scrutiny of 'established' practices and ideas. Recent educational policy has been driven hard by ideology and a consequent tendency merely to affirm the supposed benefits of, for example, unfettered competition between schools. Increasing government control over the curriculum, including direct ministerial interventions in what should be 'delivered' and how, has been accompanied by an increasing tendency to make partisan appointments in key advisory bodies and to subject to systematic derision arguments and evidence inconvenient to the policies of the day. While it is right that ITE should be rigorously directed to what schools can reasonably expect of new teachers in terms of the knowledge and skill needed to cope with the immediate tasks, it is also important that their training should not be detached from an informed understanding of the contexts in which those tasks are carried out.

November 1992

Acknowledgements

I am grateful for helpful comments on an earlier draft to members of the 'Modes of Teacher Education' research team, and from Professors Geoff Brown, Gerald Grace, Bob Moon, Richard Pring and John Tomlinson.

References

[1] Barrett, E., Barton, L., Furlong, J., Galvin, C., Miles, S. and Whitty, G. (1992) *Initial Teacher Education in England and Wales: a Topography.*

[2] Her Majesty's Inspectorate (1986) *The New Teacher in School,* HMSO and Office for Standards in Education, *The New Teacher in School.* HMSO 1993.

[3] Her Majesty's Inspectorate (1991) *Standards in Education 1989–90: the Annual Report of HM Senior Chief Inspector of Schools.* HMI/DES.

[4] Beardon, T., Booth, H., Hargreaves, D. and Reiss, M. (1992) *School-led Initial Teacher Training.* Cambridge University Department of Education.

[5] DES (1992) *Reform of Initial Teacher Training: a Consultation Document.*

[6] DFE (1992) *Initial Teacher Training: Secondary Phase.* Circular 9/92.

[7] Her Majesty's Inspectorate (1991) *School-based Initial Teacher Training in England and Wales.* HMSO.

[8] Booth, M., Furlong, J. and Wilkin, M. (1990) *Partnership in Initial Teacher Training.* London: Cassell.

10 Standards in Literacy and Numeracy

Derek Foxman
Tom Gorman
Greg Brooks
National Foundation for Educational Research (NFER)

Summary

1 Reading standards among 11 and 15 year olds have changed little since 1945, apart from slight rises around 1950 and in the 1980s. Among 7–8 year olds, however, standards fell slightly in the late 1980s. In writing performance, there was no overall change during the 1980s.

2 Less than one per cent of school-leavers and adults can be described as illiterate. Basic literacy skills are however insufficient to meet the demands of many occupations.

3 British school students are above average in geometry and statistics, but below average in number skills, compared with other industrialised countries. Britain also has a wider spread of mathematics attainment, mainly due to the weaker performance of lower attaining pupils.

4 Nationally, there was a fall in attainment among 11 and 15 year olds in number skills between 1982 and 1987, and a rise in geometry, statistics and measures.

5 Attainment both in literacy and numeracy may need to rise considerably to meet the requirements of the next century.

6 We do not have an effective system of monitoring educational standards throughout the UK. Arguments about standards will continue until such a system is in place. National curriculum assessment is not best suited to monitor national performance: for this purpose, specially-designed, regular surveys are needed, using representative samples of pupils.

7 In addition to national monitoring, we need to compare ourselves with competitor nations, some of which are setting ambitious targets for the 21st century. The debate about standards of attainment must continue, but against a background of sound evidence.

Introduction

Public concern about educational standards is not new: criticism of standards has appeared regularly since the last century and is probably due to tensions between society's changing values and requirements, and the response made by the education service. Skills in literacy and numeracy are prerequisites for full participation in our society; it is not therefore surprising that public controversy about standards often focuses on them. This Briefing asks what we mean by educational standards, and considers how they are measured and monitored. What is happening to standards in literacy and numeracy, and what will be the best way to monitor performance in future?

What are educational standards?

A 'standard' is a fixed measure against which performance is judged. A physical standard, such as a metre length, is objectively defined and is fixed over time, but educational standards in this sense, such as the letters denoting the grades attained in GCSE or the statements of attainment in the national curriculum, are less easily pinned down. Furthermore, the term 'standards' in educational discussion often refers not to particular criteria of performance but to the actual attainment of pupils: i.e. a mean score in a test or the proportion getting a question correct.

Methods of monitoring standards

Monitoring implies attempting to determine changes over

time in attainment. Five types of assessment have provided fuel for the debate on standards:

Public examinations, such as GCSE and A-level, and Scottish Standard Grade and Highers, consist of different questions each year. Nevertheless, the letter grades awarded are intended to be comparable in standard from year to year and between examination boards. But the yardsticks that the grades represent are implicit; they are carried around in examiners' heads, and there are therefore no simple methods of determining whether the grade standards remain constant. Public examinations have other limitations as devices for monitoring standards: they are taken by candidates from more than one age group, and not all of the predominant age group are entered for the examination in any one subject.

National curriculum assessment (which applies to England and Wales) was carried out officially for the first time with 7 year olds in 1991. Assessment of 14 year olds will begin in 1993 and that of 11 year olds in 1994. At these three ages, the assessments will be confined to strictly defined age groups, and all pupils in the age group will be assessed. Also from 1994, the GCSE in various groups of subjects will progressively change to become national curriculum assessment for all 16 year olds except those at national curriculum levels 1–3.

At all four ages, the assessments will consist of teacher assessments and externally set tests. The teacher assessments will vary inherently in content from school to school, and it is likely that the external tests will use different questions each year, although each question has to exemplify one of the statements of attainment which relate to a particular level in a particular subject. Since the statements of attainment are explicit, there would seem to be a lesser problem of comparability from year to year than in the present GCSE. However, as the system develops, points to watch in this regard will be the comparability of different questions supposedly exemplifying the same statements of attainment, methods of deciding when a statement of attainment has been achieved, and ways of aggregating statements achieved to attainment target level.

It is likely to be some years before the suitability of national curriculum assessment for monitoring can be fully evaluated, but it is already clear that only limited aspects of the national curriculum can be assessed in the external tests on each occasion.

There are also national assessment programmes in Scotland and in Northern Ireland, but these are more limited in scope than those in England and Wales.

Standardised tests consist of a fixed set of items relating to a particular area such as reading or mathematics. A test is initially given to a representative sample of the population whose attainment is to be measured. The results provide scores or 'norms' for particular ages of children against which the attainment of individuals can be measured. Attainment can then be monitored by repeating the test on representative samples at intervals. However, views on the nature of the content being tested may change and so the overall format of the test becomes outdated. In English, some items become outdated as language itself changes. Scores could fall as a result of these factors and be falsely interpreted as a fall in standards.

The surveys by the Assessment of Performance Unit (APU) represent the most extensive attempt to measure and to monitor performance nationally before the emergence of national curriculum assessment. The APU[1], a unit at the DES, commissioned surveys in five subjects from independent agencies between 1977 and 1990, but only those in mathematics and (English) language will be mentioned in this Briefing. These were conducted by the NFER

on representative samples of pupils in England, Wales and
Northern Ireland.

The APU surveys were very large-scale, each subject
including written, practical and oral modes of assessment
and assessing a wide range of knowledge, skills and
processes. They gave a much more detailed picture of
performance than had previously been obtained either by
standardised tests or public examinations. A number of different methods were used to monitor change in performance over the period of the surveys: the principal one was
comparing the results of the same questions used in different years. The APU programme was terminated by the
government in 1990 when the national curriculum was
introduced. The parallel programme in Scotland, the
Assessment of Achievement Programme (AAP), began in
1983 and still continues.

International surveys. The rising importance of the global
economy has produced increasing interest in comparative
standards in different countries. International studies conducted over the past thirty years have compared attainment
levels in some subjects in relation to the curricula in various countries and other factors in their schools and the
home backgrounds of their pupils. There are obvious problems in attempting these comparisons: the test questions
are likely to suit some countries more than others, transla-
tion can affect the levels of difficulty posed by specific
questions, and comparable samples of pupils are difficult if
not impossible to achieve because of the different features
of education in the participating countries. The studies are
also intermittent and the same countries do not always take
part, so that monitoring changes in comparative differences
is not easy. Despite these drawbacks there have been some
very interesting results, especially in mathematics, as
described below in section 5.

Trends in performance. In the following analysis of trends in literacy and numeracy, national curriculum assessment and public examination statistics will not be used as evidence for trends: the former because no data over time were available at the time of writing, even for 7 year olds, and the latter because although public examination statistics suggest a long-term rise in success rates, there are difficulties in interpretation.

Trends in literacy

International studies of performance in literacy which included Britain have taken place (reading comprehension in 1967, written composition in 1983), but few conclusions can be drawn from these surveys about our performance relative to other countries. Consequently, this section focuses on data from national surveys and standardised tests.

Literacy at age 7/8

For pupils in Year 3, national data are available only for England. They are available only for reading, and only for the years 1987 and 1991. In 1987, the NFER standardised a new series of reading tests, one of which was intended for pupils in Year 3. In 1991, the standardisation exercise of this test was repeated. The main finding was that average reading scores of pupils in Year 3 fell by $2^{1}/_{2}$ standardised points between 1987 and 1991[2]. This result corroborated on a national scale more localised findings, which showed a fall in particular LEAs of about one standardised score point in the average reading attainment of 7 year olds (Year 2) between 1985 and 1988, and again between 1988 and 1990.

Literacy at ages 11 and 15

For 11 and 15 year olds, national data on *reading* performance are available from several surveys using standardised pre-APU tests between 1948 and 1979, mostly conducted by NFER. APU surveys of the *reading and writing* performance of 11 and 15 year olds were conducted annually from 1979 to 1983 and again in 1988.

There was an apparent abrupt decline in average reading scores in the 1970/71 surveys, following apparently steady rises since 1948. This caused great concern about 'illiteracy' among pupils. But the decline was perceived only by overlooking the fact that most of the differences between the mean scores reported were statistically non-significant. When normal statistical criteria are applied, the proper conclusion appears to be that the aspects of reading of pupils in Year 6 and Year 11 measured by the tests then in use rose slightly between 1948 and 1952, then remained essentially unchanged until 1979.

The APU tests from 1979 were repeated in 1983, as were tests from 1983 in 1988[3]. The findings are summarised in the Table below.

		Year 6	Year 11
Reading	1973-83	Slight rise	Slight rise
	1983-88	Slight rise	No overall change
Writing	1979-83	Slight rise	No overall change
	1983-88	Slight fall	No overall change

Some findings for spelling were obtained in 1991/92 from samples of APU writing tasks undertaken by Year 6 pupils in 1979 and 1988, and by Year 11 pupils in 1980 and 1983. For the tasks examined (not a comprehensive set) an improvement in the performance of Year 6 pupils occurred and the performance of those in Year 11 remained the same. For all aspects of literacy the absolute size of the changes was small: the size of the APU samples ensured that even fairly small changes were statistically significant.

In Scotland the AAP[4] has conducted three surveys in 1984, 1989 and 1992. The results for 1992 are not yet available, but there was no change in the reading scores of Year 4 and Year 7 pupils from 1984 to 1989 and a small rise for Year 9 pupils. The same pattern was obtained for writing scores.

Literacy of adults

There have been two national performance surveys of the literacy attainments of young adults in Britain, in 1972 and 1992. The results of the 1992 survey, organised by City University, London, on behalf of the Basic Skills Unit (ALBSU), were not yet published at the time of writing. Since the tests used on this occasion were different from those used in 1972, they will provide no basis for an estimate of change over the intervening 20 years.

The 1972 survey used a version of the Watts-Vernon reading test. It was carried out as part of the continuing National Survey of Health and Development, the 1946 British birth cohort study which covered England, Wales and Scotland: the people involved were thus aged 26 at the time of the 1972 survey. This cohort had also taken the same reading test in 1961 when they were aged 15. The results[5] showed a general increase in reading scores, and an illiteracy rate 'as low as one per cent'.

Illiteracy

The best available information from the APU surveys indicates that less than one per cent of those leaving school (excluding pupils from special schools) are unable to read in the sense of being unable to answer correctly simple comprehension questions about a passage. This accords well with the adult illiteracy rate just mentioned. The APU surveys also indicate that up to three per cent of school leavers would be unable or unwilling to communicate in writing in the sense of being unable to compose a short paragraph that is intelligible on first reading.

Given these figures, it may be wondered where media reports of large numbers, usually millions, of illiterate adults in the population come from. Most such estimates between the 1950s and 1980s were based on extrapolation from the number of 15 year olds found to have a reading level at or below that of the average 7 year old or 11 year old. More recently, estimates of adult illiteracy have been based on self-report data from young adults on problems with reading and writing since leaving school. Neither form of extrapolation estimates basic literacy in the sense given in the previous paragraph.

Basic literacy is not, however, adequate for responsible involvement in the social, economic and political life of the present day, nor to meet the specialised demands of many occupations. Research in the United States has consistently found that the relationship between 'job literacy' and school-based attainment is poor. There are two main reasons for this. The first is that people with literacy difficulties usually find methods of coping with their difficulties, with assistance. Secondly, specific jobs require job-specific literacy or numeracy skills, some of which can be developed on task. Teachers cannot be expected to prepare students for specialised literacy and numeracy requirements of particular occupations. However, there is a need for literacy teaching in schools to include a higher proportion of non-literary texts, for example those addressing science topics and social studies issues.

Trends in numeracy

'Numeracy' is the term invented to parallel 'literacy' and, like it, has been interpreted in various ways. One narrow way is to assume that it relates only to the ability to perform basic arithmetical operations. Here we shall take the broader approach, meaning not only an 'at homeness' with numbers, but also the ability to make use of mathematical skills which enable individuals to cope with the practical demands of everyday life. These skills must include some knowledge of spatial representation and data handling, as well as computational ability. In school, such skills may be used to a greater or lesser extent in a number of subjects in the curriculum. Given this broad definition of numeracy it is reasonable to consider the evidence on standards in Britain from APU national surveys of mathematics, supported by data from international studies.

National surveys of mathematics

APU surveys of the mathematics performance of 11 and 15 year olds took place annually from 1978 to 1982, and again in 1987. Between 1978 and 1982, performance on items common to the two occasions resulted in a small overall increase of 1.5 percentage points at both age levels. In the interval between the surveys of 1982 and 1987 there was a very general pattern of performance changes at both 11 and 15 years, with improvements in the APU categories of geometry, probability and statistics, and measures, and a decline in number and in algebra (there were some variations in the detail of this general pattern)[6]. These changes were thought to have been influenced by changes in curriculum emphases since the publication of the Cockcroft Report[7] on mathematics education in 1982. Cockcroft, however, did not sanction a decline in number skills, but placed more emphasis on mental computation, estimation, and appropriate use of different methods of calculation than had been apparent in the curriculum.

In Scotland the AAP conducted surveys of the mathematics performance of years 4, 7 and 9 (secondary 2) in 1983, 1988 and 1991. There was a significant decline in all three year groups between 1983 and 1988[4], but it differed in extent and in different areas of mathematics between age groups. There was no further change in 1991.

International surveys of mathematics

The International Association for the Evaluation of Educational Achievement (IEA) undertook surveys of 13 and 18 year olds in 1964 and 1981. Another organisation, the International Assessment of Educational Progress, carried out two later studies in 1988 and 1991 (IAEP 1 and IAEP 2). England (or England and Wales) has participated in all four of these international surveys. Scotland has usually been represented as a separate system, but was part of the 'UK' sample in IAEP 1.

The results have demonstrated two main features of England's (or England and Wales's) comparative performance (Scotland's pattern of performance is fairly similar to England's):

- A profile of performance across topics among 13 year olds which shows England to be below average in number and above average in geometry and statistics. This profile is consistent with the changes found by APU for 11 and 15 year olds during the 1980s.

- Our top-ability students at 17+ are among the highest scores in mathematics, while our below-average younger students do less well than those in many other developed countries.

The results for 13 year olds are discussed first, since this age group is regarded as the basic one in international studies and so has been most frequently surveyed.

Mathematics at age 13
In the two IEA surveys, separated by an interval of 17 years, over 30 questions were common to both occasions in the tests for this age group. Comparison of the results reveals a general decline among the 10 educational systems participating on both occasions in all but one of the categories tested: number, measurement, geometry, statistics and algebra. The exception was algebra, in which all countries except England and Wales improved their success rates. The relative position of England and Wales

slipped in all categories between 1964 and 1981[8].

Many changes occurred between 1964 and 1981 in the organisation of education in Britain and in the content and breadth of the curriculum, which could account for a general decline in respect of the questions common to the two occasions. Nevertheless, few of these seemed inappropriate for pupils in the later study.

In the international studies carried out since 1981, the same or similar cross-topic mathematics profile has been evident. For example, comparing the surveys carried out in 1981 and 1991 (IAEP 2[9]) England's position relative to the five other countries participating in both years remains the same: first in statistics/data handling and sixth in arithmetic/number and operations. Apart from the data handling area, Hungary and France were the highest scoring countries of the six in both years.

Mathematics at age 9
The 1991 IAEP 2 survey included 9 year olds – the first international study of that age group – and the results indicate that the same cross-topic profile is evident at this age as at 13 years. The participation rate of schools was low in IAEP 2, indicating the possibility of some bias in the results. If they are valid, we should question when the lower emphasis on number begins, especially as the survey teachers' perceptions of their emphasis on calculation conflicted with the results obtained.

Mathematics at age 17+
One of the older populations surveyed in the two IEA studies consisted of students in the Upper Sixth who were studying mathematics as a substantial part of their academic programme. Our students (who were about to take A-levels) came third or fourth out of 15 countries in 1981, in each of the three topics in the test. Japan and Hong Kong were the leading nations. Eight countries participated at

this level in both 1964 and 1981, and the rank of England and Wales was just slightly worse in 1981 than in 1964.

Innumeracy
Culturally it has always been more acceptable to be innumerate than illiterate. There are no definitions of 'innumeracy' as such, but APU and other mathematics surveys have shown that there is a very wide range of performance by age 11, and that the bottom 20 per cent of 15 year olds still have a very limited grasp of even the most basic mathematical ideas. Mathematics in some form has been reaching more areas of daily life and more individuals at home and at work in recent decades and is now regarded as a subject for all to learn in school, although what aspects and in what depth remain matters for argument.

How can future changes be monitored effectively?

There are two main reasons why there has been so much controversy recently about whether or not standards are changing: irregular monitoring and the use of unsuitable monitoring instruments. At present, no effective monitoring of educational standards is occurring in England, Wales and Northern Ireland.

To be effective, monitoring needs to:
- provide an accurate picture of performance;
- give early notice of rises or falls in curriculum areas;
- detect whether changes are 'blips' or becoming trends;
- be sufficiently wide-ranging in each curriculum area to detect whether performance in different aspects of a subject is changing in different directions, at different rates;
- be able to detect, for each age group monitored, whether changes are taking place in a particular attainment band, or operating throughout the range of attainment.

In order to achieve these aims, monitoring must be reliable, and should include nationally representative samples of pupils, tackling appropriate tasks repeated at regular intervals. Unlike national curriculum assessment, monitoring does not require data from every child in the age groups concerned, only from a small sample, and each pupil involved would take only a fraction of the total assessments in a survey. The total picture would be obtained by aggregating across the sample. For this purpose, it is essential that externally set tests and not teacher assessments be used, since standardisation of conditions for all pupils taking the tests is a basic requirement for the reliability of the results. In this fashion, monitoring surveys on the one hand, and national curriculum assessment on the other, could complement each other: the latter by providing detailed information on individual pupils, and the former an in-depth picture of the knowledge and skills of the nation's children. A future effective monitoring system could be designed not only to detect trends over time in overall attainment in various curriculum areas, but also to help check that the levels of national curriculum assessment (including the new-style GCSE) are being held consistent across years – this could be done by targeting some monitoring tests at particular parts of the national curriculum.

There needs to be a continuing debate on the standards of attainment we should aim for as we move towards the 21st century. Some countries are setting ambitious targets. For instance, in the USA the National Governors' Association has adopted the following goal: 'By the year 2000, every adult American will be literate and will possess the skills necessary to compete in a global economy and exercise the rights and responsibilities of citizenship'.

In these circumstances it may not be sufficient to say that standards are not falling, or are rising slowly; it may be necessary in certain areas to progress more quickly as requirements become clearer. However, this debate must take place against a background of assured knowledge not only about how our competitors are developing their pupils' educational achievements, but also, and more importantly, about how our school pupils are performing nationally. Such knowledge can only come from a system of regular and effective monitoring.

December 1992

References

1   Foxman, D., Hutchison, D. and Bloomfield, B. (1990) *The APU Experience*. SEAC. (Lists all works published under the aegis of APU.)

2   Gorman, T.P. and Fernandes, C. (1992) *Reading in Recession*. NFER.

3   Gorman, T.P., White, J., Brooks, G. and English, F. (1991) *Language for Learning: a summary report on the 1988 APU surveys of language performance*. SEAC.

4   Scottish Education Department. *Assessment of Achievement Programme. Reports on Mathematics* (1989) *and English Language* (1990). HMSO.

5   Rodgers, B. (1986) *Change in the reading attainment of adults: a longitudinal study*. British Journal of Developmental Psychology, 4, 1–17.

6   Foxman, D., Ruddock, G. and McCallum, I. (1990) *APU Mathematics Monitoring 1984/88 (Phase 2)*. SEAC (see pages 6 and 7).

7   Department of Education and Science (1982) *Mathematics Counts (Cockcroft Report)*. HMSO.

8   Robitaille, D.F. and Garden, R.A. (1989) *The IEA Study of Mathematics II: contexts and outcomes of school mathematics*. Pergamon.

9   Foxman, D. (1992) *Learning Mathematics and Science: The Second International Assessment of Educational Progress in England*. NFER.

11 A General Teaching Council for England and Wales?

Stuart Maclure
Editor of The Times Educational Supplement
1969-1989

Summary

1 The latest proposals for a General Teaching Council (GTC) for England and Wales, backed by some 30 educational organisations including all the main teachers' unions, have once again put questions of the professional self-regulation of teachers on the agenda.

2 The powers and duties of a GTC would be set out in a Parliamentary Bill and would include establishing a Register of Teachers, laying down the conditions for compulsory registration and periodical re-registration, and administering disciplinary procedures. It would also become an important source of advice to the DFE on a wide range of policy matters relating to teacher supply and training, including in-service training and other forms of professional development.

3 A Scottish GTC was set up in 1966. It maintains a Register and regulates admissions to and exclusion from the teaching profession in Scotland and has a more limited range of advisory functions. It has become generally accepted as the authentic voice of the profession and guardian of its standards. Some real power has accrued to it within the fairly narrow limits of its legal remit but critics suggest it has been more successful as a regulator than as an adviser.

4 How would the range of functions suggested for a GTC for England and Wales relate to functions now performed by the DFE? Ministers south of the border regard the making of policy on the training of teachers and curricular issues as part of their strategic role and a Minister allowing the establishment of a GTC would be

151

creating a potential rod for his or her back.

5   It would make sense to create an independent GTC as a statutory body only if the Secretary of State were prepared to relinquish some of his or her current authority over teacher training and the curriculum. There are very real arguments for diminishing the powers of Ministers and creating more checks and balances. But these would have to be weighed against the conflict which would be thereby built into the system.

6   The case for a GTC is based on a long-term view of how the teaching profession should develop and it should not be assumed that all the functions outlined in the proposal would necessarily be introduced at once. By elevating the professional ideal, a GTC would increase the status of teaching, but only if it had some real powers. However, even with an initially limited role, a GTC might help to raise the morale of teachers and restore their standing more generally in society.

Introduction

One of the marks of a professional group in Britain is self-regulation under statute. Teachers do not have such a statutory body. Would the public benefit if they did?

For more than a century this question has been asked with more or less insistence (it was asked in the first issue of *The Times Educational Supplement* in 1910). Attempts at voluntary self-regulation have run into the sand.

The Scots achieved a General Teaching Council for Scotland in 1966 in the aftermath of a period of turbulence in industrial relations. South of the border, in the post-war period, there seemed to be little interest in such a body. There was a conflict between the idea of a General Teaching Council (GTC) and how the teachers' unions and professional associations saw their role and these differences enabled successive governments to side-step the policy issues which a strong GTC raised for them.

However, in the wake of the Scottish initiative, the Secretary of State for Education, Mr Edward Short (now Lord Glenamara), took up the idea partly influenced by the fact that in England and Wales, too, relations between the teachers and the government were at a low ebb. Short set up a working party, chaired by a senior DES official, to explore the idea with the teachers' organisations, the local authorities, the teacher-educators and others. The Weaver Report (1970) sought to bridge the gap between the unions and the Department by proposing two Councils, not one. The compromise failed to win the support of the teachers' unions and the government was happy to let the matter drop. There is the suggestion in some quarters that this was a 'near miss' for the GTC idea. In fact, there was never much enthusiasm for the idea in the DES and many of those taking part had a sense that they were going through the motions.

The Scottish General Teaching Council (SGTC)

Under the Teaching Council (Scotland) Act, 1965, the principal duties of the Scottish GTC are to:

- establish and maintain a register of all qualified teachers;
- oversee standards of entry to the profession;
- exercise disciplinary powers in relation to registration;
- advise on the supply of teachers;
- advise on the training and qualifications of teachers.

The SGTC accredits courses of teacher training, which need to carry the 'acceptable to the General Teaching Council' seal of approval, and then carries out a five-yearly review of courses once approved. The Council has 49 members in three categories – elected, appointed and nominated. There are 30 elected members all of whom must be registered full-time teachers – 11 from primary schools, 11 from secondary schools, 5 from Colleges of Education and three from further education. Elections take place every four years, all registered teachers having a direct vote. The 15 appointed members are drawn from the Scottish universities, from what has till now been the non-university sector of higher education, from the Association of Directors of Education in Scotland, from the employing authorities and from the Churches.

The four members nominated by the Secretary of State for Scotland are usually representatives of parents' organisations, industrialists, and other professional groups such as lawyers or accountants.

Strengths and weaknesses of the SGTC

After the initial excitement wore off, direct elections for the places reserved for registered teachers have generally produced low polls. Moreover, the Council has been seen by some as a place where unions and employers play out their own disputes, often combining against the Scottish Education Department. Against this caricature, defenders of the Council claim that for most of the time partisan interests are subordinated to the continuing business of the Council and that the Council works well, within its limits. The Educational Institute for Scotland, the largest Scottish teachers' union, usually takes a close interest in the elections for the teacher members. This suggests that the Institute regards it as important and would become actively concerned if it embraced policies which the Institute opposed.

However, senior officials of the Council strongly resist the idea that it is or has been a pawn of the unions. They claim that when the members of the Council put on their GTC hats they cease to act as representatives of any particular faction. If this sounds a bit too good to be true, it has to be remembered that much of the work of the Council is not contentious and most of its policies are developed over time by consensus. It is also suggested that the Council has had limited success in its broader aims of raising standards – that its real, but rather narrow, executive functions have taken up most of its energy and it has not been able to get to grips with its advisory role. There is clearly some substance in this.

But in considering what other tasks the Council might have essayed it is important to be realistic. In purely practical terms its powers are limited by the statute and it could have been given wider powers such as specific roles in the selection of candidates for teaching, or in the organisation of in-service training. But this is not how the Scottish Education Department has wanted the Council to develop

– it has suited the Department that the Council should concentrate on a narrower range of activities which trench less threateningly on government policy.

Whether the Council would have achieved more with a more extensive remit is a matter of judgement. Some would see the experience of the Council as support for the view that for such a body to flourish as an adviser there has to be encouragement from the government department which is to be advised, and some sense of expectation that the advice is likely to be acted upon. What is evident, however, is that the Scottish GTC has achieved one of the primary aims of a professional body – it has been accepted within Scotland and beyond as an authentic voice of the Scottish teaching profession and guardian of its standards – standards narrowly defined, maybe, but defined nevertheless. Some real power has accrued to the Council. The arbitrary power of the Secretary of State is curbed. He has to have regard to the Council and its decisions in making policy. He could not, for example, have introduced a 'licensed teacher' scheme on the English model even if he had wished to do so because the Scottish GTC would not have let him.

Recent proposals for a GTC for England and Wales

There were renewed efforts to establish a GTC in 1983 under the leadership of the Universities Council on the Education of Teachers together with a coalition of supporting organisations. In due time this led to the formation of a company limited by guarantee calling itself 'The GTC (England and Wales)' which in September 1992 produced a report with recommendations and a Draft Parliamentary Bill which it submitted to both the Secretary of State for Education and the National Commission on Education. What makes this the most significant GTC attempt so far is the broad base of support which it commands among teachers' organisations and the fact that it is put forward in sufficient detail to make serious discussion possible.

The Report sets out two major concerns:
- 'To safeguard the public as learners and clients in general and young people required to attend school in particular';
- To enable teachers 'to exercise a large measure of responsibility for the standards and quality of the professional service for the public'.

(a) Regulation and control
The Report argues that a government department should not decide on professional competence or personal fitness to teach without professional supervision. This applies to both handing out qualified teacher status and professional conduct. 'There is no explicit understanding of the professional conduct expected of teachers and no fully representative body which could develop such an understanding...' The recognition of non-UK qualifications provides another potential task for a GTC.

Maintaining a Register The draft Bill sets up a General Teaching Council 'which shall have in relation to England and Wales the general functions of developing, promoting and regulating the profession of teaching in the interests of the public, and the other functions assigned to it under this Act'. The Council would set up and maintain a Register of Teachers.

Admission to the Register The report states that 'the Council will decide what standards of education and training and what levels of competence and conduct should be required of new entrants to the profession...'

Disciplinary powers The GTC would have responsibility for professional discipline and standards of conduct. To be a professional teacher it would be necessary to be registered with the GTC.

The Council must have teeth. The threat of striking some-one off the register is only significant if being registered is a professional requirement. This is the same link between professional practice and registration which gives other professional regulatory bodies – including the Scottish General Teaching Council – their authority.

(b) Standards and quality
The report sets out a list of advisory functions which should be entrusted to the GTC.

Training and professional development
The Council should advise the Secretary of State on teacher training and continuing professional development. There used to be a formally constituted Advisory Council – the Advisory Council on the Supply and Training of Teachers, and its successor body – which had a recognised role as the body through which professional advice was channelled to the Education Secretary. The report states: 'It is ... unsatisfactory that a government department should make decisions on questions about the training and profes-sional development of teachers without having the advice of a competent body representing all aspects of these ques-tions...' The report foresees the need to think further about the training and professional development of teachers in further and higher education and in the pre-school area.

Accreditation of courses
The Report also argues that a GTC should have a major role in setting the criteria for the accreditation of courses of ini-tial teacher training. It notes that the remit of the Council for the Accreditation of Teachers is up for review. Its work might be brought 'within the general framework of a statuto-ry professional council...'

Induction and in-service training
'A General Teaching Council should have the responsibility of promoting and disseminating good practice in induction

in all parts of the education service, and could play a positive role in keeping under review and improving the quality of the professional development aspects of appraisal... The time is right for the General Teaching Council to assume both the advisory responsibilities left unattended since the decision not to reconvene ACSET, which by now would include an advisory contribution to the establishment of national priorities, and also the wider functions of developing criteria, promoting good practice and recommending developments which would lead to greater consistency of opportunity and expectation in whatever part of the education service a teacher happens to be employed.'

Teacher supply
In the view of the authors of the report, 'it is in the interests of any government in power and in the interests of the public that decisions about teacher supply and intake to courses of initial training should be informed by the considered and corporate advice of all parts of the education service, with the employers, those who provide schools and training institutions. The General Teaching Council should have that advisory function.'

(c) Support for proposals
When the Scottish GTC was first set up, the requirement to register gave rise to hostility among a small minority of teachers in maintained schools who objected to being forced to register (and pay an annual registration fee) as a condition of employment. The controversy over the handful of irreconcilables dominated the headlines in the first phase of the SGTC's existence but soon passed.

The authors of the latest English proposals claim that English teachers would give overwhelming support to a registration scheme. They quote some opinion surveys which support this view. They want students on education courses to be registered by the GTC and have their registration fees paid for them along with their college fees.

When the requirement to pay a registration fee comes into force for the main body of the teaching profession, the government should formally notify the School Teachers Review Body in the hope (presumably) that it might wish to increase teachers' pay to take account of the fees.

By way of political support for the proposals, they point to the recommendations of the 1990 Report of the House of Commons Select Committee on Education ('The Supply of Teachers for the 1990s'). Proposals for a GTC were also to be found in the manifestos of both the Labour and the Liberal Democrat parties at the 1992 general election.

In discussing these proposals, it is important to bear in mind that they might be brought into operation in stages and not all at once.

(d) Setting up a Council
Constitution
The proposals envisage a Council with not more than 70 members on which registered teachers form a majority. Most decisions should be taken by a simple majority, with a two-thirds majority required 'when a variation or extension of the function of the Council itself is being proposed within the framework laid down by Statute'.

- It is suggested that there should be three main groups in the Council:

i. elected registered teachers;
ii. representatives of employers of teachers and providers of schools (including the DFE), colleges and institutions providing training for teachers;
iii. persons nominated by bodies representing 'the public constituency of the education service' such as parents, governors, industry and commerce, and the trade unions.

Council members should serve for five-year periods. The

report is not definitive about the method of choosing the registered teacher members. 'We believe it would be helpful to ensure that professional associations continue to be represented. Equally, if it is considered important to have an element of direct election, with a potential electorate of nearly one million teachers we believe this should be conducted through regions... A registered teacher would have one vote, to be cast either through his or her professional association or by direct franchise in the region.'

First phase
For the first three years, funded by a government grant of £5 million a year, there would be an interim body on which the teacher representation would be 'drawn largely from professional associations while arrangements are made to register teachers'.

Fees
The report provides for a fee on registration and for periodical re-registration. After the initial period, the Council should be wholly supported by fees.

Powers and penalties
In addition to the power to strike a delinquent off the register, the Council should be able to admonish, make conditions for continuing registration, or suspend. It could make public its decisions. Appeal would be to the Judicial Committee of the Privy Council.

Committees
It would work through two main committees: an investigating committee and a professional conduct committee.

Important considerations in establishing a GTC

(a) Relationship with the Department for Education
For the past four decades, successive Education Ministers

have assumed that oversight of the supply and training of teachers was one of their principal duties under the 1944 Education Act. More recently, they have come to regard their power to decide what qualifications should be demanded of teachers – what would-be teachers should study and how they should be trained – as essential to government plans for raising the quality of the education which children receive in school.

The creation of a GTC with teeth would compromise this power. If it were within the Council's powers to determine what qualifications are required for admission to the Register or for periodical re-registration, there would be political repercussions if the policy of the Council were at variance with that of the Education Secretary. The Council might, for example, seek to raise the initial qualification threshold or to lay down new requirements for in-service training as a condition of re-registration. Such decisions would have immediate consequences for the staffing of schools and for the education budget and could not be a matter of indifference to the government.

Without a GTC, Education Secretaries have a free hand on the content of teacher training courses and how teacher training is to be organised. Having just discovered the extent of their powers, Ministers would certainly jib at handing power to an educational establishment which they blame for present shortcomings.

Practical politics, then, suggests a reluctance on the part of government to share ministerial power on teacher training. But this is not in itself an argument against a GTC. There are two opposing views about where the public interest lies.

One putative virtue of a GTC would be that it could stop misguided Ministers in their tracks. If the way to raise the quality of teachers in the long run is to recognise their professional autonomy, a GTC is a necessary prerequisite for progress. Proponents of a GTC would certainly argue that Ministers have not used their powers so well in the past that they should be allowed to hang on to them without question. Moreover, the Scottish experience must be relevant here: the SGTC has achieved this power and the skies have not fallen. But as is often the case, things may be different in Scotland because the scale of operations is smaller and cultural differences lead to a wider consensus about the role and status of teachers.

The case against is pragmatic about the realities of government and sceptical of the claims made for professional independence. How realistic is it in the present political circumstances to expect a government, Labour or Conservative, to concede real power over admission to the profession? It is by no means obvious that education would benefit if arrangements were set up which simply institutionalised conflict in an area of policy-making which all governments regard as essential to their education plans. This is not to say that a GTC might not perform a valuable self-regulatory function in regard to professional discipline to which other functions might be added in time.

What is clear is that, like the General Medical Council, a GTC would have to be completely independent of the government of the day, answerable to the Privy Council and not to any government department. Such independence is an essential prerequisite for a professional self-regulating body. Even in the initial period it would be better if the funding needed to set up the Council did not come from government funds.

(b) Advisory functions for a GTC

The proponents of a GTC recognised that political reality restricts what they can prudently ask for in the short term. Their proposals accept that on many matters the Council could only have an *advisory* role and that the Education

Secretary would wish to retain his present statutory powers. If this is conceded it undoubtedly limits the extent to
which the profession could achieve real self-regulation.
Control over admission to the craft, mystery, fellowship,
profession, is by tradition basic to professional community
and solidarity. It is also a cornerstone of professional
power. But the fact is that there would have to be a sea-
change in the attitudes and practices of the DFE before the
GTC could expect to be welcomed even in the advisory
role set out in the draft Bill.

Reference has been made to the various national advisory
councils in the past which advised on teacher supply and
training. It is a matter of fact that these came into conflict
with successive Secretaries of State and were disbanded.
The same fate overtook the two Central Advisory Councils
set up in the 1944 Education Act to advise on all aspects of
education in England and Wales. Ministers ceased to consult them or even appoint members to them after the
Plowden Report of 1967 and the Gittins report of 1968.
They were finally given their quietus in the Education
Reform Act of 1988.

Again, it may be argued that Ministers' reluctance to be
saddled with statutory advisers only underlines the need
for such independent advice – and that if this embarrasses
Ministers, then they deserve to be embarrassed. But there
are also powerful counter-arguments. It is hard enough to
change educational practices without building in obstacles.
A GTC would entrench the present professional establishment and fortify their power base. It would create a potentially formidable focus of opposition to government policy.
And if, as might seem likely, the GTC offered the teachers'
unions a new lease of professional life, there would be
wider consequences still.

Others would go further and argue as a matter of principle
that a regulatory body should not be involved in offering

advice directly to government on such matters as the supply of teachers, doctors or dentists. These questions, and the politics which attend them, would be for the professional organisations to address.

(c) The composition of the Council

On the face of it, it would seem that, for any GTC proposals to stand any chance of success, there would have to be direct elections for the teacher members, as there are in Scotland. Of course, the teachers' unions and associations would have to be allowed to put forward their slates of candidates for election and would certainly do so. The GTC proposals leave the door open for some more direct participation of the unions. This might be used to ensure all sections of the profession were represented, but might arouse its own hostility.

The GTC proposals understate the importance of a strong minority of lay members on the Council – members chosen by the Secretary of State to represent the public interest. Once appointed it would be essential that all members of the Council, lay and professional, should be – and be seen to be – responsible individuals, and not delegates of any organisation or pressure group.

It is one thing to believe that, in many of the executive functions of the Council, the members of the Council will act responsibly and set their union affiliations to one side. No single group of teachers would form in a majority in the Council. But it is quite another to be confident that, if called on to consider wider issues about teacher supply and training, they will rise above the sectional interests which diminished the value of the advice offered by previous advisory bodies on teacher supply and training. Teacher-trainers have their logs to roll no less than other groups of teachers.

(d) Political change

It could be argued that some of the difficulties which contemporary Ministers would have with a powerful GTC are only temporary. It is certainly right to take a long-term view about the virtues of a GTC. But the desire to have a strong central control in English and Welsh education goes back several decades and extends to both the major political parties. It is now embedded deeply in the DFE. Power over teacher training and supply is not an element in the exercise of this central control which any political party will readily relinquish.

Conclusion

The great mistake would be to take an exaggerated view of what a General Teaching Council could achieve in the circumstances which prevail in England and Wales. But because it could not do everything, it does not mean it could do nothing. There could still be an important if limited role for such a body, starting with responsibility for professional discipline. But no-one should expect it to become a powerful and innovative body; nor can it, by itself, provide an elixir to revive teacher morale. This said, it should again be emphasised that a GTC's aims are long-term. It might be that with a more limited brief and modest expectations, a start could be made. Such a body could help to sustain the professional status of teaching. It would provide an alternative professional focus in the public mind to that offered by the teachers' unions. By elevating the professional ideal, it might in due course influence the character of the unions and professional associations themselves.

January 1993

12 The Issue of Class Size

Peter Mortimore
Peter Blatchford
Institute of Education, University of London

Summary

1 There is a widespread belief amongst parents, teachers and others that pupils learn most effectively in small classes. This is reflected by the fact that one of the main reasons cited for choosing independent schools is their smaller classes.

2 Class sizes are much higher in primary schools than in secondary schools, despite younger children being more dependent than older pupils on adult help. The way that schools are resourced, which leads to this situation, needs to be questioned.

3 International data show that pupil-teacher ratios in the United Kingdom at the primary level compare unfavourably with almost every other industrialised country but are fairly near the average at the secondary level.

4 Research evidence on the benefits of smaller classes is not entirely clear-cut, but from recent work in the US it appears that pupils educated in smaller classes during the first four years of schooling out-perform pupils in larger classes and maintain their academic advantage and demonstrate increased participation two years later. Children from disadvantaged backgrounds benefit most from smaller classes.

5 To determine the best use of teachers' time and the size of teaching groups in secondary schools, it is suggested that the principle of *fitness for purpose* should be applied.

6 The benefits of a reduction in class size would be maximised by a review of teaching methods.

7 A British research study on the long-term effects of different sizes of class on the attitudes, achievement and behaviour of pupils is long overdue.

Introduction

The issue of class size is not simple: parents believe smaller classes are beneficial and usually cite small classes as one of their main reasons for choosing independent schools[14]. Teachers – not surprisingly – also favour small classes. Yet the published research evidence, according to the Director of the National Foundation for Educational Research, '... has been conflicting, inconclusive and disappointingly meagre'[3]. This Briefing explores this conundrum by examining variations in class size and in pupil:teacher ratios (PTRs) found within the UK and abroad, and by reviewing the experimental evidence drawn mostly from American studies about the effects of different sized classes on pupils' attainment.

Available statistics

It is not easy to obtain an accurate picture of class size. This is partly because a range of different measures is used – collecting data in different ways at different times – and also because both schools, and the classes in which pupils are taught, are subject to frequent change. Transfers of pupils between teaching groups, changes of teachers, the arrival or departure of groups of pupils and revisions to the timetable can have an effect on the size of teaching groups. In this Briefing, we define a 'small' class as having 20 or fewer pupils and a 'large' class as having more than 30, although we are aware that, in many cases, actual classes are considerably smaller and larger than these.

In order to obtain a general picture of whether classes are

getting larger or smaller, the UK Government's Education Departments collect annual snapshots of sessions but, unfortunately, strict comparisons between countries are not possible since information is collected at different times of the year. PTRs, which provide a measure of the total teaching resource available to the school, are usually calculated by dividing the total number of (full-time equivalent) pupils on the school's roll by the (full-time equivalent) number of teachers. It is a different measure from the average class size, for it takes no account of differences in teachers' preparation or marking periods, or of variations in non-contact time within the school day. It has to be borne in mind that the pupil element of the PTR is usually a smaller figure than that of the average class size (a school with a PTR of 16.6:1 may, for example, have average class sizes of 19 or 20 pupils). Information on PTRs, but not for class size, is collected for independent schools.

Class size

With all these caveats in mind, what variations can be found in the measures provided by the various government departments? The latest complete published data are for 1991, but provisional figures for 1992 appear to be very similar.

Table 1: Average class size by country and phase (1991)[13]

Phase	England	Wales	Scotland
Primary	26.8	23.1	24.7
Secondary	21.0	19.2	18.5

Table 1 shows that class size in primary schools varied between the three countries, with Wales having the smallest (23.1) and England the largest figures (26.8). The figure for Scotland fell midway between the two. The average difference between England and Wales of over three pupils per class is substantial. In secondary schools, the difference between the largest figure (England) of 21.0 and the smallest (Scotland) of 18.5 again indicates a variation of between two and three pupils, on average, for each class. The relatively low Scottish average size probably reflects the fact that the conditions of service for Scottish teachers include a 'normal maximum' figure (33 for primary and the first two years of secondary, and 30 for other pupils), as well as an 'upper limit'.

In order to investigate the extent of the variation in more detail, we have examined trends, over time, in the average class sizes for English primary and secondary schools. The figures have been disaggregated in Table 2 to show the proportions of classes falling into three groups (1–20 pupils; 21–30 pupils; 31+ pupils).

Table 2: Primary class size (England)[7]

Class size	1982	1987	1989	1990	1991
% 1-20	20.4	16.8	14.8	13.5	11.9
% 21-30	57.1	62.6	65.5	65.9	66.0
% 31+	22.5	20.6	19.7	20.6	22.1
Average class size	25.4	25.8	26.1	26.4	26.8
Number of classes	154,431	142,793	145,210	146,499	146,583

After a long-term decline in the number of pupils due to a falling birth rate, numbers have been increasing in English primary schools since 1985. The average class size over the ten-year period 1982 to 1991 increased by 1.4 pupils. The proportion of classes with over 30 pupils dropped to below 20 per cent in 1989 before returning in 1991 to a level close to the figure found ten years before. The greatest change found in the table, however, concerns the proportion of classes with 20 or fewer pupils. This percentage has almost halved over this period (from 20.4 to 11.9), indicating that many of the smallest classes have been phased out and the proportion of the middle-sized classes (21–30) has been increased accordingly.

Table 3: Secondary class size (England)[7]

Class size	1982	1987	1989	1990	1991
% 1-20	45.3	46.9	48.3	47.2	45.0
% 21-30	45.7	46.5	46.2	47.5	49.8
% 31+	9.0	6.6	5.5	5.3	5.2
Average class size	21.3	21.0	20.6	20.7	21.0
Number of classes	169,313	150,133	137,464	132,753	130,372

In secondary schools where, over the ten-year period 1982 to 1991, the number of pupils fell by just under 25 per cent, the overall average class size has changed very little, as can be seen in Table 3. Perhaps because of the impact of falling rolls, the proportion of classes of over 30 has fallen (from 9.0 to 5.2) and that of classes between 21 and 30 has risen over the same period (from 45.7 to 49.8). The proportion of small classes (20 and below) grew to over 48 per cent of all classes in 1989 before returning to a similar level (45 per cent) to that found ten years before. It is difficult to interpret these secondary findings, however, because, in general, sixth form classes are approximately half the size of those with pupils younger than 16, as can be seen in Table 4.

Table 4: Pre-and Post-16 Average class sizes (England)[8]

Age group	1982	1987	1989	1990	1991
Pre-16	23.0	22.7	22.3	22.5	22.8
Post 16	10.7	10.3	10.8	10.9	11.2

Over the period there has been very little change in the ratio between average class sizes of the pre- and the post-16 groups. The reasons for schools and LEAs maintaining such a difference in resourcing levels are the nature of advanced level work (with its very heavy preparation and marking requirements), the uneven distribution of advanced level students between schools, and the difficulty of maintaining reasonably-sized groups whilst offering a wide choice of subject options. The difference between the resourcing in school sixth forms and earlier years has long been questioned but no overall solution has been identified. It is somewhat paradoxical that the youngest pupils in the system – the infants who are least able to act independently and, therefore, most dependent on adult help – usually experience some of the largest class sizes. As these pupils progress upwards and become more independent, their class size is often reduced until – as young adults and potentially autonomous learners – they are taught in the smallest groups that they have experienced. Current sixth form groups are even smaller than many groups in higher education. This policy of resourcing according to age, so that older pupils generally experience smaller classes, needs to be re-thought, but we doubt whether the LEAs – faced with the possibility of schools opting out – would be able to institute change. This could only happen, we believe, with the support of the Department For Education (DFE) and of any funding bodies established to deal with grant-maintained schools. It remains to be seen, too, whether the new system of locally managed schools, in which delegated powers have been given to governing bodies, will affect class sizes from 1992 onwards.

Other data on class size made available by the DFE show that there are also substantial differences between LEAs. For example, in 1991 the proportion of primary school pupils in England in classes of over 30 varied from over 56 per cent (Redbridge) to below 2.5 per cent (Lambeth). Such large-scale variation is caused by a variety of factors to do with the amount of money allocated to the LEA by government, the impact of falling rolls, the level of local income from rates or community charge, local policies on the deployment of teachers, variations in the time allowed for other activities, local traditions and the relative take-up of available places in any one school. Finally, it is worth noting that, as a recent Parliamentary Answer has shown, in January 1991 over 10,000 pupils were recorded as being in classes of over 40[12].

What is seldom included in official tables, however, is any information on the number or role of people other than teachers present in classrooms. Yet in some schools recent policies have encouraged the employment of an increasing number of classroom assistants to carry out a range of support tasks under the direction of the teacher[16]. In other schools, parent volunteers have been welcomed into classes in order to provide general learning support and help with specific tasks such as hearing pupils read. In these circumstances, the official size of the class may provide only a partial – although important – view of the opportunities available for pupils to interact with adults.

Pupil:teacher ratios (PTRs)

Turning to the other measure of teacher availability, the PTR, Table 5 shows national differences for primary and secondary as well as for non-maintained (independent) schools.

Table 5: Average number of pupils per teacher (Pupil: Teacher ratio) in the UK by Country and Phase (1991)[13]

Phase	England	Wales	Scotland	N. Ireland	UK
Primary	22.2	22.3	19.5	22.8	22.0
Secondary	15.5	15.4	12.2	14.9	15.2
Non-maintained	10.8	9.8	10.4	11.0	10.7
All schools	17.3	18.2	15.2	18.1	17.2

In 1991, the average ratios for England, Wales and Northern Ireland were similar in both primary and secondary schools. The figures for Scotland, however, were considerably lower for each phase of schooling: 2.7 pupils per teacher fewer than the lowest other primary or secondary figure. The figures for non-maintained schools cannot be compared directly with either of the top two rows of the table since they are aggregates of both primary and secondary schools. However, an approximate comparison can be drawn by considering the two bottom rows of the table (the *all schools* row includes the non-maintained schools but their overall effect is not large; reducing, for example, the figure for England only from 17.4 to 17.3). This comparison shows that, on average, the difference between the pupil component of the ratio in maintained and non-maintained schools in England is 6.5 pupils. Put another way, teachers in independent schools have to teach, on average, only about 60 per cent of the number of pupils of their maintained sector equivalents.

Another interesting feature of Table 5 is the difference found between Scotland and Wales. Given the considerably fewer Scottish PTRs, it is perhaps surprising that the average class size, noted earlier in Table 1, is not even smaller. The difference, for instance, between the average PTR and the average class size for Scottish primary schools is 5.2 pupils, whilst that for Welsh primary schools is only 0.8 pupils. The implication is that Welsh primary teachers – possibly because of a large number of small rural schools – have considerably less school time for activities other than classroom teaching, than do their Scottish counterparts.

Within England, as with class size, there are also considerable differences in PTRs between LEAs. In 1991 Westminster had the most generous (17.1) and Kent had the highest ratio (24.3) at primary level. Kensington and Chelsea had the most generous (12.9) and Durham the highest ratio (18.8) at secondary, although it should be noted that some LEAs (such as Durham) provide some or all of their post-16 education in tertiary colleges not included in the analyses – thus raising their PTR.

International comparisons

International figures are even harder to interpret as – in addition to the points already noted – there are differences between countries in the length of the school year, the hours of day in which a pupil is taught, the usual teaching loads of staff and the nature of their other duties. Such information is seldom available in a comparable format. Nevertheless, OECD international data enable approximate comparisons with the UK to be drawn (see Table 6). They show that primary PTRs varied markedly from an average of 11.1 pupils to one teacher in Sweden, to 31.1 in Turkey (a difference of 20 pupils) and, in secondary schools, from an average of only 8.3 pupils in Belgium to 22.7 in Turkey (a difference of over 14 pupils). In general, countries that had a generous PTR in one sector also had a generous figure in another. Most countries, like the UK, had more generous PTRs in secondary than in primary schools; but in the Netherlands, New Zealand and Sweden this pattern was reversed and primary, rather than secondary, schools had more favourable staffing ratios. The UK had one of the highest PTRs at primary level (22.0 compared to an OECD average of 18.5) but was in the 'middle' group, close to the OECD average, for secondary PTRs (15.0 compared to 15.2).

Table 6: Average number of pupils per teacher (1988)[8]

Phase	PTR: 20 or more	PTR: 15-20	PTR: less than 15
Primary	Turkey, Ireland Japan, UK	New Zealand, Netherlands, Australia, US, France, Canada	Luxembourg, Italy, Denmark, Austria, Sweden
Secondary	Turkey, Norway, Netherlands, New Zealand	Japan, Ireland, UK, US, Canada	France, Australia, Sweden, Denmark, Luxembourg, Austria, Italy, Belgium

Research on the effects of class size

Considering its importance, there is a dearth of British research on the *effects* of class size. When results have been reported, they have usually been part of a wider study. For instance, Rutter *et al* found little evidence of the impact of class size in their study of secondary schools[20] but Mortimore *et al* found evidence of smaller classes being associated with the greater progress of the youngest 8 year old pupils and with better performance in mathematics[15]. Most recently, the evaluation of the 1991 Standard Assessment Tasks for 7 year olds noted an increased likelihood of higher achievement in small classes. Typically, however, only correlations or associations have been reported between class size and average pupil attainment, with little or no firm evidence on the *impact* of a particular class size on the achievements of its pupils. It is widely recognised that results from these correlational studies are difficult to interpret, because they do not control for intake (for example, lower attaining pupils can be concentrated in smaller classes)[2,11].

The situation is very different in North America where much research has been conducted on this topic and several comprehensive summaries and meta-analyses of research data are available. Glass *et al* argued that '... a clear and strong relationship between class size and achievement has emerged' and they claimed that the smaller the class, the higher the pupil's achievement with teacher morale and pupil attitudes improving in smaller classes. These claims, however, have not gone unchallenged. Another thorough review of research criticised the idea that an optimum class size can be specified in isolation from other factors, such as the age of pupils or subject matter being taught[19]. The authors argue that within the range of 23–30 pupils, class size seems to have *little* effect on pupil performance beyond the early years and they suggest that it is the lower achievers in the early years who benefit most from smaller classes.

In order to test reliably the effectiveness of reductions in class size, studies are needed which compare the progress of pupils and teachers who have been randomly allocated to classes of different sizes. To control for school effects, it would also be preferable to conduct comparisons on different sized classes within schools. The most recent and comprehensive evidence of this sort comes from a major state-wide intervention in Tennessee (project STAR – Student Teacher Achievement Ratio), which included over 7,000 pupils in 79 schools. This project compared student achievement in three types of classes: small classes (13–17), regular classes (22–25) and regular class sizes with a full-time teacher aide. Pupils were followed through from kindergarten (age five) to third grade (age eight). The results show that pupils in the small classes group – at all four age levels – significantly outperformed pupils in the other two groups in mathematics and reading, with the biggest effects being found in the first year of compulsory schooling (grade 1). Moreover, the positive effects of small classes remained two years after the pupils had returned to their regular sized classes; that is, in grades 4 and 5[17,1] The research also found that small classes brought about improvements in pupils' participation in school; again, even two years after entry into regular classes. There is also evidence that disadvantaged minority pupils benefited most from small classes, and that the initial 'boost' they received seemed to be maintained, at least, until grade five[9,24].

Whilst not disputing these results, critics have argued that the gains in pupils' attainment do not justify the expense of employing more teachers[22,23]. These critics agree with proponents of class size reductions that the most significant effects are found with pupils who are in the first year of schooling, but they go on to point out that the effects seem to decrease thereafter. However, this decrease is predictable in the sense that the experience of the initial class reductions was a one-time event: ensuing years are a continuation, not a new experience. Moreover, the fact that benefits were evident some years after the initial intervention, and after entry into regular classes, deflects some criticism of the costs involved.

One reason for the limited benefits from small classes found in some studies may be that teachers maintain their old methods of teaching and do not take advantage of the new opportunities smaller classes can offer[21]. It is difficult to know whether it is the opportunity for more individual attention for pupils, more opportunities for pupils to become involved in practical learning tasks, or enhanced teacher motivation and satisfaction in small classes, which indirectly benefit pupils. It makes little sense, therefore, to consider class size in isolation from teaching practices, because the potential benefits of reducing class size will only occur if teachers alter their behaviour and classroom organisation. Research from the US offers little doubt that very small classes (below 17 pupils) can help attainment, but the limited duration of the projects prevents the crucial question of long-term effects being answered definitively.

There is surprisingly little discussion of why class size reductions are expected to have a positive effect on pupils' learning. One exception is the recent survey of teacher time and curriculum manageability which found that teachers in larger classes (especially in those over 28 pupils) spend significantly more time in preparation.[4] Given that one important component of any learning situation is the *time* of the teacher available for individual pupils, it is hard to believe that smaller teaching units cannot *promote* better progress. Certainly this view is supported by those parents who cite this reason for paying for independent schools. Such a view is also buttressed by practice in other countries which have more generous PTRs and legal class size limits.

Parents and teachers remain convinced that children learn better in smaller classes[5]. Unfortunately, few studies have sought to elicit the views of pupils, possibly because, unless they had *experienced* different sized classes, it would be difficult for them to make an informed judgement. Yet such a judgement could be very illuminating, not only from the point of view of whether pupils learn more easily in classes of a particular size, but also as to whether they feel happier, believe they are less likely to be bullied and are more confident about speaking up for themselves and participating in practical activities.

Conclusions

1   From the American experimental evidence, it appears that small classes (below 17 pupils) can lead to increased gains in learning in the first six years of school and, especially, in the first year of compulsory schooling and with disadvantaged or very young pupils.
2   Reducing (even radically) class sizes, however, appears to make little difference to the achievement of pupils unless the teachers alter their style of teaching in order to exploit the opportunities of the smaller group.
3   Primary school PTRs in the UK (except for Scotland) are among the least favourable in the OECD countries and are increasing, while secondary PTRs are close to the OECD average.
4   Both PTRs and class sizes are likely to be affected by current innovations such as the delegation of budgets, the increasing amount of administration carried out by senior staff, and the consequences of open enrolment.
5   Post-16 pupils are usually taught in the smallest groups, frequently less than half the size of those of the youngest pupils in primary reception classes.
6   Independent schools usually have much smaller classes at both primary and secondary levels.
7   Within their school budgets, heads and governors will have only limited ability to vary staffing levels. More radical changes – or shifts within existing resourcing (for example, from post-16 classes to younger pupils) – could be achieved only by LEAs or other funding agencies and would need the support of the DFE.

Recommendations

1 Resourcing on the assumption that older pupils generally need smaller classes should be questioned. In British primary schools – and especially at Key Stage 1 – class size remains important; and consideration should be given to reducing this and to the introduction, in England and Wales, of an upper limit on reception and Year 1 classes.

2 Whilst it is important to continue to monitor the size of teaching groups in secondary schools, the principle of fitness for purpose should be used to determine the best use of teacher time and the size of the group.

3 Reductions in class size, whether initiated at DFE, local or school level, should always be accompanied by a review of teaching methods, classroom management and in-service training in order to maximise potential benefits.

4 A carefully controlled British research study on the long-term effects of different size classes on the attitudes, achievement and behaviour of pupils is long overdue and should be commissioned by the DFE.

March 1993

References

1 Achilles, C.M., Nye, B.A., Zaharias, J.B. and Fulton, B.D. (1993) *The Lasting Benefits Study* (LBS) *in grades 4 and 5 (1990–1991): A Legacy from Tennessee's Four-Year (K-3) Class-Size Study (1985–1989), Project STAR.* Paper to North Carolina Association for Research in Education.

2 Burstall, C. (1979) *Time to Mend the Nets: A Commentary on the Outcomes of Class-size Research.* Trends in Education 3, 27–33.

3 Burstall, C. (1992) *Playing the Numbers Game in Class.* Education Guardian 7th April.

4 Campbell, R. and Neill, S. (1992) *Teacher-time and Curriculum Manageability Key Stage 1: Third Report of Research into the use of teacher time.* AMMA.

5 CASE (1992) *Briefing on Class-size.* Campaign Briefing Number 2, June.

6   DES (1992) *Statistical Bulletin 2/92.*

7   DES *(1982–1992) Annual Statistics for England.*

8   DFE (1992) *Statistical Bulletin 13/92.*

9   Finn, J.D. and Achilles, C.M. (1990) *Answers and Questions about Class Size: A State-side Experiment.* American Educational Research Journal 27, 3 pp 557–577.

10 Glass, G., Cahen, L., Smith, M.L. and Filby, N. (1982) *School Class Size.* Beverly Hills California, SAGE.

11 Gray, J. (1981) Times Educational Supplement 3 July.

12 Hansard (1992) *Parliamentary written answers,* 13th November.

13 HMSO (1992) *Regional Trends.*

14 ISIS (1992) *Annual Census.* Independent Schools Information Service, London.

15 Mortimore, P., Sammons, P., Stoll, L., Lewis, D. and Ecob, R. (1988) *School Matters: The Junior Years.* Wells, Open Books.

16 Mortimore, P., Mortimore, J., with Thomas, H., Cairns, R. and Taggart, B. (1992) *The Innovative Uses of Non-Teaching Staff in Primary and Secondary Schools Project, Final Report,* London, Institute of Education/The Department For Education.

17 Nye, B.A., Achilles, C.M., Zaharias, J.B., Fulton, B.D. and Wallenhorst, M.P. (1992) *Small is far better* Paper to Mid-South Educational Research Association, Knoxville, Tennessee.

18 OECD (1992) *Education at a Glance* Organisation for Economic Co-operation and Development, Paris.

19 Robinson, G. and Wittebols, J. (1986) *Class-size research: A Related Cluster Analysis for Decision Making.* Arlington, Virginia, Educational Research Service.

20 Rutter, M., Maughan, B., Mortimore, P. and Ouston, J. (1979) *Fifteen Thousand Hours.* Wells, Open Books.

21 Shapson, S.M., Wright, E.N., Eason, G. and Fitzgerald, J. (1980) *An Experimental Study of the Effects of Class Size.* American Educational Research Journal 17, 2 pp 141–152.

22 Slavin, R. (1990) *Class Size and Student Achievement: Is Smaller Better?* Contemporary Education 62, 1 pp 6–12.

23 Tomlinson, T. (1990) *Class-size and Public Policy: The Plot Thickens.* Contemporary Education 62, 1 pp 17–23.

24 Word, E., Achilles, C.M., Bain, H., Folger, J., Johnstone, J. and Lintz, N. (1990) *Project STAR Final Executive Summary: kindergarten through third grade results.* Contemporary Education 62, 1 pp 13–16.

13 An Alternative Approach to Parental Choice

Michael Adler

Reader in Social Policy and Member of the Centre for Educational Sociology, The University of Edinburgh

---

Summary

1 The evidence from a decade of open enrolment in Scotland suggests that parental choice has led to an inefficient use of resources, widening disparities between schools, increased social segregation and threats to equality of educational opportunity.
2 Although there have been gainers as well as losers, the balance sheet suggests that parental choice has been a 'negative sum game' in which the gains achieved by some pupils have been more than offset by the losses incurred by others and by the community as a whole.
3 It is likely that the outcomes of open enrolment in England will be even more problematic.
4 Recent legislation has not achieved an optimal balance between the rights of parents to choose schools for their children and the responsibilities of government to promote the education of all children.
5 An alternative approach to education policy which takes choice seriously but attempts to avoid the most unacceptable consequences of recent legislation is outlined, the main components of which are as follows:
   (a) Within limits, schools would be encouraged to develop their own distinctive characteristics.
   (b) Decisions about school allocation should seek to promote children's interests (rather than parental preferences) and would involve teachers and older pupils as well as parents.
   (c) Decisions about school allocation would be made for all children (and not just for a minority). Where the

number of applicants for a school is greater than the number of available places, priority would be given to those whose cases are most strongly supported.
(d) Local authorities would be expected to formulate admissions policies for schools. This would provide a measure of protection for schools that lose pupils.

Introduction

The aims of this Briefing are (i) to outline and compare English and Scottish legislation relating to parental choice, (ii) to review the findings of research on the effects of parental choice in Scotland where legislation was introduced more than ten years ago, (iii) to assess the likely effects of parental choice in England in the light of the 1988 Education Reform Act and subsequent policy developments, and (iv) to put forward an alternative approach to parental choice which takes choice seriously but seeks to avoid some of the most unacceptable consequences of recent legislation.

Parental choice north and south of the border

The 1944 Education Act and the 1945 Education (Scotland) Act gave local authorities a broad discretion to determine school admissions. This created few problems until the mid-1970s when widespread dissatisfaction with state education and political opposition to the extension of comprehensive schooling prompted the Conservative Party, which was then in Opposition, to champion parental choice. The Conservatives were returned to office in 1979 and soon introduced legislation to this effect, first for England and Wales and, soon afterwards, for Scotland.

The changes brought about by the parental choice provisions in the 1980 Education Act and the 1981 Education (Scotland) Act can be interpreted in a number of ways, for example:

1. As a shift away from an authority-wide approach to school admissions (which enables education authorities to prevent overcrowding and under-enrolment, deploy resources in an efficient manner and pursue their own conception of social justice) towards a parent-centred approach (in which parents decide what is best for their children and parents' concerns have priority over those of the education authorities).

2. More generally, as a shift away from a collective-welfare orientation (which focuses on the achievement of collective ends, is primarily concerned with the overall pattern of decision-making and recognises the necessity for trade-offs between the various ends the policy is trying to achieve) towards an individual-client orientation (which focuses on each individual case, assumes that individuals are capable of deciding and acting for themselves and precludes the possibility of trade-offs).

3. As the first stage of a two-stage deregulation of the educational system which seeks to undermine the role of the local authority and replace bureaucratic and political forms of accountability with market-like relationships between schools and parents. In this two-stage process, the second stage comprises the delegation of powers and responsibilities from education authorities to individual schools and a greater involvement of parents in their management.

Until 1988, deregulation had proceeded further in Scotland than in England and Wales. This is because the parental choice provisions in the 1981 Education (Scotland) Act were considerably stronger than those in the 1980 Education Act and Scottish education authorities had much weaker powers to control school admissions than local education authorities in England and Wales.

The position in England and Wales was completely

changed by the provisions of the 1988 Education Reform Act. This strengthened the rights of parents and reduced the powers of local education authorities, introducing a form of 'open enrolment' similar to that which has existed in Scotland since the early 1980s. Local education authorities are now prohibited from imposing their own intake limits and from turning away pupils unless a statutorily-defined number is exceeded. It also introduced a substantial degree of delegated financial management. Thus, in England and Wales, all secondary schools and most primary schools now receive budgets from the local authority which, subject to meeting their statutory obligations, they are free to spend as they wish. By contrast, local authorities still determine school budgets in Scotland and School Boards only have minor and largely consultative powers[13].

Considering these two sets of developments together, it is clear that demand-side deregulation in England and Wales has caught up with its earlier development in Scotland while supply-side deregulation has been taken a good deal further. The 'uncoupling' of schools from local authorities and the replacement of bureaucratic and political forms of accountability by market-like relationships between parents and schools has been taken a stage further in England and Wales than it has in Scotland. How long this disparity will be allowed to continue is a matter for conjecture but the recent publication of new guidelines for the devolved management of schools in Scotland suggests that the gap is set to close.

The impact of parental choice in Scotland

Since a form of 'open-enrolment' has existed in Scotland for more than a decade and there have been a number of pieces of research on the implementation and impact of parental choice in Scotland, it is clear that much can be learned from the Scottish experience. The latest available figures indicate that 14.9% of pupils in the first year of primary school and 11.5% of pupils in the first year of secondary school were the subject of a 'placing request' (for an alternative to the designated school)[14]. There were considerable variations between regions with substantially higher rates in the more urban authorities, where a number of schools may be within fairly easy reach, and correspondingly lower rates in the more rural authorities, where geographical considerations effectively preclude a choice of school for most parents. Since 1982/83, the first year in which the legislative provisions were implemented in full, the number of placing requests has increased by about 50%. Although most of these placing requests were granted, there has been a significant fall in the success rate from 97.8% in 1982/93 to 89.3% in 1990/91 due, mainly, to the closure of school annexes, the removal of temporary accommodation and the imposition of *de facto* intake limits to prevent overcrowding.

About 10% of parents whose requests were turned down appealed to a statutory Education Appeal Committee. These committees, which contain a majority of councillors, can hardly be described as independent and it is not therefore surprising that few appeals are successful at this stage. A very small number of parents made a further appeal to the courts. However, most of these cases have been deserted by education authorities which have preferred conceding to the individual parent to losing the case and having to reconsider those of all the other parents whose requests for the school in question had been turned down. Most of the cases that have actually been heard by the courts have been decided in favour of the parents.

Research carried out between 1983 and 1986 by Adler *et al* assessed the significance of the parental choice provisions introduced into Scotland by the 1981 Education (Scotland) Act[2]. The main findings are set out in the panel below.

1. In the cities, the proportion of placing requests was much higher than in the country as a whole. In several cities, it was 20–25% and in some city areas, it was more than 50%. These requests came from right across the social class spectrum. However, although there was no overall relationship between social class and the exercise of parental choice, there were often strong relationships at the local (school) level.

2. Avoidance of the local (catchment area) school was important for a majority of parents who made a placing request in each of our case-study areas.

3. For a majority of these parents, choice involved finding a satisfactory alternative to the local school rather than making an optimal choice from a wide range of possible schools.

4. In requesting schools for their children, parents claimed that they were influenced much more by geographical and social factors, for example proximity and discipline, and by the general reputation of the school, than by educational considerations, for example the curriculum, teaching methods or examination results. Moreover, they relied on rather limited and second-hand information about the schools concerned.

5. Appeal committees tended to uphold the authorities while the courts, on the whole, upheld the parents.

6. Because of declining school rolls and because most intake limits have not been challenged in the courts, few schools have been really overcrowded. However, some were certainly full to capacity, while a rather larger number of schools were chronically undersubscribed. Nevertheless, there have been very few school closures.

7. On the whole, the schools which gained most pupils were formerly selective schools in middle-class areas, while the schools which lost most pupils have been those that served local authority housing schemes in deprived peripheral areas.

8. There was considerable evidence of 'band wagon' effects, and little evidence of the market functioning as a self-correcting mechanism. Success in attracting pupils often led to further success while schools which lost pupils found it very difficult to prevent the outflow continuing.

Many of the findings have been confirmed by more recent research. Echols *et al* have shown that the schools which were selected tended to be formerly selective schools with above-average attainment levels and pupils from higher socio-economic backgrounds, and that the incidence of choice was a function of the opportunities available in the local community[6]. Willms *et al* have demonstrated that parents tended to choose schools with better (unadjusted) examination results and higher socio-economic status pupils[16]. However, parents found it difficult to gauge the 'added value' that a school would contribute to their child's examination performance[11]. Consequently, parents' choices only marginally benefited their children in terms of better examination results. Thus, although parents' choices appear rational in the sense that they increase their children's performance in examinations, the effects are not as great as they would appear at first sight to be. Moreover, the moderate gains for some pupils are associated with high costs for others (in particular pupils at schools in deprived areas which lose a substantial number of pupils) and for the system as a whole. Although there is no *a priori* reason why parental choice should increase social segregation, the available evidence suggests that it does and that this is likely to result in greater inequalities in attainment.

The balance sheet

Evidence from a decade of open enrolment in Scotland suggests that parental choice has resulted in a rather inefficient use of resources since expenditure per pupil is much higher in a school with a small roll than a school with a large one[3]. It has also led to marked differences between schools since, even without formula funding, schools which lost pupils also lost staff and resources and could no longer offer comparable educational opportunities. Combined with increasing social segregation, parental choice poses a serious threat to equality of educational opportunity with potentially very serious implications in a democratic society. In Scotland it has already led to the re-emergence of something resembling a two-tier system of secondary schooling in the big cities. This is different from the old, two-tier system which existed prior to the introduction of comprehensive schooling in that the lower tier now caters for a minority of children whereas before it catered for the majority. The existence of a small number of rump schools located in the most deprived areas of the big cities is clearly a serious cause of concern.

Although there have clearly been gainers as well as losers from the Scottish legislation, the balance sheet suggests that the gains have been relatively small compared with the losses. Those who have gained have done so at the expense of others and, by and large, those who have lost have been those who could least afford to do so. Thus, parental choice in Scotland appears to have been a 'negative sum' game in which the gains achieved by some pupils have been more than offset by the losses incurred by others and by the community as a whole. The result of aggregating individual choices, which may themselves be rational, is a situation which can fairly be described as irrational. Moreover, the problems outlined above can only become greater as the incidence of placing requests continues to increase as it will almost certainly do. This is partly because education has many of the characteristics of a 'positional good', i.e. something which is desired because of the status associated with having it[8]. Since the scarcity value of a positional good diminishes as the number of people choosing it increases, 'first order choices' provoke 'second order choices' as people attempt to retain their higher status.

Widening disparities in educational provision can also be attributed to other legislative developments. Of particular importance here are the provisions in the 1988 Education Reform Act (replicated for Scotland, in the 1989 Self-Governing Schools etc. (Scotland) Act) which allow parents to decide, in a secret ballot, whether they wish their child's school to opt out of local authority control and become a grant-maintained (England and Wales) or a self-governing (Scotland) school funded directly from central government. Although the final decision rests with the Secretary of State, proposals to change the status of the school require the support of a majority of parents. Opted-out schools may not change their character or their admissions arrangements immediately or without the approval of the Secretary of State, but the future direction of policy is quite clear. This has recently been made quite explicit in the White Paper which seeks to promote much greater diversity and specialisation in schools, to further diminish the role of the local authority and actively to encourage opting out[5]. The aggregate effect of these changes is almost certain to increase the extent of parental choice of school.

A vital question is whether the impact of parental choice of school in England and Wales in the 1990s will resemble the impact of parental choice of school in Scotland in the 1980s. Unfortunately, there are several grounds for thinking that it will be considerably more problematic. First, there is less of a tradition of collectivism in England than in Scotland and, for this reason alone, the incidence of parental choice in English urban areas will probably turn out to be higher than in Scotland. Second, the existence of much larger ethnic minority populations in many English cities raises the prospect of ethnic segregation on a scale that simply could not exist in Scotland where the ethnic minority population is very much smaller. Where, for example, white and Asian parents want their children to go to schools with children from similar backgrounds, it would appear that there is little a local authority can do to prevent this[4]. Third, the policy context is very different. The publication of examination results will affect schools' reputations (whether deservedly so or not) and will almost certainly boost choice while the introduction of formula funding will make it much more difficult for local authorities to support schools that may be in need of a measure of protection. Although resources may be used more efficiently, they may also be used less effectively. Fourth, since more than 300 schools in England have already opted out of local authority control while none in Scotland has so far done so and the White Paper (referred to above) only applies to England and Wales, diversity and, hence, the rationale for choice are both likely to be more pronounced in England and Wales than in Scotland.

An alternative approach

It does not follow from the arguments set out above that parents should be deprived of their rights to express a preference for the schools they wish their children to attend. In any case, it would be extremely difficult in practice to bring this about. However, a better balance between the rights of parents to choose schools for their children and the duties of education authorities to promote the education of all children is clearly needed. In the remainder of this Briefing, five proposals which, taken together, could help to secure a better balance between these concerns are briefly outlined[1].

1. As a prerequisite, the fiction that all primary and comprehensive secondary schools provide an identical set of educational opportunities and the aspiration that they should strive to do so should both be abandoned. Over and above the common core curriculum, schools should be encouraged to develop particular curricular strengths. Schools should also be encouraged to develop and promote their own particular teaching styles, institutional ethos and extra-curricular activities. These different school characteristics would, in part, reflect the views of Governing Bodies and School Boards, in part, those of the headteacher and the teaching staff, but

education authorities would have an important role to play in preventing all schools from adopting the same set of characteristics and ensuring an appropriate degree of diversity.

2. In order to ensure the widest possible access to a range of schools with different characteristics, school catchment areas should be abandoned. Although open enrolment implies that parents may send their children to any school, most children still attend the school serving the catchment area in which they live. This is because most education authorities still use catchment areas and because parents are required to take the initiative if they do not want their child to attend the catchment area school. In towns and cities, school catchment areas often do not represent local communities or neighbourhoods. Where they do represent local communities or neighbourhoods, they constitute the major source of inequality in educational attainment at school level and thus the major obstacle to equality of status and parity of esteem between schools.

3. Much more thought needs to be given to the interests which the right of school choice is trying to protect. At present, the legislation seeks only to protect parents' interests in choice. However, since parents act as agents of their children but are not all equally effective in this regard, children's interests need to be considered directly. This would entail efforts to ensure that children attend those schools which are best suited to their particular personalities and talents. Teachers and parents will often have different views as to what these are: it is therefore important to find some means of involving them both in decision-making. A recent IPPR report refers to the need to emphasise co-operation rather than competition[12]. This would call for improved parental participation in decision-making rather than increased avoidance of unsatisfactory schools, or using

Hirschman's terminology, mechanisms which enhance 'voice' rather than 'exit'[9]. Discussions between teachers, parents and, in the case of older pupils, the pupils themselves would enable all of these parties to examine each other's reasoning, and decide what the child's interests are and how they can best be furthered. They would lead to recommendations for a particular school (or schools) in much the same way that careers guidance (at a later stage) leads to recommendations for further education, training or employment.

4. Instead of providing an escape-route for a minority of parents who do not wish their children to attend the local (catchment area) school, legislation would seek to enhance the interests of all children by setting up procedures for assessing their needs and identifying the schools at which they are most likely to thrive. Where the number of pupils who are matched with a school in this way exceeds the number of places available, priority would – subject to local authority policy on the composition of the school (see below) – be given to those pupils whose cases are most strongly supported through the procedures outlined above. This should ensure that schools are chosen for children rather than vice versa.

5. A greater measure of protection would be given to schools which have lost pupils and to the pupils who attend these schools. One way of achieving this would be to enable education authorities to set limits on the admission of pupils to schools which have gained pupils where there are good reasons for so doing. Scottish research indicates that the imposition of admission limits on the most popular schools can provide a measure of protection for less popular schools although these limits lack statutory force[2]. Local authorities would still be responsible for formulating a set of general policies, for example in relation to minimum, opti-

mum and maximum school sizes and appropriate ability, social or racial mixes for schools.

The proposals outlined above challenge a number of
beliefs which are strongly supported on the left and the
right of the political spectrum. Thus, on the one hand, they
reject the view that all schools (and all teachers) should be
able to cater equally well for all children and attach less
importance to the links between schools and the communities in which they are located; on the other hand, they
reject the view that parents always know what is best for
their children and question the appropriateness of internal
markets in education.

Proposals 1 and 2 bear some resemblance to policies which
are currently being pursued by the government although
they differ quite markedly from them in that they envisage
a much more important and continuing role for local
authorities. Proposals 3, 4 and 5, on the other hand, are
rather different in their emphasis in that they seek to promote co-operation in place of competition and to offer a
greater measure of protection to the most vulnerable
schools and pupils. Taken together, the five proposals constitute an alternative approach to education policy which
takes choice seriously but attempts to avoid the most unacceptable consequences of recent legislation, and to produce
better balance between the rights of parents to choose
schools for their children and the duties of local authorities
to promote the education of all children for whom they are
responsible.

Although they differ in some respects from proposals outlined in NCE Briefing No. 7 (see p.89)[15], e.g. in the
attempt, within limits, to foster diversity, in the involvement of primary school teachers in the allocation of children to secondary schools and in the procedures for selecting children for schools which are oversubscribed, it is significant that they have several common features, e.g.

requiring all parents to make a choice, providing help and advice to parents and paying for children's transport to and from school.

Conclusion

Liberal economic theory assumes that individuals are the best judges of what is in their own interests. Whether or not this is true, it is fairly clear that parents are not necessarily the best judges of what is in their children's interests. However, this situation is not one which parents can themselves remedy. The problem is structural rather than motivational. Institutional changes which would enable all parents, with the assistance of teachers, to make more informed choices about the types of school which would best promote their children's learning and thus further their children's interests, and which would re-emphasise some of the legitimate collective policy concerns which have been eclipsed by the construction of a 'quasi market' in education need to be introduced[7,10]. It would be fanciful to suggest that the task is going to be easy, but it would similarly be defeatist to conclude that, because it is clearly going to be difficult, it should not be attempted.

March 1993

Acknowledgements
I am very grateful to my colleagues Andrew McPherson, David Raffe and Doug Willms, and to Josh Hillman for their very helpful comments to an earlier draft of this Briefing.

References

1 Adler, M. (1993) *Parental Choice and the Enhancement of Children's Interests*. In Munn, P. (ed.) Parents and Schools: Customers, Managers or Partners? London: Routledge.

2 Adler, M., Petch, A. and Tweedie, J. (1989) *Parental Choice and*

Educational Policy, Edinburgh: Edinburgh University Press.

3 Audit Commission (1986) *Towards Better Management of Secondary Education*, London: HMSO.

4 Bradney, A. (1989) *The Dewsbury Affair and the Education Reform Act 1988* Education and the Law, 1(2), 51–57.

5 Department for Education and Welsh Office (1992) *Choice and Diversity: a New Framework for Schools*, Cm.2021, London: HMSO.

6 Echols, F., McPherson, A. and Willms, J. (1990) *Choice among State and Private Schools in Scotland*, Journal of Education Policy, 5(3), 207–222.

7 Glennerster, H. (1991) *Quasi Markets for Education?* Economic Journal, 101 (September), 1268–1276.

8 Hirsch, F. (1977) *Social Limits to Growth*, London and Henley: Routledge and Kegan Paul.

9 Hirschman, A. (1970) *Exit, Voice and Loyalty: Responses to Decline in Firms, Organisations and States*, Cambridge, MA: Harvard University Press.

10 Le Grand, J. (1991) *Quasi Markets in Social Policy*, Economic Journal, 101 (September), 1256–1267.

11 McPherson, A. (1992) *Measuring Added Value in Schools*, NCE Briefing No.1, London: National Commission on Education.

12 Miliband, D. (1991) *Markets, Choice and Educational Reform* (Education and Training Paper No.3), London: Institute for Public Policy Research (IPPR).

13 Munn, P. (1991) *School Boards, Accountability and Control*, British Journal of Educational Studies, 39(2), 173–189.

14 Scottish Office Education Department (1992) *Placing Requests in Education Authority Schools*, Statistical Bulletin, Edn/B6/1992/13, Edinburgh.

15 Walford, G. (1992) *Selection for Secondary Schooling*, NCE Briefing No.7, London: National Commission on Education.

16 Willms, J. and Echols, F. (1992) *Alert and Inert Clients: the Scottish Experience of Parental Choice of Schools*, Economics of Education Review, 11(4), 339–350.

14 Special Needs Education: The Next 25 Years

Professor Klaus Wedell
Institute of Education, University of London

Summary

1 During the 1970s and up to the late 1980s there was remarkably rapid development both in understanding children and young people's special educational needs (SENs) and in their education.
2 The role of environmental factors in contributing to SENs was recognised. It became evident that SENs occurred in a continuum from the most severe to those less so, many experienced by pupils in ordinary schools; about 20% of pupils were involved at some point in their schooling.
3 The 1981 Act asserted the right of children and young people with SENs to be educated as far as possible with their peers in ordinary schools; it remains a challenge for all schools to extend their flexibility so as to respond to pupils' learning needs in the future.
4 Recent educational legislation has, in conjunction with fiscal constraint, increased the difficulties that LEAs and schools face in meeting their obligations to pupils with SENs and has fragmented responsibility for ensuring that SENs are met.
5 Examples are cited of good practice which point to potential future developments:
   a. making better use of available resources through collaboration between teachers, schools and authorities;
   b. improved practice in schools, such as collaborative learning groups for pupils with different learning needs, 'teacher support teams', realising the

potential of computer-aided learning, better partnership with parents;
c. more effective teaching through emphasising curriculum-based teacher assessment for monitoring pupil achievement and planning progress.

Introduction

How can one gauge the potential scale of development of special needs education over the next 25 years? One way is to look back over a similar period to see what has been achieved. This shows that principles and practice relating to the education of children and young people with special educational needs (SENs) have developed more during this period than have those in most areas of education. Unfortunately, recent education legislation has put some achievements of the past at risk and legislation currently proposed could possibly jeopardise future development. One should none the less consider the means of making progress in this field. This Briefing aims to cover three areas, with coverage confined to the school years:

- the development of special needs education over the last 25 years;
- the implications of recent and proposed legislation; and
- the scope for future development.

The development of special needs education over the last 25 years

It is easy to forget that, in the UK, the right to education of all those with SENs was not recognised until the 1970 Act. This legislation brought pupils with the most severe learning difficulties, who had been termed 'ineducable' and had therefore been cared for and educated within the NHS, under the responsibility of the Local Education Authority (LEA). The Act reflected developments in thinking in other countries as well as in the UK about the role of education in providing access to equal opportunities. In 1978, the Warnock Committee summarised thinking about SENs up to that time, and made the points shown in Panel 1[4].

PANEL 1: The Warnock Committee's views

1. The aims of education are the same for all children. The means needed to achieve these might be different for pupils with SENs, as might the extent to which the aims can be reached.

2. SENs are not caused solely by deficiencies within the child. They result from interaction between the strengths and weaknesses of the child, and the resources and deficiencies of the environment. SENs occur in a continuum of degree of severity, and so it is not meaningful to attempt to draw a hard and fast line between the 'handicapped' and the 'non-handicapped'.

3. All schools have a responsibility to identify and meet pupils' SENs and all children and young people with SENs should be educated alongside their peers as long as their needs can be met and it is practicable to do so.

4. Parents, and as far as possible the children and young people with SENs themselves, have the right to share in the decisions about how their needs are met.

The concept of the 'continuum' of SENs was derived from studies which showed that, in addition to the 2% of pupils who received their education largely in special schools and units, a further 18% of pupils might require some form of special needs education at some time in their schooling. Education in general therefore had to take account of pupils' diversity of learning ability. The interactive causation of SENs, the recognition of the right to integration, and the rights of parents in decision-making were included in the first Act to be concerned specifically with SENs, which was passed in 1981 and implemented in 1983. The Act defines SENs as those which require additional or different provision from that 'made generally' within an LEA. The LEA also has to identify those children whose needs require provision which it can only offer on an individual basis, whether in the child's school or in a special school or with other support. For such a decision, a multiprofessional assessment of the child has to be carried out by LEA-designated personnel, with the needs and provision to be set out in a 'Statement' to be reviewed annually. Parents must be given an opportunity to comment on any provision the LEA proposes and can appeal if they disagree. The current Education Bill proposes that appeals be considered by Tribunals, which would replace the existing variety of arrangements.

In the light of the Warnock Committee's rejection of the label of 'handicap', the then Department of Education and Science (DES) subsequently ceased to collect data on pupils by category of handicap. In order to plan provision for SENs as they occur, it is of course still important to have information on the prevalence of hearing, visual or motor impairment, problems in language development, emotional and behavioural difficulties, difficulty in learning ranging from specific difficulties with reading, for example, to severe and general learning difficulties, and combinations of any of these. The last 25 years have seen changes in the incidence of disabling conditions as the result of advances in preventive medicine and in obstetric practice. The former has drastically reduced the incidence of, for example, hearing impairment; the latter has, to varying extents, led to the survival of children with more severe and multiple disabilities.

The Warnock Committee made a number of crucial recommendations which were not incorporated in the 1981 Act, and have still not been instituted. The Committee recommended that parents of children should be offered a 'named person', who could guide them in planning appropriate provision for their children. Another recommendation was that *all* teachers with designated responsibility for special needs education should have a recognised qualification appropriate to their work. In the years following the 1981 Act, a small number of research projects was commissioned to study how special needs education had changed from the publication of the Warnock Report onwards. The following are some of the changes reported up to the middle or late 1980s in studies of samples of LEAs:

- 66% of LEAs increased staff supporting pupils with SENs in ordinary schools between 1978 and 1983[11].
- 54% of LEAs increased expenditure on special needs relative to inflation between 1983 and 1987, a reflection of the fact that the 1981 Act had been introduced without additional funding[12].
- 76% of LEAs reported an increase in pupils with SENs taught in nursery, primary and secondary schools between 1983 and 1985. There was a general shift from segregated to less segregated provision for pupils with all forms of SEN except for emotional and behaviour problems[12].
- Data from LEA returns to the DES showed that, between 1982 and 1987, there was an overall drop from 1.53% to 1.41% in the percentage of pupils aged 5–15 in special schools in England. This study also revealed wide variations between different LEAs, with some showing significant increases[20].

The above findings show that most LEAs responded to concern about meeting the SENs of pupils in ordinary schools. There was, overall, a move to reducing the extent to which pupils with SENs were segregated. However, it has to be remembered that these general trends smooth over significant variations between different LEAs.

The implications of recent legislation

When introduced as a Bill, the 1988 'Education Reform Act' made barely any reference to how special needs education was to be furthered or even maintained. Schools' funding was to depend predominantly on the number of their pupils and they would compete for pupils through their position in league tables of aggregate achievement in the national curriculum. Both these provisions constituted a potential disincentive for schools to admit pupils with SENs and to allocate resources to support them. At the same time, LEAs were required to delegate increasing proportions of their funds to schools, thus reducing the amount available for central services to support pupils with SENs. Community Charge-capping and the loss of funds allocated to 'opted-out' grant-maintained schools further reduced LEA budgets. A number of studies illustrated the effect of these problems on schools and LEAs:

- the National Foundation for Educational Research (NFER) found that, already in late 1991, 15% of a sample of 81 LEAs reported that schools had made cuts in special needs co-ordinator posts and in learning support departments[10].
- an unpublished study for the Economic and Social Research Council found that 85% of a sample of 946 secondary teachers in 4 LEAs were concerned about the resource implications for pupils with SENs[23].
- the Audit Commission and HMI found that, in a small sample of headteachers interviewed, 52% judged that the resources to meet pupils' SENs were insufficient, although 69% claimed that they were not limiting their admission of pupils with SENs.

There is a considerable body of anecdotal evidence suggesting that both ordinary and special schools are finding it difficult to meet pupils' SENs. The trend is reflected in increases in the percentage of pupils with statements of special needs in LEAs. If schools cannot fund the resources they need to meet pupils' SENs, the Statement procedure offers a way of obtaining additional resources from the LEA. Thus:

- it was reported that between 1990 and 1992, the average percentage of pupils who had been 'statemented' rose from 2.0% to 2.4%, despite the fact that most LEAs had policies intended to limit increases[9];

- a study of Department for Education (DFE) data on the percentage of children in special schools showed that there was a new rise from 1.02% to 1.04% between 1988 and 1991 among primary school children, while the trend for secondary school children continued downwards from 2.09% to 2.05%[21];

- a survey carried out at the end of 1991 found that 50% of LEAs reported an overall increase in pupils placed in special schools[16];

- a DFE report expresses concern about the number of pupils excluded from schools. This matches other reports of a marked increase in exclusions[5]. It is important to distinguish among these those pupils who are regarded as having SENs, usually those with emotional or behaviour disturbances. But it is significant that data obtained over a two-year period showed that 12.5% of excluded pupils had Statements, indicating that even the designated resources were not proving sufficient for these pupils.

The Bill published in November 1992 poses further problems for meeting pupils' SENs. It envisages a progressive limitation of the LEA's scope to co-ordinate support in its area for pupils' SENs, as the proportion of its 'opted-out' schools increases. If and when the proportion reaches 75%, the LEA's responsibility for SENs will be limited to pupils with Statements. At this point, the Bill would also stop provision for SENs being administered as a continuum. It would also make it impossible for LEAs to submit to the Secretary of State their plans for meeting the full range of pupils' SENs in their area, as required in Circular 7/91. The crucial need for LEAs to co-ordinate provision was stressed by the House of Commons Select Committee on Education in its 1987 report on the functioning of the 1981 Act. The Committee concluded that special needs provision was too complex to be left to the responsibility of individual schools.

Under the Bill, grant-maintained schools would come under a national Funding Agency for Schools (FAS), which would presumably share responsibility for pupils with SENs with the LEA. This would add to the already existing difficulty in achieving co-ordination of responsibility for meeting SENs between education and non-education agencies serving different geographical areas[12]. A further agency, the Office for Standards in Education (OFSTED), now has the general responsibility for supervising the quality of education offered. It will delegate this responsibility to inspection teams whose tenders it accepts. Although the procedures to be adopted by these teams include inspection of special needs provision, there are no assurances that the teams will have the necessary level of expertise. The teams will not be responsible for ensuring that any required improvements are achieved.

The Bill and the 1988 Act thus fragment responsibility for ensuring that the range of pupils' SENs are met. In response to representations made to it, the government has amended the Bill to require that all schools supply information about how they meet their pupils' SENs, and has also permitted LEAs to continue to offer some specialist services for pupils with SENs. Many of the detailed requirements regarding provision for pupils' SENs will be covered in a 'Code of Practice' yet to be agreed. It remains to be seen what this will contain and how its requirements will be funded. It is paradoxical that, while the Bill increases the uncertainties about how pupils' SENs can be met effectively, its main specific provisions on SENs focus on revising procedures to enable parents to appeal if they are dissatisfied with the provision made for their children.

The future

The Audit Commission and HMI showed that there has been much to criticise as well as to praise in the past and present education of pupils with SENs[2]. In general, however, the evidence indicates that following the Warnock Report there was a period of considerable advance, but since the time of the 1988 Act there has been a deterioration in provision for pupils with SENs. The current Bill, as it stands at the time this paper is being written, might well continue this trend. The provisions of the recent legislation have been termed 'reforms', and so one would have expected them at least to promote the good which has been achieved. Referring to the proposals for special needs education in the Bill, the Chairman of the Select Committee on Education (Sir Malcolm Thornton) is quoted (*TES* December 11th 1992) as saying 'If we really believe that SENs are going to be given a better deal under the new legislation than under the old system, then this is the biggest triumph of hope over experience that I have ever encountered'.

It is paradoxical that a number of the aims espoused by the recent legislation are ones which would be regarded as reasonable, were it not that the means chosen to implement them are potentially counter-productive and potentially harmful to pupils with SENs. The following are some examples:

1   The aim of giving schools flexibility by allowing them to manage their own budgets is to be commended. However, if the cost of meeting pupils' SENs is included, then under present circumstances the integration of pupils with SENs may be hindered. When funds are short and schools' budgets depend on competition for pupil numbers, a school's commitment towards 'expensive' and potentially 'popularity reducing' pupils is put

under strain, and at worst becomes incompatible with practicalities of funding.

2   Greater regard for the cost-effectiveness of services could lead to more considered use. However, this does not imply that special needs services can be operated on market-economy principles. Forcing specialist services to depend on purchaser-provider relationships with individual schools makes them too sensitive to the ability of schools to afford them. Quality services for pupils' SENs can be quickly lost, but would take long to rebuild. This will need to be considered in guidance about the amendment to the Bill allowing LEAs to continue to offer specialist services.

3   The promotion of parental involvement in democratic decision-making about the education of their children should be encouraged. There must, however, be safeguards for parents of children with SENs who are by definition in a minority. With pupil-led funding in times of constrained finances, schools wishing to maximise their resources may favour policies supporting the interests of the majority of parents, thus jeopardising the rights of the few.

4   The aim of making funding formulae for schools 'transparent' and 'easily understood' might seem desirable, but not if the formulae are *educationally* meaningless. For example, a recent consultation paper on funding GM schools proposes that the cost of meeting their pupils' SENs should be based on the proportion of pupils who obtain free meals in any given school, because this is an easily derivable figure. The Audit Commission and HMI showed that many LEAs have developed collaborative audit procedures which offer not only a direct means of assessing the various levels of support schools provide for pupils' SENs, but which also form an essential part of the development of whole

school policies on meeting SENs[2]. These procedures may not be 'transparent', but they can make a direct contribution to raising school effectiveness.

From the point of view of special needs education, perhaps the main paradox is that the current legislation proposes means which do not further its aims to provide for pupils' diverse educational needs. Seen from 25 years hence, it will seem inexplicable that, although we recognised our failure to meet diversity, we did not recognise the reasons for this failure.

It is not the task of this paper to prognosticate on the future of education in general. However, from the point of view of the education of pupils with SENs two points emerge. First, many writers on special needs education in this country[1] and in the USA[19] have pointed out that the continuum of pupils' SENs merges into the range of diversity of ability identifiable in all pupils, and consequently special needs education must be offered more as an extension of education in general. Second, special needs education has for long been organised to achieve flexibility of response to pupils' diversity *within* schools, both ordinary and special schools. The extent to which flexibility has been achieved in ordinary schools is illustrated in the Danish concept of the 'school for all'[14]. It is significant that, in Denmark, only about 0.5% of pupils have to be offered education in segregated provision.

Progress in the education of pupils with SENs in the next 25 years will be inextricably linked with developments in educating all children and young people. These developments will start from the recognition that schools cannot meet the diversity of their pupils' needs with the rigidity of preordained classes of standard size, each staffed by a teacher required to provide standard pedagogical approaches to an over-detailed curriculum. Seen from 25 years on, it will seem incredible that we did not use the scope for organisational and pedagogical flexibility which already exists to respond to the particular demands both of the various aspects of a broad and balanced curriculum and of pupils' learning needs. These varied demands call for flexibility in using the range of teacher expertise, non-teaching support, size of pupil grouping, and instructional media including micro-processors. They also call for the participation of pupils, parents and the community, and the involvement of supporting specialist education, health and social services personnel.

Educational approaches for pupils with SENs offer many indications about how these kinds of flexible response to pupil needs and curricular demands can be achieved. Panel 2 shows three areas.

PANEL 2: A flexible response
1. *Making better use of available resources*
   - The Audit Commission and HMI reported how schools in some LEAs participate in decisions about the equitable sharing of resources for pupils with and without Statements[2]. As a result, schools are led to consider their own needs in relation to the needs of other schools.
   - Schools which group themselves into partnerships to share resources for their pupils' SENs have been the subject of a recent study[8]. Such schools have increased their capacity to meet pupils' SENs through mutual support in developing whole-school policies and through sharing the expertise available both in their own schools and from specialist support services. The partnerships often span the phases of schooling, and so ensure continuity in the way in which individual pupils' needs are met.
   - Ordinary schools have set up links with special schools to exchange pedagogic and subject expertise between staff, and to allow flexible movement of pupils between the schools[13]. This flexibility can counter the potential segregation of pupils in special schools, and widen the interpersonal experience of mainstream pupils.
   - In-service materials have been developed to enable Education, Health and Social Services staff to collaborate in organising special needs provision, in order to meet pupils' needs more effectively and also to avoid wasteful overlapping and interference[8].

---

2. *Matching pedagogical practice to the needs of pupils and the demands of a broad and balanced curriculum*
   - 'Teacher support teams' have been formed in schools to mobilise the varied expertise of staff in schools to help individual teachers facing problems in meeting their pupils' needs[17].
   - The contributions of teachers and classroom assistants have been made more effective through systematic planning of their respective roles to maximise support for pupils in the classroom[3].
   - In many curriculum areas children with different learning needs have been shown to learn more effectively if they are grouped to collaborate in each others' learning[18].
   - Parents have made a major contribution to their children's learning through collaboration with teachers. This has been demonstrated in a variety of studies including some of children learning to read and others concerned with the development of personal competence in children with severe learning difficulties[22].
   - The contribution of computer-aided learning for pupils with SENs has been amply demonstrated across a range of curriculum areas[15]. Flexible 'shell' programmes have made it simpler for teachers to match programmes to individual pupils' learning needs, and 'talking' computers have extended scope for responsiveness. Micro-processors have also revolutionised methods of helping children with motor or sensory disabilities to overcome communication barriers.

3. *Effective teaching depends ultimately on teachers being able to respond flexibly to pupils' learning*
   - Teachers need a clear framework of curricular progression against which to monitor pupil progress, and efficient ways of recording what pupils have achieved.
   - Pedagogic practice in the education of pupils throughout the range of SENs has long been grounded in curriculum-based assessment, and a variety of user-friendly means of record-keeping has been devised. The introduction of the national curriculum has offered a so-far unrealised opportunity to build a relevant and realistic framework of progression in the curricular areas covered, and this could contribute to improved curriculum-based assessment.

Conclusions

The examples in the panel show that practices in the education of pupils with SENs already indicate how an educational context could be created which could respond to pupil diversity. A further crucial requirement is that the requisite spectrum of teacher expertise is available to match pupils' SENs. This in turn demands that opportunities are assured for teachers to acquire appropriate forms and levels of professional qualification, one of the aims of the Warnock Report which has not yet been achieved.

Progress in education for the next 25 years has to start with a recognition of children and young people as they are. From this a context can be created which meets the full range of pupils' SENs along the lines of the principles originally stated in the Warnock Report. It is clear that effectiveness cannot be achieved without a commitment to providing the necessary means, but the examples given show that concern for the efficient use of resources does not have to be neglected. Perhaps the most significant finding of all is that many of the necessary developments depend on creating a climate which encourages the collaborative sharing of responsibility. Will it be possible to pursue the vision of these developments through the present turbulence in education?

May 1993

References

[1] Ainscow, M. (in press) *Towards effective schools for all.* National Association for SENs.

[2] Audit Commission/HMI (1992) *Getting in on the Act/Getting the Act together.* HMSO.

[3] Balshaw, M. (1991) *Help in the classroom.* Fulton.

[4] DES (1978) *Special Educational Needs, the 'Warnock Report'.* HMSO.

[5] DFE (1992) *Exclusions* – a discussion paper.

[6] DFE (1992) *A common funding formula for grant-maintained*

schools.

7   Evans *et al* (1989) *Decision-making for SENs.* Institute of
Education.

8   Evans *et al* (in press) *Clusters, the collaborative approach to meeting SENs.* In Riddell, S. and Brown, S. (eds.) *Children with SENs:
Policies and Practice into the 1990s.* Routledge.

9   Evans, J. and Lunt, I. (1992) *Developments in special education
under LMS.* Institute of Education.

10 Fletcher-Campbell, F. with Hall, C. (1993) *LEA support for special
needs.* NFER-Nelson.

11 Gipps, C. *et al* (1987) *Warnock's Eighteen percent.* Falmer Press.

12 Goacher, B. *et al* (1988) *Policy and provision for SENs.* Cassell.

13 Jowett, S. *et al* (1988) *Joining forces: a study of links between special and ordinary schools.* NFER-Nelson.

14 Hansen, J. (1992) *The development of the Danish Folkeskole,
towards a school for all.* European Journal of Special Needs
Education. 7.

15 Hawkridge, D. and Vincent, T. (1992) *Learning difficulties and
computers.* Jessica King.

16 Lunt, I. and Evans, J. (1991) *SENs under LMS.* Institute of
Education.

17 Norwich, B. and Daniels, H. (1992) *Support from the team.*
Managing schools today 1 (6) 30–31.

18 Slavin, R.E. (1989) *Co-operative learning and student achievement,*
in: Slavin, R.E. (ed.) School and classroom organisation. Erlbaum.

19 Stainback, W. and Stainback, S. (1984) *A rationale for the merger
of special and regular education.* Exceptional Children 51 (2).

20 Swann, W. (1987) *Integration statistics.* Centre for Studies on
Integration in Education.

21 Swann, W. (1992) *Segregation statistics.* Centre for Studies on
Integration in Education.

22 Wolfendale, S. (ed.) (1989) *Parental involvement.* Cassell.

23 Wrigley, V. and Clough, P. (1992) Personal communication.

15 Promoting Careers: Guidance for Learning and Work

A.G. Watts

Director, National Institute for Careers Education and
Counselling (NICEC); co-founder, Careers Research
and Advisory Centre (CRAC)

Summary

1   Careers education and guidance are now higher on the
    public-policy agenda than ever before. This can be
    related to changes in the nature of learning and work,
    and of career development.
2   The case for radical improvements in guidance provi-
    sion is supported by its benefits to individuals and to
    social equality, but also by evidence concerning its eco-
    nomic benefits.
3   Careers education and guidance should be an integral
    part of the curriculum in schools and of the funding pro-
    vision for post-compulsory education. Within schools,
    there should be an explicit entitlement. Within post-
    compulsory education, the role of guidance should
    include feedback on learners' unmet needs.
4   Career development should be an integral part of all
    employment provision. Investors in People and similar
    programmes are currently providing welcome support to
    this notion, but much more needs to be done.
5   Alongside guidance services within education and
    employment, there should also be access to guidance
    from a neutral, independent base. Such services can
    provide broader-based guidance from a more impartial
    perspective; they can also help to ensure coherence
    and continuity of guidance provision. A big expansion of
    guidance services for adults is needed, funded on the
    principle of core provision for all and more comprehen-
    sive provision for those unable to pay.

6   Recommendations are made for the establishment of a
National Council on Guidance for Learning and Work,
for improvements in training for guidance practitioners,
for the exploitation of computer-aided careers guidance
systems, and for the development of a culture of evaluation in the guidance field.

The changing role of guidance

Career choices determine how we spend a major part of our lives and much of the contribution we make to the society in which we live. They also determine, to a significant degree, the kind of people we become.

Guidance services exist to help people with these choices. In the past, their role has been a limited one. Choices have been determined largely by social forces and by selective processes within education and employment. Guidance services have tended to be a kind of switch mechanism at the transition from education to employment. They have accordingly tended to be marginal in position and low in status.

Now the situation may be changing. The debate stimulated by the CBI report *Towards a Skills Revolution*[1] has helped to place guidance higher on the public-policy agenda than ever before. The CBI report viewed guidance as a key part of a strategy designed to upgrade skill levels and improve national competitiveness. It also emphasised that career development (and by implication careers guidance) should be *for all* and should be *lifelong*: in other words, that all individuals should be encouraged to review their skills and their career directions regularly throughout their lives.

This change of policy perspective is linked to more profound changes within education and employment which are reflected in the shift of attention to the concepts of learning and of work. The shift of concepts is significant in three respects:

- Their *breadth*. Learning takes place in many settings, not just educational ones. 'Learning' covers education *and* training: it does not deny the distinction between them, but it encourages them to inter-penetrate one another. 'Work' covers employment and recognises its crucial importance, but covers other work too: self-employment, for example, and all the household work and voluntary work, not to mention shadow-economy work, which sustain communities and enrich their quality.

- Their *nature*. 'Education' and 'employment' tend to describe institutional structures: they are, in that sense, bureaucratic, industrial-society concepts. 'Learning' and 'work' are essentially about processes and are owned by individuals: they are more potent concepts for a post-industrial society.

- Their *relationship*. Education tends to be seen as preceding employment. Learning and work cannot be seen in that way. One works to learn; one learns to work. They are symbiotic: they depend upon one another. Both are continuing processes. In the post-industrial world, a society that wishes to work must be a learning society.

The concept of 'career' is being redefined along similar lines. Increasingly, it is viewed in broad terms, not as a structure (e.g. a career *in* engineering), but as a process, to describe an individual's lifetime of learning and work. This view changes radically the role of careers guidance. If 'career' is a process owned by the individual, just as 'learning' and 'work' are, then guidance needs to be ongoing, and central not peripheral.

These shifts reflect changes in the 'psychological contract' between the individual on the one hand, and education and employment systems on the other[2]. Employers no longer want to take responsibility for long-term commitments to individuals. Educational institutions increasingly want to view individuals as independent learners. Pressures are being exerted on both sets of institutions to be more responsive to individual needs and demands. Individuals are moving more frequently between educational institutions, between employers, and between the two. Their relationships with these institutions are open to more regular review. Guidance is a key means of empowering individuals within this process. It is the lubricant that activates and channels the individual's energies, and enables both education and employment systems to respond to, and draw from, those energies (see figure below).

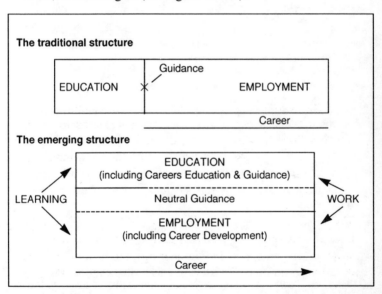

The case for radical improvements in guidance provision is justified by the benefits it brings to individuals and to social equity. But it is further supported by evidence concerning its public economic benefits[3]. Guidance can assist the efficient operation of the labour market in three main ways:

- by supporting the *individual decisions* through which the labour market operates;
- by reducing some of the *market failures* of the labour market (for example, reducing drop-outs from education and training, and mismatches between supply and demand);
- by contributing to *institutional reforms* designed to improve the functioning of the labour market.

The Audit Commission and HM Inspectorate have recently underlined the role of guidance in reducing waste within educational provision for 16–19-year-olds[4].

Who benefits?

Potentially, careers guidance offers benefits:
- to *individuals*, in enabling them to cope with and derive maximum benefit from the complex range of educational and vocational choices with which they are presented;
- to *education and training providers*, in increasing the effectiveness of their provision by helping learners to be linked to programmes which meet their needs;
- to *employers*, in helping potential employees to come forward whose talents and motivations are matched to the employer's requirements;
- to *government*, in making maximum economic use of society's human resources.

Careers guidance services can accordingly play a significant role in fostering:
- efficiency in the allocation and use of human resources;
- social equity in access to educational and vocational opportunities.

They also have a particularly important function in reconciling these roles with the value attached in democratic societies to the rights of individuals to make free choices about their own lives.

A three-pronged strategy

What is needed is a national strategy on guidance for learning and work with three facets:
- careers education and guidance as an integral part both

of schools and of post-compulsory education, offering regular opportunities for pupils and students to explore the relationship between what they are learning and their career development;
- career development as an integral part of all employment provision, offering trainees and employees regular opportunities to review their current work, their future aspirations, their skill requirements, and ways of meeting these requirements;
- access to *neutral careers guidance* at points when individuals wish to review objectively possibilities for movement between educational institutions, or between employers, or between the two.

Careers education and guidance in schools

Careers education and guidance should occupy a pivotal role in schools. It should link the school to the economic system, the needs of pupils to the needs of the wider society, and the individual pupil's present to his or her future.

The core of a school's careers programme is careers education within the curriculum, designed to develop the skills, knowledge and attitudes which will enable pupils to make and implement career decisions both now and in the future. Careers education has four main components[5]:
- *self awareness* – acquiring understanding of the distinctive characteristics (abilities, skills, interests, values) that define who one is and the person one wishes to become;
- *opportunity awareness* – acquiring understanding of the world of work, the opportunities it provides, the demands those opportunities make, and the rewards and satisfactions they offer;
- *decision learning* – acquiring skills for making career decisions;
- *transition learning* – acquiring skills for implementing career decisions and managing career transitions.

Careers education and guidance are officially defined within the National Curriculum as constituting one component of five cross-curricular themes, from age 5 to age 16[6]. These themes are, however, structurally weak; the notion of cross-curricular themes is attractive in principle but difficult to implement, and can erode specialist provision without putting anything of substance in its place; the crucial support services from LEA advisers and the like are beginning to disintegrate; and the Technical and Vocational Education Initiative (TVEI), the contractual nature of which is largely responsible for keeping careers work actively on schools' agenda, has now passed its resource peak and is due to end in 1997.

What is needed is a clear statement of entitlement[7] which is visible to pupils and parents, is made accountable by identifying a careers co-ordinator responsible for making sure it is delivered, and is regularly evaluated as part of school inspections. This entitlement should include:
- a formal, progressive careers education curriculum, defined in terms of input (minimum amount of curriculum time) and/or of learning outcomes (which should be assessed where possible);
- access to high-quality information, including use of information technology;
- experience of work, integrated into the curriculum, including at least two weeks' work experience (broadly defined) in the final period of compulsory schooling;
- access to individual guidance, delivered by persons trained in its techniques;
- regular opportunities to engage in recording achievement and action planning.

Curriculum provision should start from age 5 to develop pupils' concepts of work roles and to counteract restrictive stereotypes related to social background and gender which can form at an early age. Specific timetabled provision – whether on a stand-alone basis or integrated into a programme of personal and social education – should start at age 13 at the latest. This provision should be complemented by longer blocks of time (for experience-based activities) linked to cross-curricular infusion of careers concepts: a declared policy and support structure are needed to manage such infusion. It is also important that tutors and parents should be actively involved in the careers programme.

Every secondary school should have a careers co-ordinator. It is a crucial role. Co-ordinators need to be of sufficient seniority to carry out their managerial role, and to be adequately trained. A recent survey found that less than a third of the teachers responsible for careers guidance work in schools have a professional qualification in guidance, and concluded that 'the quantity of careers guidance training remains a national disgrace'[8]. This requires urgent attention if quality careers programmes are to be developed in all schools.

Careers education and guidance in post-compulsory education

Traditionally, the sector of education in which guidance has been least well developed is further education (FE). This has been because of the (often false) assumption that students have already committed themselves to particular career paths by their choice of (vocational) course. The growth of non-vocational courses and of courses concerned with broad forms of vocational preparation has however changed this situation, and careers education elements are often now included in such courses. Indeed, some FE courses are in effect extended careers education and guidance programmes: this applies, for example, to courses designed for those returning to study or paid employment after child-rearing, or for the unemployed. Moreover, the growth of modular courses and of credit accumulation and transfer systems means that guidance is now required on a continuing basis to help students to build up and review their individual modular programmes, particularly as some of these choices may have important vocational implications. The new funding arrangements for further education attach considerable importance to guidance at entry to, during, and on exit from, learning programmes[9].

Within higher education, most traditional universities have well-established careers services of their own. These provide very effective information and placement services, as well as guidance interviews. An increasing number also set up careers education programmes, either as part of the curriculum or outside it. If such programmes are to grow, however, it seems desirable for teaching departments to take more ownership of them, using the careers service as a resource. The Enterprise in Higher Education programme has encouraged developments of this kind[10]. At the same time, some of the former polytechnics have very limited career services: sometimes one adviser for several thousand students. Clearer guidelines for adequate provision are needed from funding bodies. Each higher education institution should have a clear policy on its delivery both of careers education and of individual guidance.

A key role for guidance in all post-compulsory education, particularly in adult and continuing education, is providing feedback on learners' needs which are not met by existing provision. Guidance can thus not only help individuals to choose between the opportunities available, but also encourage educational providers to adapt to learners' requirements.

Career development in employment

Career development within employment is a major current growth area. The government's Investors in People initiative, alongside the emerging structure of National Vocational Qualifications, is providing strong support to appraisal schemes and the like which incorporate guidance purposes. This is now being enhanced by the Skill Choice initiative which includes encouragement for employers to offer their employees 'skill check' credits. In addition, employers are increasingly incorporating access to guidance as part of out-placement packages.

The National Record of Achievement, including attention to action planning as well as recording past achievement, is being introduced not only in schools and colleges but also by some employers. It potentially provides a basis for life-time learning and progression.

The implementation of such methods is still however limited, particularly among small and medium-sized companies. While a promising start has been made, much more needs to be done before help with career development becomes a reality for all or even most employees.

The need for neutral guidance

The potential advantages of guidance services within education and within employment are:
- They have more continuous contact with the individuals based in their organisation, and so are able to deliver more sustained guidance than any external service could do.
- They are likely to be in a stronger position to influence their organisation to alter its opportunity structures in response to individuals' needs and demands, as revealed through the guidance process.

On the other hand:
- Many people spend significant parts of their lives outside education and employment (because they are

unemployed, for example, or engaged in child-rearing).

- Guidance services within particular organisations do not usually have a sufficiently broad view of opportunities outside that organisation.
- Organisations can have vested interests in the outcomes of individuals' decisions, which can make it difficult to provide guidance that is neutral. HMI, for instance, have criticised the tendency in some schools to bias guidance at 16 to encourage students to stay on (with the capitation advantages this brings to the school) rather than to move on to learning opportunities elsewhere[11]. Employers, too, are likely to be reluctant to encourage valued employees to explore opportunities in other companies.

It is therefore crucial that there should also be access to the broader and more impartial perspective which a neutral guidance service can bring.

Delivering neutral guidance

The Careers Service has a statutory remit to provide a neutral guidance service, free of charge, for individuals in full- or part-time education. The new Trade Union Reform and Employment Rights Act is designed to give it greater freedom to extend its services to other groups, perhaps on an all-age basis, though the extent of public funding for this is uncertain. It is also important to recognise that there are other guidance agencies that offer neutral guidance, including educational guidance services for adults (usually free of charge) and private guidance agencies (fee-charging).

Arguably, there is an important role for neutral guidance services to play not only in direct guidance delivery but also in supporting guidance activities within education and employment, and in ensuring the overall continuity and coherence of guidance provision. The Careers Service has in recent years played a strong role of this kind in relation to careers programmes in schools and colleges: a crucial by-product is to make its neutral guidance more accessible to students. The removal of the Careers Service from the control of LEAs under the new Act could gravely weaken its relationship to schools and colleges. In implementing the legislation, care needs to be taken to ensure this does not happen, and indeed to strengthen and broaden its supportive role. In the long run, a stronger and more consistent structure than that envisaged by the Act is likely to be needed, with active and balanced involvement of education providers and employers, if quality and genuine neutrality are to be assured.

A massive expansion is also needed of neutral guidance services for adults. Existing provision is limited and poorly publicised, and totally inadequate to meet the potential demand. The government's current response is through experiments in guidance vouchers. It is unclear to what extent this represents an attempt to stimulate a real market in guidance which will encourage financial investment in such guidance from individuals and employers, or a new form of public provision which is likely to be more politically acceptable and more consumer-centred than the old. There is a danger that the attempt to establish a *market in guidance* based on competition between guidance agencies and on customer payment may undermine the establishment (as it is in Germany, for example) of publicly-funded guidance as a *market-maker*: in other words, a cost-effective way of making labour markets (and education and training markets) work[3] may be in jeopardy. At the very least, effective quality-assurance mechanisms are needed plus assured publicly-funded provision for those unable to pay (e.g. the unemployed, the unwaged, and the low-waged), plus some core provision for all. The latter might include, for example, information services, access to computer-aided careers guidance systems, and some professional support to help individuals define the further help they need.

Recommendations

In addition to the proposals made above, it is recommended that:

1 A National Council on Guidance for Learning and Work should be established to define and monitor quality standards and to provide strategic leadership for guidance in support of lifelong career development for all[12].

2 Improvements should be made in training for guidance practitioners, drawing upon the work of the new Lead Body for Advice, Guidance and Counselling in developing nationally recognised standards of competence. (In France, *conseilleurs d'orientation* are now required to have a three-year psychology degree, followed by a two-year specialist diploma and a year's on-the-job training; in some cases in Britain it is possible to practise with no formal guidance training at all.)

3 More investment should be made in exploiting the use of computer-aided careers guidance systems. Such systems have considerable potential for increasing access to guidance and improving its quality, particularly if careful attention is paid to integrating them into broader guidance programmes.

4 Encouragement should be given to developing a culture of evaluation in the guidance field, encompassing standards and performance indicators for management purposes, support for self-reflective practitioners, and effective partnerships with researchers.

July 1993

References

1 Confederation of British Industry (1989) *Towards a Skills Revolution.* CBI.

2 Herriot, P. (1992) *The Career Management Challenge: Balancing*

Individual and Organisational Needs. Sage.

3 Killeen, J., White, M. and Watts, A.G. (1992) *The Economic Value of Careers Guidance.* Policy Studies Institute.

4 Audit Commission and Her Majesty's Inspectorate (1993) *Unfinished Business.* HMSO.

5 Law, B. and Watts, A.G. (1977) *Schools, Careers and Community.* Church Information Office.

6 National Curriculum Council (1990) *Curriculum Guidance 6: Careers Education and Guidance.* NCC.

7 Confederation of British Industry (1993) *A Credit to Your Career.* CBI.

8 Cleaton, D. (1993) *Careers Education and Guidance in British Schools.* Institute of Careers Guidance/National Association of Careers and Guidance Teachers.

9 Further Education Funding Council (1992) *Funding Learning.* FEFC.

10 Watts, A.G. and Hawthorn, R. (1992) *Careers Education and the Curriculum in Higher Education.* CRAC/Hobsons.

11 Her Majesty's Inspectorate (1992) *Survey of Guidance 13–19 in Schools and Sixth Form Colleges.* Department of Education and Science.

12 Ball, C. (ed., 1993) *Guidance Matters: Developing a National Strategy for Guidance in Learning and Work.*

16 Raising Standards in Deprived Urban Areas

Michael Barber

Professor of Education at Keele University and
formerly Head of Education and Equal Opportunities
Department at the National Union of Teachers

Summary

1 Standards of education in Britain's deprived urban
  areas are too low, as demonstrated by GCSE results,
  assessments at age seven, and HMI Reports.
2 Not only are spending cuts having a detrimental effect
  but recent reforms are encouraging the tendency of
  markets to redistribute resources from the weak to the
  strong.
3 Individual schools can buck trends only in the short
  term. LEAs' powers are too constrained for them to
  tackle successfully and strategically the educational
  problems of deprived urban areas. A national strategy is
  urgently required to challenge educational disadvantage
  in these areas and to build on the many examples of
  good practice around the country.
4 A range of possible solutions for raising standards in
  deprived urban areas is proposed including:
  (a) real growth in spending at small but predictable
      annual increments over a long time scale, with
      resources distributed towards areas of greatest
      need and linked to reform targets;
  (b) a local organisation to co-ordinate child-centred
      services, to support schools, to promote innovation
      and experiment, and to co-ordinate business,
      education and community involvement, intervening
      where a school consistently fails according to
      recognised criteria;
  (c) community-oriented strategic school development
      plans, and recognition and development of the

potential of teachers, other staff and other adults in the community;

(d) universally available child care and nursery education, primary schools concentrating on basic skills, a range of strategies to improve pupil motivation in secondary schools, a wider range of after-school educational opportunities, and encouragement of specialisation of schools (with a return to selection by overall academic ability being ruled out);

(e) continuation of the improved participation in post-compulsory education.

Standards in deprived urban areas

There is no doubt that standards of education in Britain's deprived urban areas are too low. The bottom 30 local education authorities (LEAs) in the league table of GCSE performance are all in urban areas, many of which suffer substantial deprivation[4]. A similar picture emerges from the league table of LEA performance in standard assessment tasks for seven year olds[5]. This evidence confirms the judgement of Her Majesty's Inspectorate (HMI) that 'the poorest schools are those in the inner city taking children from disadvantaged backgrounds...'[8] Social class appears to be the single most important influence on educational achievement. This is evident from the evaluation of the SATs for seven year olds in 1991 and 1992[11,12]. Another analysis of the 1991 SATs suggests that 'about 37% of variation in performance is explained by the level of social status'[13]. If, therefore, Britain's educational performance is to improve substantially over the next decades, a concerted national policy for improving education in deprived urban areas is essential.

Background to the task

The phrase 'deprived urban areas' is a shorthand. It is taken from the most comprehensive recent survey of government policy for urban areas[15]. As the authors point out, 'we understand the objections to the term "deprived areas"; we use it because... to most people it conveys better than any alternative the kind of place we are examining'.

Deprived urban areas have:

- higher absolute rates of unemployment than other areas;
- on average, over 20% of the population claiming income support/supplementary benefit, as against a national level of 11.5%;
- 'housing conditions [that] have deteriorated since 1977'.[15]
- a high incidence of racism, including an increasing amount of racial violence;
- high crime rates, in part related to the growth of the 'drugs culture'.

There is little evidence that life is improving in Britain's urban areas and a good deal to suggest it is deteriorating[15]. None have yet reached the state of complete breakdown which appears to have occurred in Los Angeles, but as an image of the future of some of Britain's deprived urban areas it remains a potent symbol. This is not intended to suggest in any deterministic sense that educational failure is inevitable for many pupils in deprived urban areas. Nor is it to argue that the *aims* of education should be different in an urban area. On the contrary, it is to argue that if pupils from these areas are to be given an opportunity of education even remotely equal in quality to that of their counterparts elsewhere, then a national strategy is required to challenge educational disadvantage and to build on the many examples of good practice around the country.

At present there is considerable evidence that national policy is having the opposite effect. This is certainly the case in relation to expenditure levels. There is clear evidence of real reductions in expenditure in the last two or three years though the effect so far on classrooms, as opposed to LEA services, has been limited. One major consequence has been a dramatic reduction in spending on discretionary services such as adult education, under-fives, the youth service and discretionary student awards.

However, the problem is not solely, or even mainly, an issue of resources. With the exception of the relatively small grants for truancy and literacy purposes, the basic assumption behind government policy is that its general educational strategy will benefit all areas, including deprived urban areas. Even if this proves true, the huge gap in terms of achievement would remain. There is little or no evidence yet of the success of recent policies in terms of educational outcomes. HMI, reporting on the National Curriculum[9] and on local management of schools (LMS)[10], found no evidence that either had yet raised standards. In April 1993 they reached a similar conclusion about grant-maintained schools.

Although it is early days to conclude that these policies have failed, certain preliminary conclusions can be drawn:
- 'markets' have a tendency to redistribute resources from the weaker to the stronger;
- schools in deprived urban areas are more likely to require the external support which is currently being reduced;
- there is no policy element designed consciously to counteract the disadvantage faced by pupils in deprived urban areas.

It seems reasonable to conclude, therefore, that current national education policy by itself is unlikely to solve or even alleviate the huge educational difficulties facing deprived urban areas.

Furthermore, the ability of LEAs to solve the problems is constrained by:
- tight expenditure restrictions;
- central government's determination to reduce their powers;
- in some cases, their own inefficiency as organisations and the lack of co-ordination between them and other relevant service organisations;

- the destructive rather than creative relationship between local and central government which characterised the 1980s.

In spite of these restrictions, some LEAs have achieved notable successes, particularly at tertiary level.

Individual schools also can, to use Peter Mortimore's phrase, 'buck the trends'[1]. The effective schools research of Rutter, Mortimore, Smith and Tomlinson, and others shows that some schools in urban settings are far more effective than others. Nevertheless, focusing solely on in-school factors associated with success will not lead to salvation across the system. The evidence shows all too clearly that urban schools suffering a change of leadership, high teacher turnover, a rapid change in student population or other pressures can descend rapidly from success to failure.

On a more positive note, there have been some recent trends that are encouraging for schools in deprived urban areas. The current review of the National Curriculum may lead to its becoming more flexible. It should lay down the basics and leave greater opportunity for inner city schools to relate their curriculum to their particular locality and pupils. Sensible assessment based on national criteria at regular intervals is essential. Inner city schools need to be able to compare themselves to schools elsewhere, and to national standards. There is encouraging evidence that at last strides are being made towards major improvements in post-16 participation rates. It is also significant that the government is prepared to invest in this growth area even at a time of public expenditure cuts. This and the development of innovative access courses have assisted in improving the numbers moving from deprived urban areas into higher education.

A package of possible solutions

Level of resources
Both the adequacy and predictability of available resources need to be addressed. A possible solution would be to develop a ten-year strategy which involved sustained growth at small, real, and predictable rates (e.g. 1% to 3% per annum), integrally linked to the targets for the implementation of reform. Then schools could provide the consistent strategic development which would underpin improved education.

Allocation of resources
Resources should be redistributed towards areas of greatest need. This can be achieved through the Department of the Environment Standing Spending Assessments at national level and through the LMS formula at local level. When there is a national Common Funding Formula it too could be used to redistribute, although unless it is sensitive to local circumstances it may fail to be sufficiently precise. An essential element of the investment programme should be its relationship to the achievement of reform targets at school and other levels in the system. Careful evaluation procedures would, therefore, be essential.

Providing local direction
Current government policy seems designed to reduce the LEA to undertaking those functions which neither schools nor private sector agencies are prepared to take on. It underestimates the need in deprived urban areas for both a creative force and a support network. Solving the problems of deprived urban areas requires some local organisation which can:
- support schools during periods of transition (e.g. change of head, excessive staff turnover) or other turbulence (e.g. an influx of refugees, an economic setback such as the shutdown of a major local employer);

- set targets and evaluate progress;
- design an appropriate funding formula;
- contribute to (but not dictate) each school's planning process;
- co-ordinate the business (e.g. compacts) and voluntary sector contribution;
- ensure innovation from sources other than central government.

These roles are over and above the special education responsibilities which the government has decided to leave in local hands. The need to encourage innovation at all levels (a factor insistently made in the literature on successful management) should be emphasised.

A multi-agency approach

Education reform could have significant benefits, but it would be misleading to suggest that it alone can bring about the dramatic improvement of standards that is required. There is a need for a co-ordinated strategic policy involving those responsible for health, housing, social security, business, training, education and resourcing. There is some evidence from the USA that school districts which have made advances on education reform are developing structures for inter-agency collaboration or child-centred services. San Diego's New Beginnings Initiative and the Minneapolis Youth Co-ordinating Board are examples of a variety of services jointly promoting 'child-based reforms'[3].

Business involvement

The recession has weakened partnerships between schools and business. Nevertheless, the potential benefits have been demonstrated in the 1980s. Work experience (currently in danger of collapse), properly integrated into the curriculum, should be seen as essential. The original compacts worked well, the watered-down successors less so. The potential of partnership remains to be developed.

Experimentation should be encouraged; for example, certain types of business unit such as design studios could operate from within school buildings. The benefit to pupils in providing a wider range of role models could be substantial.

Reform-focused negotiation

There is ample evidence from Australia and the USA, as well as the UK, that school-based models of management (such as LMS) are broadly positive once there is sufficient money in the system and assuming the formulae allow for redistribution. To unlock their full potential two further steps are required: first, teachers, headteachers and governors need training for their respective management and governance roles; and, second, schools need to develop genuine partnership with parents and the local community. Research shows that when parents understand what their children should be learning, how children should learn it and how they can assist their children, then standards rise[6]. Community compacts could help to reduce the substantial gap in understanding between teachers and parents and unlock the potential of partnership[7].

The example of Cincinnati in Ohio is instructive. There, leadership of the reform programme has rested with the local teacher union in alliance with business and the (largely black) local community. This combination has shifted a sometimes reluctant school board towards radical change. Traditional negotiations over salaries and conditions have been replaced by problem-solving negotiations which link reform to investment. Both school district and teachers have obligations but see 'the improvement of educational standards as the most important issue on the bargaining agenda' (*Cincinnati Enquirer*, 16 December 1984). The focus has been on partnership and the professionalisation of teaching. Outcome data provide no clear evidence as yet, but relatively high levels of community satisfaction suggest that the reforms are having an impact.

So far these kinds of development have not occurred in Britain. While governing bodies here have balanced representation of parents, teachers and community, their potential, particularly in deprived urban areas, has not been realised. The key to this will be the extent to which headteachers and teachers involve governors and parents in education policy development. Each school's development plan could set out not only a three-to five-year strategy but also annual targets. They could become the focus of problem-solving negotiation between staff, governors and representatives of parents. Some targets might relate to pupil achievement or the implementation of reform in the school. Others might involve changes in the community's attitude to the school (e.g. agreed levels of attendance at parents' evenings). The school development plan could thus become a 'community compact' or, to use the American phrase, 'a trust agreement'. This would provide agreed goals and a practical strategy for achieving them.

Support for inner city teachers

Teachers in the inner city need to have pride and to found all their work on high expectations. Making full use of teachers' potential is of the highest possible priority. To avoid their being ground down by the pressures of inner city teaching, teachers need:

- recognition (why not, amongst other things, billboard advertisements such as one in the USA reading 'Greenfield Thanks its Teachers'?);
- opportunities to visit schools in different circumstances, here and abroad;
- regular opportunities for professional development in which they have a role in determining priorities, for example achieved by giving teachers in deprived urban areas professional development vouchers worth, say, £300 a year;
- investment in their own initiatives for innovation, research and development.

Headteachers in particular need training before and after taking up their post. The new DFE support for headteacher mentoring is welcome. Headteachers and teachers need to become far more integrally linked with the education departments of higher education institutions. Involvement in the selection and training of future members of the profession and in writing and research could provide the opportunities for renewal that professionals who commit themselves to working in deprived urban areas deserve. It will be through means such as this, rather than salary attractions alone, that recruitment and retention of good quality teachers will be ensured.

Support from other staff

The success of schools depends not only on teachers, but also on other staff. Teaching or classroom assistants, who make a major contribution in urban schools, need to be included in school improvement strategies and offered a worthwhile career path. The use of other adults in the community (e.g. business people, PhD students living locally, parents with a range of talents which they might offer) could also make significant contributions as 'teaching associates'. The Paul Hamlyn Foundation pilot projects on this theme may bear important fruit. There is also evidence of schools moving towards employing more non-teaching administrative staff to relieve teachers of administrative burdens and thus to devote more time to teaching. This trend could enable resources to be used more effectively.

Emphasis on nursery education

There is powerful evidence that nursery education and quality child care can make a significant contribution to improved educational standards, particularly for those from disadvantaged backgrounds (see NCE Briefing No. 8, p.103)[16]. They should be made universally available in deprived urban areas.

Emphasis within primary education

In primary schools, an emphasis on literacy, numeracy and the skills and attitudes which enable further learning ought to be paramount. The early feedback on the reading recovery programme which central government has funded is very positive and consideration should be given to its expansion. A comparable programme for numeracy would also be beneficial. HMI reports state that teachers set too many tasks that are insufficiently demanding[9]. A revised National Curriculum could encourage higher expectations; for example, the introduction of National Curriculum science, if supported by further in-service education, will prove to be a major step forward. The growth of pupil:teacher ratios in urban areas, where children have extraordinarily diverse needs, ought to be reversed. More powerful still would be opportunities for teachers to see peers at work in other schools in different areas.

Pupil motivation in secondary education

The biggest single problem in secondary schools is low levels of pupil motivation. This is exacerbated in deprived urban areas by the large number of pupils who already suffer from low self-esteem. Hence the peer-group pressure often seeks to undermine aspiration to high levels of academic achievement. Various developments in recent years need to be considered in thinking of this crucial problem.

- GCSE, in its present form, with its emphasis on what pupils are able to do and its coursework element, appears to have been successful in improving motivation.
- Programmes specifically designed to build pupils' self-esteem have been designed in the USA. These involve emphasising pupils' success and careful preparation of teachers to find ways of encouraging success for all pupils without in effect rewarding poor quality work.
- Cognitive Acceleration through Science Education (CASE) developed at King's College, London, focuses on encouraging pupils to develop new ways of thinking

and indeed to reflect on the way they have been thinking. The results of a longitudinal study revealed substantially enhanced progress among those involved in the programme[2].

- Whole school policies on behaviour also appear to assist, particularly where their basis is rewarding and encouraging success, and avoiding the downward spiral of crime and punishment. Teacher training and commitment are essential; the decline in the constructive use of the lunch hour in many schools provides endless opportunities for poor behaviour and affects the attitudes of pupils to learning for the worse.

- Carefully structured modular programmes can have a motivational effect through offering short-term achievable objectives rather than distant and apparently unachievable goals. The possibility this approach offers of a rich and varied curriculum is also beneficial. One way to improve motivation is to offer all pupils an area in which they can shine.

- Programmes such as Ted Sizer's Coalition of Essential Schools are making headway. They do so by encouraging a team of 6–8 teachers to take responsibility for, say, 150 students. The team meets daily and plans the curriculum and pastoral care of students. The cost in teacher planning time is outweighed by significant rewards in terms of pupil motivation, a coherent curriculum across subjects and individual care and attention.

A longer learning day
Schools should be closely linked to a range of after-school youth activities (e.g. sport, drama, etc.) staffed by appropriately trained adults. After-school enrichment programmes and homework or 'prep' clubs can have many more educational benefits than alternatives like the television or some of the more dubious attractions of the street.

Building on a school's strength
The evidence relating to selection according to overall aca-

demic ability is extremely negative. While those selected for a 'grammar school' path may be positively motivated, there is plenty of evidence of the negative effects on motivation and self-esteem of not being selected. At a moment in history when the economy demands that a high proportion of young people achieve success, widespread reintroduction of selection according to ability could be devastating particularly in deprived urban areas.

Specialisation is a different issue. Given a National Curriculum, specialisation cannot lead to the kind of narrowing of the curriculum that might have resulted in the past. In America, in places like Cincinnati, schools with 'an alternative programme' have been introduced with the express purpose of attracting a wide social and racial mix of pupils into deprived urban areas. Often the most successful have been those which specialised in a particular philosophy of education (e.g. Montessori), rather than a curriculum area. The results overall have been mixed, with the magnet school often succeeding at the expense of other less well-provided-for schools. In St Louis attempts were made to avoid this outcome by providing for Quality Education Programmes in the non-magnet schools[3]. The success of Harlem District 4 where the introduction of wide diversity and choice was followed by substantial educational progress cannot be ignored.

In spite of their progressive origin and their potential to prevent ghettoes developing in at least some inner-city areas, schools which specialise have found little favour in this country for three reasons: first, those that have been developed, like the CTCs, have been funded to levels undreamed of in most schools; second, they appear likely to open up selection according to ability by the back door; and third, at age 11 most pupils cannot be expected to know what will motivate them for the next seven years. It may be that over the long term, each of these three problems could be solved. In the short term, a school developing a specialism would need additional investment during an innovation period, but over the long term no school should be funded preferentially. The second objection would be overcome if selection according to overall academic ability was not acceptable as a criterion in admissions policies. The third objection loses much of its potency so long as the National Curriculum applies to all such schools, or if the specialisation is one of philosophy rather than of curriculum. Pimlico School in London, with its music specialism, for example, has operated successfully in a comprehensive context for many years. Certainly in inner cities the idea that a school should build on its strengths and indeed offer the facilities it develops for wider community use is attractive; so too is the possibility of a school which offers an approach based on a different philosophy of education.

Dealing with failing schools
If the strategy for the regeneration of urban education is on course then failing schools should be rare. Nevertheless, there will be occasions where schools consistently underperform. Such schools are an infringement of children's rights. Some but not all of them will be in deprived urban areas. The idea that failing schools should be allowed to die in the market place is disastrous, above all for the young people within them. A coherent policy would require clarity about what constitutes failure. Two sets of criteria could be used: firstly, there could be relatively objective data based on value-added analysis of national assessment and of funding formulae; secondly, there could be more selective information on the extent to which a school has met the objectives set out in the school development plan negotiated with its governors and parents.

In the extreme circumstances of a consistently failing school, the proposal of the Massachusetts Business Alliance for Education should be considered: '... under-performing schools should be required to receive increased technical assistance from the state. If after receiving such assistance, a school continues to under-perform, then state education authorities should declare it "educationally bankrupt".'[14] LEAs (or failing them, OFSTED) need stronger powers to intervene and where necessary to establish a task group to bring about improvement.

Continuing to improve participation in post-compulsory education

Despite recent improvements, deprived urban areas fall a long way short of national averages, which themselves fall short of standards set by our international competitors. The combination of a confusion of qualifications and inadequate attitudes to training and education among employers is damaging and needs to be challenged. Much more progress is needed in increasing numbers moving from deprived urban areas into higher education, not only for the young people who will benefit directly but also because of the effect that much larger numbers reaching this academic level would have on aspirations locally. Higher education should develop further its more flexible approaches to admissions and attach greater weight to school recommendations and records of achievement. In the short term, business-funded scholarships for inner city pupils to Oxford, Cambridge and other universities could encourage high aspirations and help to change the climate in schools.

July 1993

References

1 Barber, M. (ed., 1992) *Education in the Capital* Cassell.

2 CASE (1990) *Better Learning: A Report from the CASE Project* King's College, University of London.

3 Cibulka, J., Reed, R. and Wong, K. (eds., 1992) *The Politics of Urban Education in the United States* Falmer.

4 DFE (1992) *School performance tables: public examination results.* DFE.

5 DFE (1992) *School performance tables: Key Stage 1 assessments.* DFE.

6 Fullan, M. (1992) *The New Meaning of Educational Change* Cassell.

7 Holden, C., Hughes, M. and Desforges, C. (1993) *What do parents want from assessment?* In Education 3–13 (Vol. 21, No. 1).

8 HMI (1992) *Report of the Chief Inspector* HMSO.

9 HMI (1992) *The Implementation of the National Curriculum* HMSO.

10 HMI (1992) *The Implementation of LMS* HMSO.

11 Leeds University (1992) *Report of the ENCA Project.* SEAC.

12 Leeds University/NUT (1993) *Assessment and Testing of Six and Seven Year Olds* NUT.

13 London Research Centre (1992) *Pupil attainments and social status* LRC.

14 Massachusetts Business Alliance for Education (1991) *Every child a winner* Boston.

15 Policy Studies Institute (1992) *Urban Trends:* 1 PSI.

16 Sylva, K. and Moss, P. (1992) *Learning before school* National Commission on Education Briefing No 8.

17 Financial Support for Students in Higher Education

Maureen Woodhall

Reader in Education Finance, Institute of Education, University of London, and Research Fellow, Department of Education, University of Wales, Aberystwyth

Summary

1 Higher education (HE) is a profitable investment, both for the country as a whole and for individual students. Access to HE for both young people and adults should be expanded, but the taxpayer cannot be expected to bear the full cost of financing it.

2 In 1991–2 the government spent £2 billion on student awards. The system provides financial support for an elite but fails to meet the needs of many students, particularly mature or part-time students or those taking lower level courses who are not eligible for mandatory awards. Many students now face financial hardship, while at the same time the wealthiest students enjoy free tuition and the high cost of student awards means that the number of university places has to be severely rationed.

3 Student loans were first introduced in 1990 and 37% of all eligible students took a loan in 1991–2. Loans have been attacked for discouraging participation in HE but a new Higher Education Contribution Scheme (HECS) in Australia has not deterred students.

4 A new system should be established, which combines means-tested grants and loans and targets support towards those students with greatest need. It should offer equality of opportunity for all who can benefit from HE, including part-time as well as full-time students and others who are currently excluded.

5   The fairest and most efficient way for graduates to repay their loan would be through income-related payments, collected through an income-tax surcharge (as in Australia) or through a supplement to National Insurance Contributions.

Introduction

The need for expansion and wider access to higher education (HE) in Britain is widely acknowledged. Bodies such as the Council for Industry and Higher Education (CIHE), the Royal Society of Arts (RSA) and the Institute for Public Policy Research (IPPR) have all recently argued for increased opportunities for HE, including much wider access for adults and students from working-class families, greater institutional diversity and an adequate system of funding to secure the maintenance of quality of teaching and research along with wider access[1]. Numbers of full-time and part-time students in universities and colleges have increased rapidly in recent years, as Professor A. H. Halsey showed in NCE Briefing No. 6 (see p.77). The proportion of 18–19 year olds going on to HE rose from one in eight in 1979 to just over one in four in 1992, and government's plans, set out in the 1991 White Paper *Higher Education: A New Framework*, are for this proportion to rise to one in three by the end of the century[2]. Current economic problems mean that government has called a temporary halt to the rapid expansion of the past few years; the latest public expenditure plans call for a period of consolidation in which participation is maintained at current levels, but assume that from 1996 renewed growth will enable Britain to achieve the target of one in three young people in HE by the year 2000.

The debate about how to finance the expansion of HE has focused on two issues: finance for institutions, and how to achieve the right balance between public and private contributions; and financial support to enable students to meet the costs of tuition and living expenses. The two are of course closely related. If students are expected to pay tuition fees, financial support for needy students will be vital, unless HE is to be confined to those wealthy enough to pay from their own or their parents' resources. Even when tuition is free, there will be students who need financial help to meet the cost of maintenance, books and travel. If students have to pay tuition fees as well as living costs, a more extensive and generous system of support will be needed. Any attempt to finance expansion of HE by shifting costs from public to private sources will have major implications for student support.

The present system of student support

Until 1962, financial support for students was the responsibility of local education authorities (LEAs), apart from a small scheme of state scholarships awarded on grounds of academic merit. The result was that students in different parts of the country received different levels of assistance and in 1960 the Anderson Committee recommended a national system of mandatory grants for all full-time students[3]. This system remained largely unchanged until 1990, when government introduced loans to supplement grants, whose value had declined until, in 1989, the maximum grant was worth 25% less in real terms than in 1962. All full-time and sandwich course students who are studying for a first degree or comparable qualification are entitled to a mandatory award from their LEA, provided that they have not previously received an award for another course and are ordinarily resident in the UK. (Since 1980 all overseas students have been required to pay 'full-cost' fees.) Mandatory awards cover tuition fees in full for all students, and provide a means-tested maintenance grant which is normally dependent on parents' income. Students taking non-degree courses (for example in music, dance, BTEC national certificate or diploma, City and Guilds and other vocational courses) may receive a discretionary award, but there are considerable variations between LEAs both in the proportion of students receiving discretionary awards and in the level of support. Some LEAs give discretionary awards to part-time students or others who are not eligible for mandatory awards, but the number of such awards has fallen in recent years as LEA expenditure has been subject to capping, and there are wide variations in both number and level of awards. In the case of mandatory awards LEAs are reimbursed in full by the DFE.

During the 1960s and 1970s the system worked well for most full-time students although critics pointed out that it discriminated against part-time students, those studying non-degree courses and others who for various reasons had to rely on discretionary rather than mandatory grants, and it meant that most students were financially dependent on their parents, not all of whom were able or willing to pay their assessed contributions in full. There were several proposals for change, including the introduction of loans to replace or supplement grants. The idea of loans had first been considered, and rejected, by the Robbins Committee in 1963, and loans were fiercely opposed by the NUS. The system came under increasing strain, however, during the 1980s as the number of students, and therefore the cost of student support rose, the value of the maintenance grant failed to keep pace with inflation, the expected parental contribution increased and there was mounting evidence that many students did not receive the full parental contribution assumed in their grant calculations.

Government argued that a combination of grants and loans would:
- support the broadening of participation in HE at the same time as sharing the cost of students' maintenance more equitably between taxpayers, parents and students themselves;
- increase economic awareness and self-reliance among students;

reduce, over time, the increasingly unsustainable burden of direct public expenditure on student grants[4].

It justified proposals for new arrangements by arguing that the financial benefits of a university degree, in terms of higher lifetime earnings, make HE a profitable personal investment, and a system of pure grants meant that 'taxpayers in general – poor and middling as well as rich – are contributing to the living costs of students who in many cases come from, and as graduates are likely to occupy, the more advantageous positions in society'[4]. It also pointed out that a comparison with other countries showed that UK expenditure on student support was substantially higher, as a percentage of the education budget, than elsewhere, even though the participation rate in Britain was lower than in many other industrialised countries. Student support accounted for over 20% of current public expenditure on HE in the UK in 1984, compared with about 10% in France and the Netherlands, 8% in the USA and 3% in Italy and Germany. The most recent available comparison (for 1986) confirms that Britain spends more, per student, on student support than other industrialised countries. Moreover, this support is concentrated on a relatively narrow range of courses and students.

There was bitter controversy about the introduction of loans. The NUS organised strong opposition and the banks refused to participate, as government had originally intended. Nevertheless, a loan scheme funded by government and administered by a specially created Student Loans Company was established and began operation in 1990. At the same time government withdrew student access to housing benefit, income support and unemployment benefit. In order to meet the needs of students facing exceptional hardship, Access Funds of £25.5 million were established, to be administered by HE institutions, to provide additional support in the form of discretionary bursaries or loans.

In 1990, government introduced another significant change, designed to provide an incentive to institutions to expand by linking their income more closely to recruitment and shifting the balance of funding from grants from the Funding Councils (which reflect notional, rather than actual student numbers) to tuition fees paid through student award arrangements. Fees were increased from about £500 in 1989 to £1,600 in 1990 and since 1991 there have been three rates. In 1992–3 annual home student fees are £1,855 for classroom-based courses, £2,770 for laboratory/workshop based and £4,985 for medical, dental and veterinary courses. For students with mandatory awards this change made no difference, since all such students have their fees paid in full. It did have an impact, however, on students who do not qualify for a mandatory award because they have previously been in HE or do not meet residence requirements. In some cases, a student who wants to transfer from one university to another, to re-enter HE after dropping out of an unsuitable course or to acquire a second qualification, could face annual fees of nearly £3,000 for a science or engineering course and nearly £5,000 for medicine, but be ineligible for a mandatory award. This represents a significant barrier to access at a time when many adults wish to retrain or upgrade their skills in response to redundancy.

Table 1: Current Systems of Student Support in UK

Value of student support (1992-3) for students outside London[a]	
Basic Grant	£2,265
Student Loan[b]	£715
Number of Mandatory Awards (England & Wales, 1990-1)	496,900
Number of Discretionary Awards (1990-1)	107,000
Number of students taking a loan (1991-2)	261,100
Eligible students taking a loan (1991-2)	37%

Source: DFE

Notes: (a) In 1992-3 the basic grant for students in London was £2,845, and the loan £830. For students living in the parental home the grant was £1,795, and loan £570;

(b) For a full year (i.e. including a long vacation). Students in the final year of study could borrow £525 (in London, £605; living at home, £415).

Table 1 summarises the current arrangements for student support. Students in London are entitled to slightly higher grants and loans than those studying elsewhere, while those who live at home, rather than in university halls of residence or private lodgings, receive less. In addition there are various additional allowances for disabled students, older students (aged 26 or over at the start of their course) and those with dependants. The size of an individual student's grant depends on parental income and their 'assessed contribution' which is deducted from the basic grant. Students whose parents have low incomes (below £13,630 in 1992–3) receive a full grant, but in most cases parents are expected to contribute towards students' living expenses, even if the student is married. Table 2 illustrates the assessed parental contribution at different income levels in 1992–3. Students from the wealthiest families receive no maintenance grant, but have their fees paid in full. In 1990–1 nearly 500,000 full-time students received mandatory awards and a further 107,000 students received discretionary awards, while 3,600 received awards for post-graduate study. The total cost of maintenance grants plus fees was £1.7 billion.

Table 2: Examples of Assessed Parental Contribution (1992-3)

Residual Income (£)	Assessed Contribution (£)
13,630	45
15,000	169
20,000	717
25,000	1,354
30,000	2,129
35,000	2,923
40,000	3,716

Source: DFE
Note: 'Residual income' is calculated by deducting from gross income allowances for dependent adults, interest payments and pension contributions which qualify for tax relief, etc.

In 1991–2 the Student Loans Company made a total of 261,000 loans, worth £139 million, and collected repayments of £3.1 million; administrative costs, including the development of a computerised system for managing loan disbursement and recovery, amounted to £13.7 million. These figures demonstrate that it will be many years before the student loan scheme generates any savings. In fact, government's own calculations, when loans were introduced, suggest that it will be well into the next century before the loan scheme breaks even. Graduates are expected to begin to repay their loans (by direct debit) in the April after the end of their course, unless their income is less than 85% of average earnings (this threshold is currently about £1,000 a month). By July 1992 31% of borrowers had been granted deferment, on grounds of low income, 3% were slightly in arrears and 9% were in default (defined as two or more instalments overdue)[5]. By December 1992 the number in default had fallen to 6%.

Weaknesses of the present system

Since the revised system of student support was introduced in 1990 it has been subject to increasing criticism. Government claims it is one of the most generous systems of support in the world, but acknowledges that 'this apparent generosity is a mixed blessing'[4]. The result of the heavy reliance on grants and the fact that all students with mandatory awards have their fees paid in full, together with the increasing pressure on public funds, means that the supply of places in HE has to be severely restricted by the Treasury.

Even so, there is mounting evidence that the full grant plus loan is not adequate for many students' financial needs. The House of Commons Select Committee on Education in 1992 received considerable evidence of financial hardship among students. One reason is that the introduction of student loans, the freezing of the grant and the withdrawal of student eligibility for social security benefits coincided with a drastic fall in the number of part-time or vacation jobs – on which students traditionally relied to supplement their grants – as a result of the recession. The result is that many students now face substantial debts (in addition to their student loans) and there are fears that this will lead to increased drop-out. A survey by the CVCP in 1992 showed that students facing the greatest financial problems included those in private rented accommodation, who often have to pay rent for 52 weeks (whereas the student grant covers only the academic year), mature students and those with dependent children, who previously relied on income support but are no longer eligible and cannot even claim free school meals for their children. Mature students are likely to be particularly affected, since they face higher costs such as child care, but although many were previously employed and paying national insurance contributions they can no longer claim unemployment benefit or other support, even during vacations. Yet government projections of student numbers assume an increase in the proportion of mature students.

Student resistance to loans seems to be declining, and the proportion taking a loan, which was substantially below predictions in the first year of the scheme, rose to 37% in 1991–2, but there are still widespread complaints about administrative complexities and misunderstanding of the fact that the loans have a real interest rate of zero. This means that the debt is index-linked, so that a graduate repays the amount borrowed in terms of constant purchasing power, but no further interest is charged. This aspect is not understood by many students or their parents, and there are other misunderstandings. The scheme allows deferral of repayment for graduates who are unemployed or have low incomes and does not take account of a spouse's income. It also allows those who interrupt their career while raising children to postpone repayments during that period and opponents still voice fears that the prospect of a 'negative dowry' will discourage women from entering HE.

A more fundamental problem with the existing student loans, emphasised by critics such as Nicholas Barr[6], is that they are 'mortgage-type' loans, which graduates are normally expected to repay in equal instalments; they thus represent a heavier burden in the early years of their career and are more likely to deter students than 'income-contingent' loans, where repayments are related to income and the borrower undertakes to repay a fixed percentage of income. This alternative is discussed further below.

The real weakness of the current system of student support is that despite the introduction of student loans it is still so costly in terms of public expenditure (total expenditure on fees, maintenance grants and loans was £2 billion in 1991–2 and projected to rise to £3 billion by 1993–5), that it acts as a brake on expansion while at the same time leaving many students facing real financial hardship. It also fails to meet the needs of mature students, part-timers and those from the most disadvantaged homes and fails on equity grounds. The distinction between mandatory and discretionary awards means that poor students who do not qualify for a mandatory award are excluded, or receive very little support, while all mandatory award holders have tuition fees paid in full, even if they come from the wealthiest families. Recent research suggests that the average value of HE subsidies (in the form of free tuition) that benefit families in the top income bracket is ten times greater than those received by families in the bottom income bracket; this reflects the fact that children from 'professional' and 'managerial' homes are four times more likely to go to university than those from working-class families[7].

Student support in other countries

Britain is unusual in providing both free tuition and maintenance grants for the majority of students. Tuition is free in most European countries, but in France and Germany the proportion of students receiving support for living expenses is much lower than in Britain, while the Netherlands and Scandinavian countries rely far more heavily on loans than grants. In Japan only about 12% of students receive financial support, entirely through loans, and students in both public and private universities pay fees. In the USA the pattern of HE finance and student support is very complex. Most universities and colleges charge fees, but the level varies considerably depending on the type of institution and whether it is public or private. Students finance both fees and living expenses through a combination of means-tested grants, loans and 'Work-Study' (a scheme under which the federal government sub-sidises part-time jobs for students on the university or college campus), as well as parental support and their own earnings. There has been increasing reliance on loans in recent years in the USA; in 1990–1 65% of total federal government student aid of $21 billion was in the form of loans, and about five million students received loans totalling nearly $14 billion, mostly from private banks backed by government guarantees. President Clinton has recently proposed a new form of student support under which students would receive financial assistance in return for community service, and he has also proposed income-contingent repayment of loans and a new scheme which would enable students to borrow directly from the federal government rather than from private banks. Both these proposals are likely to prove controversial and may well face opposition in Congress.

Other countries have recently made fundamental changes. In 1989 Australia introduced a new Higher Education Contribution Scheme (HECS) under which all students must pay a contribution equivalent to about 20% of aver-age university costs. This can either be paid as a fee at the start of each academic year or be deferred until after gradu-ation, when it is collected by means of an income tax surcharge of between 2% and 4% a year, depending on earnings. It is therefore often described as a 'graduate tax', but in fact it is a loan, collected through the tax system, rather than a true graduate tax. When a graduate has met the full liability, under HECS, the obligation to pay extra income tax is cancelled, whereas a graduate tax would mean a continuing obligation throughout a graduate's working life. Thus, even the highest paid graduate does not pay more than his or her full HECS contribution (indexed to inflation), while students who can afford to pay an 'up front' fee receive a discount (recently increased from 15% to 25%).

When HECS was first announced it provoked student protest, but it is now widely accepted as a fair way of funding expansion, and it has had no deterrent effect on demand for HE[8]. The money collected each year (AUS $200 million in 1992) is paid into an educational trust fund and used to finance recurrent and capital grants to universities. Students still receive means-tested grants towards their living expenses, under a scheme known as AUSTUDY, but since 1992 they may opt to receive a higher level of support, as a loan, which is also collected through an income tax surcharge.

In a five-country comparative study of student support in 1986, Johnstone pointed out that all countries, regardless of political system, must share the costs of HE between four funding partners: parents, students, taxpayers and institutions (colleges and universities, which may receive donations or endowments to help students)[9]. At that time the student's share in Britain was unusually low compared with Sweden, Germany or the USA, which all rely mainly on loans. The introduction of student loans in the UK coincided with a shift towards greater reliance on loans in several other countries, including Japan and Australia[10]. Even in China students can now receive loans to help finance their living expenses[11] and the African National Congress recently proposed student loans and means-tested tuition fees for South Africa.

Despite their widespread use, however, student loans in their present form do not generate substantial savings for the taxpayer, since most schemes are highly subsidised (loans are often interest-free or charge low rates of interest) and there is often substantial default. In 1988 17%, on average, of Americans with student loan debt did not repay their loans, because of unemployment, low earnings or other reasons; the proportion of defaulters from private vocational schools was 27%[12].

Options for change

Several recent proposals in this country have suggested ways of enabling students to meet an increased share of HE costs in order to finance expansion. Barden, Barr and Higginson reviewed student loan options for the CVCP in 1991 and concluded that it is unrealistic to assume an increase in taxpayers' share of HE costs and that the fairest and most feasible option is a student loan with income-contingent repayments, collected through additions to income tax or national insurance contributions (NICs)[13]. There have been proposals for increased or even full cost tuition fees; some institutions are currently examining the feasibility of charging 'top-up' fees to supplement publicly funded fees and grants and the London School of Economics (LSE) recently considered the introduction of supplementary fees of £500 a year. There have been proposals to give students vouchers to help finance such fees, and vouchers could be means-tested so that disadvantaged students received vouchers of above average value. Many vice-chancellors apparently favour a contribution scheme modelled on the Australian HECS, or even a full-scale graduate tax under which graduates with high incomes would pay more than the costs of their education, while low earners would pay less and the unemployed would pay nothing[14]. Howard Glennerster and Nicholas Barr at LSE are currently developing proposals for loans with income-contingent repayments and a 'user-charge' to be paid by employers of graduates. They estimate that revenue from such a scheme could be between £1.2 billion and £9.2 billion (in 1993 prices) depending on the future growth of incomes and the level of employer contributions[15].

Such options could not only lead to a more equitable system of student support but also generate additional resources for HE. These resources could help fund expansion of student places and also provide additional support for the most needy students, who now often face financial hardship, and those who now do not qualify for grants or loans, including part-timers and those taking non-degree courses. In NCE Briefing No. 5 David Finegold proposes a strategy to break out of the 'low-skill equilibrium' that has plagued Britain for so long (see p.63). One essential ingredient of such a strategy is to abandon a system of financial support which is confined to full-time students taking conventional degree-level courses in HE and which discriminates against students in other forms of education or training.

Recommendations

It is now widely recognised in Britain and other countries that the entire burden of financing HE cannot be left to the taxpayer alone. Both access and quality would inevitably suffer. HE is a profitable investment both for the country and for individual students. Britain urgently needs to expand HE and to find a fairer way of sharing the costs – of both tuition and student maintenance – between the taxpayer, parents, employers, and students themselves. This requires changes in the balance between tuition fees and institutional grants as well as between grants and loans for student maintenance. It also requires an end to the inequitable distinction between mandatory and discretionary awards, which means that wealthy students receive free tuition at the taxpayers' expense while some needy students are denied support because they are doing a different course or choose to study part-time. One way to achieve this would be to introduce an Australian-style income contingent contribution, to be paid by all students (or graduates), regardless of whether they studied full-time or part-time, for a degree or lower level qualification. This could be collected through a surcharge to income tax or NICs, which would protect the unemployed or low paid and have the advantages of income-related repayment without the disadvantages of a true 'graduate tax' – that highly paid graduates would have to pay more tax, throughout their lives, than those with equally high earnings but no HE.

A fair and flexible system of student support should:
- provide a combination of means-tested grants and repayable loans to help students meet the costs of both tuition and maintenance;
- target support where it is most needed by providing more for those with the greatest financial needs (e.g. mature or disabled students);
- support both full-time and part-time students;
- support both degree level and other higher and further education courses, in acknowledgement of the increasing diversity of post-school education;
- collect debts by equitable and cost-effective means; i.e. income-related repayments collected through the income tax or National Insurance system.

July 1993

References

[1] See CIHE (1992) *Investing in Diversity.* CIHE; Ball, C. (1990) *More Means Different: Widening Access to Higher Education.* RSA; and Finegold, D. *et al* (1992) *Higher Education: Expansion and Reform.* IPPR.

2 H.M. Government (1991) *Higher Education: A New Framework.* Cm 1541. HMSO.

3 Ministry of Education (1960) *Grants to Students.* Cmnd 1051. HMSO.

4 Department of Education and Science (1988) *Top Up Loans for Students.* Cm 520. HMSO.

5 Student Loans Company (1992) *Annual Report.*

6 Barr, N. (1989) *Student Loans: The Next Steps,* Aberdeen University Press.

7 See Evandrou, M. *et al* (1993) *Welfare Benefits in Kind and Income Distribution.* Fiscal Studies, Vol. 14, No. 1, pp. 57–76; Smithers, A. and Robinson, P. (1991) *Beyond Compulsory Schooling: a Numerical Picture.* CIHE.

8 Chapman, B. and Chia, T. (1993) *Income Contingent Charges for Higher Education:* Paper presented at International Symposium on the Economics of Education, British Council, Manchester, May 1993.

9 Johnstone, B. (1986) *Sharing the Costs of Higher Education.* New York: The College Board.

10 Woodhall, M. (1989) *Financial Support for Students: Grants, Loans or Graduate Tax?* Kogan Page.

11 Shouxin, L. and Bray, M. (1992) *Attempting a Capitalist Form of Financing in a Socialist System: Student Loans in the People's Republic of China.* Higher Education, Vol. 23, No. 4, pp. 375–387.

12 US Department of Education (1991) *Beyond Defaults: Indicators for Assessing Proprietary School Quality*

13 Barden, L., Barr, N. and Higginson (1991) *An Analysis of Student Loan Options.* London: CVCP.

14 Lincoln, I. and Walker, A. *Increasing Investment in Higher Education: The Role of a Graduate Tax* (forthcoming).

15 Barr, N. and Glennerster, H. (1993) *Funding a Learning Society.* Paper presented at a seminar at LSE, May 1993. See also CVCP Newsletter, May 1993 for a summary of the Barr-Glennerster proposals and the Australian HECS.

18 Local Democracy for the Learning Society

Professor Stewart Ranson
School of Education, The University of Birmingham

Summary

1 The main aim of educational policy-makers should be to establish the conditions in which a 'learning society' can flourish. Such a society is more likely to grow from a foundation of strong local democracy, which allows citizens to play an active part in developing the goals in education, than from a system which concentrates power at the centre.

2 Recent education reforms have sought to replace the post-war 'social democratic' tradition with the principle of the market place, giving primacy to the individual 'consumer' and seeking to raise standards by encouraging competition between schools.

3 Markets will not solve our problems. A better way forward would be to develop a system of governance which builds upon the achievements of the 'social democratic' approach as well as those of the more recent reforms.

4 The powers of Whitehall should be reduced. But this must not mean a return to detailed and hierarchical control by LEAs.

5 The LEA (or its successor body) of the future will need strategic planning and resourcing powers. Increasingly, however, its style of working must be to seek to influence and to work in partnership with institutions and others in the community, rather than to direct.

6 For the 'learning society' to succeed, we must strengthen community and family support for and interest in education. Three initiatives are proposed:
   • community forums, to enable parents, employers and

local groups to take part in decision-making about local provision;

- local authority grants to support community education initiatives proposed by the forums;
- area officers to help stimulate community involvement in education and support the development of local projects.

Introduction

In periods of social transition education becomes central to future well-being. Only if learning is placed at the centre of their experience can individuals continue to develop their capacities, institutions be enabled to respond openly and imaginatively to periods of change, and the differences between communities become a source of reflective understanding. The challenge for policy-makers is to promote the conditions for such a 'learning society': this should enable parents to become as committed to their own continuing development as they are to that of their children; men and women should be able to assert their right to learn as well as to support the family; learning co-operatives should be formed at work and in community centres; and preoccupation with issues of the purpose and organisation of learning should then result in extensive public dialogue about reform.

Such a society can only grow if supported by a framework of national governance based on a strong system of local democracy that allows citizens from many backgrounds to play an active part in developing their communities, including the education institutions which meet their needs. Only such a new structure can provide the foundation for sustaining the personal development of all.

While a number of recent reforms to the government of education may well contribute to the learning society others seem likely to frustrate its realisation. Recent education reforms have sought to replace the post-war 'social democratic' tradition with the principle of the market place supported by power concentrated in Whitehall. Markets, however, will only fragment local communities, while centralised power engenders inertia. A better way forward would be to develop a system of governance which supports the purposes of the learning society, building upon the achievements of the 'social democratic' approach as well as those of more recent reforms.

The post-war 'social democratic' approach

This system developed over the post-war period lasting for thirty years with the support of a cross-party consensus on the organising principles needed to govern education. All children should have an equal chance to develop their full potential so that opportunity will not depend upon parental wealth but on need and achievement. The 1943 White Paper's emphasis on placing 'the child (at) the centre of education' guided policy for the next generation. Selection at 11+ denied opportunity and presented an artificial barrier to personal development. Policy-makers came to learn what every parent knows: that capacities and confidence are not fixed but grow over time. The introduction of comprehensive schools from the late 1950s, for children of all abilities and social backgrounds, reinforced this understanding. All should now have access to the same forms of knowledge and understanding that underpin common life chances. A form of governance as partnership evolved between Whitehall, town hall and the profession that accorded responsibility in relation to task, prevented any one partner from monopolising power and ensured co-ordinated planning and resource redistribution to meet the needs of young people.

This period was one of considerable progress; for example, 'major improvements in exam performance were achieved by the average ability students and they were mostly achieved in comprehensive students...'[6] Nevertheless there were limits. Under-achievement persisted in too many areas and could be connected to some of education's organising principles: passive learning and, especially, an examination system which for many emphasised failure rather than achievement. If motivation is the key to learning then systems of education need to reinforce a sense of purpose: i.e. active learning in the classroom leading towards the contribution that young people are to make to their society. The support of parents and community is essential ('it takes a whole village to educate a child') as is 'a future' that lends purpose to learning. But parents were not part of the post-war partnership, just as the public were not encouraged to play a wider role in society as active citizens. It was the age of professionalism. The challenge for our time is to rebuild the public domain as an important foundation for the learning society.

Education in the market place

The response of the present government to this challenge has been to place the parent as consumer at the centre of its policy-making. Standards of education will be raised, it is claimed, by giving parents the power of choice in order to encourage competition between schools. Public information should be available to guide parents and strengthen the accountability of schools as they deliver the new National Curriculum designed to provide a better definition of what is taught and learned. The 1988 Education Act inaugurated many of these reforms in the local system of education: schools, granted their own budgets, could now allocate resources to meet their needs in this context of 'market pressure'. The local education authority (LEA), withdrawn from detailed control of schools, could then concentrate on overall strategy, support to schools and assuring the quality of their performance.

Since 1992, however, the definition of the problem appears to have shifted. Now, the very idea of a local *system* of education is questioned and with it the role of the LEA. All schools are exhorted to become autonomous from local government. One American study, influential here, makes explicit the underlying reasons, blaming local democracy for the purported failures of schools[3]. Adversarial politics, it is argued, leads to the winning party imposing rules to secure its policy preferences, such as equal opportunities, on unwilling schools. Freed from such 'bureaucratic controls' autonomous schools can respond flexibly to market signals, fulfil customer wants and raise standards. The 1993 Education Act, in removing the LEA from the face of legislation and questioning the need for an Education Committee, brings into question not just the need for a local *system* but, more significantly, the value of *local democracy* to education.

Some of the government's reforms have gained support in the profession and the community: the need to create a national framework for the curriculum, or to focus more rigorously on the quality of learning, or to delegate more decision-making capacity to schools. Arguably, however, other aspects of policy, principally the trend to accord primacy to the market at the expense of local government, seem likely to damage education.

Markets, despite the rhetoric, deny opportunity for many: supporters as well as opponents acknowledge that they create inequality. In education they work so that competition forces schools to see each other as rivals striving to gain the advantage that will secure survival. The emerging research evidence suggests, however, that from this rivalry emerges a hierarchy of esteem with schools increasingly inclined to 'select' and 'exclude' pupils in order to produce a school population likely to shine in the national league tables (see NCE Briefings Nos. 7 and 13, on p.89 and p.183)[1,2,7,10]. In this market hot-house only some parents are likely to see their children admitted to their chosen schools: those with time, resources, knowledge and confidence to 'promote' their children; or those with 'able' children. Children with 'special' needs may struggle to secure a place in schools at the apex of the hierarchy that begins to celebrate 'academic' distinction above other learning achievements. Some schools may seek to specialise in providing for this market 'niche'. For policymakers this illustrates 'choice and diversity'. Others believe this policy is covertly restoring a selective system in which access to good education is confined to some schools where the social characteristics of parents will determine the chances of admission.

Although the market (a parent rejecting one school for another) may jolt this or that school into improving its relative position in the league table, it also inescapably entrenches the importance of the table (and as NCE Briefing No. 1 on p.1 showed, 'raw' league tables take no account of 'value-added' by school). In this context, some schools, by definition, *will always* suffer invidious comparison. That is what competition creates. It is a zero-sum game in which if there are to be winners there are sadly always going to be losers. Individually, schools and parents are forced to play a game which may well disadvantage them and leave them powerless to change the rules. The power of resources is valued above the authority of reason. A system of governance is thus created in which public policy is removed from public deliberation, choice and action, the only processes through which a community can devise a system of education that can meet the learning needs of all.

Markets cannot resolve the predicaments we face; indeed they ensure that we stand no chance of solving them. These predicaments – the restructuring of work, environmental erosion, the fragmentation of society, opportunity for all – are issues of well-being, rights and justice which cannot be resolved by individuals acting in isolation. Markets will merely exacerbate these problems which are public in nature; all citizens should have a right to contribute to their analysis and resolution.

Democracy in public education

Only the democratic and consultative processes of the public domain can help our society tackle these difficult problems. As Dunn argues: 'In the face of the obscure and extravagantly complicated challenges of the human future, our most urgent common need at present is to learn how to act together more effectively'[5]. Far from being a burden upon a community, a system of local democracy is a key institution which can provide it with the freedom and justice to create the conditions for all to flourish.

The arguments for democratic local government or at least statutory community participation in management of education develop in three stages:

1. Learning is inescapably a *system*: a process which cannot be contained within the boundaries of any one institution. Discovery and understanding occur at home, in the community, on a scheme of work experience as well as in college or school. Progress, furthermore, will unfold more securely between stages of learning when the providers of learning at each stage are mutually comprehending and supporting. Improving achievement depends for its realisation upon a wider system of learning: one element cannot be treated in isolation from another if each is to contribute to the effective working of the whole. All young people should be provided with opportunities to realise their powers and capabilities. Accepting that there are differences between schools, we must aim to ensure that every school has the appropriate number of pupils and the provision of resources and teachers to support a balanced and comprehensive curriculum (with choices at key stages to respond to diversity of need). These are characteristics which have

to be managed at the level of the system as a whole, as well as the school.

2. Education systems are more effective if managed locally, as well as nationally and at the level of the institution. Different tasks need their appropriate tier of management. The 1993 Education Act, by removing the LEA from its constitutional role in Section 1 and by abolishing the requirement to establish an Education Committee, brings into question the local management of education within a national framework. A local system of management is needed to ensure understanding of local needs, responsiveness to changing circumstances, and efficiency in the management of resources within geographic boundaries consistent with identifiable historical traditions.

3. Such local systems need to be properly accountable and this requires location within a local framework. Education should be a public service for the whole community rather than for particular parents, young people and employers, who have an immediate and proper interest in the quality of the education provided, and so it must be responsive and accountable to the community as a whole. The significance of learning for the public as a whole suggests the indispensable location of the service within a local government framework which enables all local people to express and reach consensus on their views and to participate actively in developing the processes of their education service. A learning society – enabling all to contribute to and respond to significant changes – will depend for its vitality upon the support of local institutions which take responsibility for all members of the community.

Developments which have become preconditions for the educational progress of many young people – a gender neutral curriculum, bilingual teaching, multicultural education, comprehensive schooling – did not emerge from Whitehall, nor from isolated individuals, but instead from local discourse and public action. The task now is to reconstitute the conditions for a learning society in which all are empowered to develop and contribute their capacities.

Reforming the local governance of education

A flourishing public domain requires the vitality which local governance brings to education[4,8,9]. Upon the LEA, or any organisation which succeeds it, lies the inescapable task of re-interpreting national purpose to local need and generating within the community a sense of shared purpose.

The Local Education Authority (or its successor body)

A more sophisticated system of governance is needed to realise this demanding task. The local body of the future should, therefore, become a strategic authority complemented by a framework of community councils and institutional governing bodies. This will establish a foundation for democracy and representation to ensure decision-making is more accountable, being grounded in wide public discussion.

While future reforms should restore the institutional unity of such a body (by seeing that grant-maintained schools and city technology colleges come under its overall authority), the tradition of hierarchical control should remain a thing of the past. The local authority will relate to a more diffuse system of councils, institutions and agencies with delegated decision-making powers appropriate to their functions and responsibilities. Although it should be accorded greater 'steering capacity' than under the 1988 Education Reform Act, it must, nevertheless, largely seek to *influence and to work in partnership with* education institutions rather than to direct them.

The functions of a local body should provide strategic leadership that will encourage local education partners to develop a shared understanding of learning quality, public service and accountability. The functions should include:

- *Promoting a vision of the learning society* for all throughout their lives, celebrating diversity of culture, and being committed to the long-term process of transforming the way people think about themselves and their powers and rights. It entails reforming local education so as to give access to a curriculum which empowers learners to develop their capacities and gain the confidence to play their public role as citizens in the development of their society.
- *Strategic planning and resourcing*: to ensure cohesion and direction by requiring development plans from every part of the service. These should express specific objectives while taking account of the local authority's mission. Specific grants targeting policy priorities and formulae for funding institutions and centres based on need rather than the per capita (quasi-voucher) system can ensure that resources support policy.
- *Support*: increasingly, the task for local bodies will not be to provide services but to offer support to the providers enabling them to realise their priorities.
- *Evaluating quality* by monitoring, evaluating and developing the quality of all its institutions and services, identifying good practice and achievement in the learning process, and acting as the catalyst and promoter of excellence by sponsoring research and innovation.
- *Partnership*: a process of working in partnership with a multiplicity of organisations. It requires the LEA to develop a culture of shared responsibility and collaborative working which encourages institutions to trust in more permeable boundaries.
- *Enabling participation* with parents, employers and the wider public to ensure services are provided which meet their needs; to report on (and hopefully assure them of) the quality of those services and most signifi-

cantly to engage the public in a discussion about the purposes and process of education in the learning democracy.

The Institutions

Future reforms need to build upon the achievements of the 1988 Act in strengthening the authority of schools and colleges, although not as independent islands but as bodies looking outward to the learning needs of the community as a whole. Schools would continue to be led by strong governing bodies, whose elected membership represents all the local partners, including parents, students and the local communities, and whose principal functions would be to prepare, within the guidelines laid down by the local supervisory body, a development plan that supports the distinctive needs of the institution.

A priority must be for schools to work as partners with parents and the community, as the key to improving pupil motivation and achievement, while service to and involvement of the public reflects the broader responsibility of school and college to promote education within the community. Best practice in a number of schools suggests that effective strategies include:

* Welcoming parents into the life of the school and establishing a new style in which schools will listen to and respond to parents. The great mystique of teacher autonomy needs to be unmasked.
* Parents being viewed as complementary educators, in school and home. For example contributing to reading schemes has an acknowledged influence upon motivation, confidence and attainment scores.
* Developing shared understanding of the curriculum. Teachers, pupils and parents as well as others need to know what is intended and how it is to be pursued and achieved. This could lead to greater dialogue in curriculum design; listening to parents and members of the community can enrich the curriculum with local knowl-

edge and experience as well as enhance a school's cultural understanding.

- Parents being seen as partners in assessment of children's learning progress through regular communication.
- Parents being seen as partners in evaluation and accountability with schools having the confidence to report to parents about pupil and school performance, and to listen to and include the 'accounts' of parents.

Parents and the Community

A robust 'periphery' of local democratic participation will be needed to support the learning society as much as a strong local body or the State. Schools and colleges must contribute towards such an area and community perspective, committed to working together so that they are more effective in listening to and responding to the needs of the community. If the principle of participation and local responsiveness is to be firmly established then mechanisms need to be developed to help identify local needs, facilitate participation and contribute to the co-ordination of local services. These mechanisms could take three forms:

1. *Community forums.* Some schools have in the past introduced such forums to extend community participation, and in some authorities forums have been established for specific purposes, for example to review proposals for school reorganisation, or more generally to consider educational issues. A stronger democracy suggests the need for community forums with a wider remit to cover all services enabling parents, employers and community groups to express local needs and share in decision-making about provision to meet them.

2. *Grant-giving capacity.* Public dialogue about change in the community is properly a primary responsibility of local forums but they should be able to exert influence. This could be achieved by a limited resource-giving capacity (delegated by the local authority) to support

the learning needs of individuals and groups within the community. This would be an important strategy in enfranchising and empowering community education and would reinforce service providers' responsiveness to local needs.

3. *The enabling role of an area officer.* Mutual co-operation in services will sometimes happen spontaneously. It is likely to be accelerated with the support of an area officer or adviser who encourages parental and group involvement in identifying learning needs and in deciding upon and organising appropriate development projects. Monitoring and evaluating progress are crucial activities in the role. It is a networking role, in which the officer, or local community representative, works to link up the parts of the service so that the Authority and its institutions can make an integrated response to the needs of parents and the community.

Conclusion

The current political system encourages passive rather than active participation in the public domain. A different order of values, giving all people a firm sense of purpose in their lives, can create the conditions for motivation in the classroom. It would encourage individuals to value their active role as citizens and thus their shared responsibility for the common-wealth. Active learning in the classroom needs, therefore, to be informed by and to lead towards citizenship within a participative democracy. Teachers and educational managers, with their deep understanding of the processes of learning, can, I believe, play a leading role in *enabling* such a vision to unfold not only among young people but also across the public domain. Reformed governance of education is needed to support the needs of a new age for a learning society in which all can develop and contribute their powers and capacities. Such a society is more likely to grow from a foundation of strong local democracy.

July 1993

References

1 Adler, M. (1993) *An Alternative Approach to Parental Choice*. NCE Briefing No. 13.

2 Ball, S. (1992) *Schooling, Enterprise and the Market*, AERA Symposium Paper.

3 Chubb, J. and Moe, T. (1992) *Politics, Markets and America's Schools* Washington, Brookings.

4 Cordingley, P. and Kogan, M. (1993) *In Support of Education: The Functioning of Local Government,* London, Jessica Kingsley.

5 Dunn, J. (ed., 1992) *Democracy: the Unfinished Journey, 508 BC to AD 1993*. Oxford University Press.

6 Glennerster, H. and Low, W. (1990) *Education and the Welfare State: does it add up?* In Barr, N. *et al (eds.) The State of Welfare: The Welfare State in Britain Since 1974*. Clarendon.

7 Jonathon, R. (1990) *State education service or prisoner's dilemma: the hidden hand as a source of education policy,* British Journal of Educational Studies, Vol. 38, No. 2, 16–24.

8 Ranson, S. (1992) *The Role of Local Government in Education: Assuring Quality and Accountability*. Harlow, Longman.

9 Ranson, S. and Tomlinson, J. (eds. 1993), *School Co-operation: New Forms of Local Governance,* Harlow, Longman (forthcoming)

10 Walford, G. (1992) *Selection for Secondary Schooling* NCE Briefing No. 7.

19 Moral and Spiritual Education

The Revd Dr Kenneth Wilson
Principal, Westminster College, Oxford

Summary

1 Education is less than complete unless it pays attention to the moral and spiritual dimensions of human life.
2 Self knowledge, mutual understanding and the nature of the human being lead to the search for justice, truth and beauty. These enliven any total curriculum.
3 To appreciate human experience as it is, the history and expression of religious enquiry must figure prominently in the curriculum.
4 The breadth and significance of the purposes of education as conceived by the 1988 Education Reform Act (ERA) will not be met by the National Curriculum as presently constructed. Provision for religious education (RE) and collective worship are required of every maintained school but are not part of the National Curriculum.
5 There are practical problems in meeting the intentions of the ERA.
   • RE syllabuses are developed without appropriate attention to the purposes and structure of the whole curriculum, thus isolating the teaching of RE, with damaging consequences.
   • There are insufficient teachers of an appropriate calibre. Collective worship, in particular, requires much careful preparation and attention to intellectual, aesthetic and moral questions.
6 However, there is a common value system, which begins to command the assent of a large majority of UK society as outlined in the text. What is needed is the development of an understanding of the whole curriculum which takes full account of these common values and the place of RE within it.

7 The discussion of the framework for RE should be set within the Christian tradition, because attention to traditions found in Great Britain is most likely to enlighten the minds and hearts of the average British child. But, part of the framework will involve drawing attention to the truth, claims and moral perspectives of other religious traditions.

8 A curriculum for RE consistent with the provisions of the ERA, in addition to being informative and morally sensitive, should provide knowledge of a religious text, religious history, religious values and should draw on other areas and perspectives of the curriculum.

9 In order to be effective, RE should be included within the National Curriculum, maintaining a clear distinction between religious and moral education, and should be planned and assessed accordingly. But this would inevitably require more and better trained teachers and more resources, an issue upon which society and government must decide.

Introduction

Education is less than complete unless it pays attention to the moral and spiritual dimensions of human life. Indeed, comment about their importance has come increasingly to the fore in current debate about the future of our society. To put it no higher, it is not possible to stress all the components which go to make up an education, without raising questions about the nature of what it is to be human. History is important, but it does not provide a full education. Mathematics is central to the description and understanding of quantities, order, structures and their relationships, but it does not constitute an account of the whole of reality. Not even science, let alone technology, can of itself and in its own terms, quench the desire to ask questions about oneself and the world in which one finds oneself. To talk of education as a whole, it is necessary to refer to its moral and spiritual perspectives.

It is, of course, true that schooling of itself is unlikely to provide the totality of moral and spiritual education. The family, the wider local society, combined with experiences of membership of voluntary associations, as well as the media and cultural activity will all have their influence. But without a self-conscious, critical focus on the moral and spiritual dimensions of life in formal education, they will lack the serious attention which they require in the long-term interests of individual and social well-being.

Justice, Truth and Beauty

It is natural for all human beings from their earliest experiences as children and young people to be curious about themselves. Not all persons behave the same way in similar circumstances. Some are brave in the face of physical danger, others lie in order to achieve their ends or to escape blame. Some enjoy the company of others, while there are those who enjoy their own company. Some are intellectually brilliant, others who lack that ability nevertheless have strength of character and are, as we say, 'born leaders'. And such observation of others leads individuals to ask questions about themselves, and to essay the difficult task of learning to control themselves. Self-knowledge must be an aim for any formal education.

By the same token, so must mutual understanding be an aim. Everyone needs to be able to build up a picture not only of how he or she interprets the behaviour of others, but also how others see his or her behaviour. What is going on here? What did he intend? Why did she think I meant that? Furthermore, these questions concern groups, communities, families, tribes, professions, nationalities, races, religions, the sexes, as well as individuals and persons. What works and what does not? How in the affairs of the world may we arrange things well? How are we to understand, value and interpret our experience?

The spiritual in many minds is associated with what, since it cannot be defined, is assumed to be nebulous and therefore utterly valueless. The truth is quite different. The spiritual is the term we use to refer to the essence of what it is to be human. Of course, the question of human nature is itself debatable. Is there such a thing as human nature? However, there are features of human experience which tend to point to the essence of the human even if it is not definable and therefore continues to remain debatable.

Thus, human beings are naturally curious; we want to know why and how things occur, we want to know how best and most completely to describe our experience, we want to know what goes with what in building up a picture of things, and we want to know the meaning and significance of life. But it does not stop there, because we are active and not merely contemplative beings: we want to know what happens if we choose to behave in one way rather than another, we want to know how the world looks to others and how we could or should go about changing our perspective on the world. Also, for the most part, we want to work with others rather than against them.

By attending to these fundamental concerns of self-knowledge, mutual understanding and the nature of the human being, there is encouraged the search for justice, truth and beauty. And any education system worth its salt will want to encourage that. The normative and the descriptive are properly seen to be ingredients of a good education.

Religious Enquiry

It is in religious terms and in the context of religious practice as well as in theological thought, that these questions have been explored most consistently and completely and have been expressed. In particular, curiosity about the place of human beings in the universe, of one human being in relation to another and of a person's knowledge of himself or herself lies at the centre of questions about the nature of God and his responsibility for the universe as we know it, in every religious tradition. If one is to explore and take account of what it is to be an affectionate loving human being, in a world which one does not control, in which one's experience is from time to time ambiguous, it is, if not necessary, at least desirable to pay attention to the possibilities which are opened to each person by relating the human to the divine. It is an opportunity which should not be missed. Just conceivably the spiritual is a dimension which enables us to continue to explore what it is to be human and how to enable it to flourish. The understanding of the human will be transformed by thinking of it in the light of the best knowledge of the world that we have, and in relation to what is meant by 'God'. There is no way to do this apart from attending to religion and the human experience of it.

In the world as we know it, for a child to be religiously, even theologically, illiterate is to lack perspectives on what it is to be human and therefore to be in danger of being ignorant of the emotional, intellectual, metaphysical, aesthetic and moral worlds which are in principle open to us. And who would want to deny these possibilities to the growing child?

The Basic Curriculum

The 1988 Education Reform Act (ERA) reaffirms the legal requirement of the 1944 Education Act that both religious education (RE) and collective worship must find their place alongside the National Curriculum in any school curriculum that is to satisfy the terms of the Act. Indeed, it is (albeit in brackets) so stated in Part 1, Chapter 1 and paragraph 1 of the Act. Furthermore, it must be supposed that the next paragraphs ((2) a and b) identify the full range of the curriculum. Thus,
- (2) The curriculum for a maintained school satisfies the requirements of this section if it is a balanced and broadly based curriculum which:
  - (a) promotes the spiritual, moral, cultural, mental and physical development of pupils at the school and of society; and
  - (b) prepares such pupils for the opportunities, responsi bilities and experiences of adult life.

It could hardly be plainer: the National Curriculum does

not and could not of itself cover the needs of the pupils or society in all particulars but with the addition of RE and collective worship (to be called significantly the 'basic curriculum'), we shall at least be able to deal also with the spiritual and moral dimensions.

Yet these could be thought to involve one of two things. First, the addition of discrete areas of the curriculum and specific experiences to compensate for their lack in the National Curriculum. Second, a reconceptualisation of the total curriculum so as to provide for a basic integration which would offer a National Curriculum including RE and collective worship, so as to deliver a total educational experience to pupils which was spiritually and morally nourishing. But can we now do this? Does there exist an understanding of the curriculum in its totality 'balanced and broadly-based' which enables a school genuinely to fulfil its responsibilities for RE and collective worship so as to provide for the spiritual and moral needs of pupils and of society?

The consultation paper on Religious Education and Collective Worship (D.f.E. 1992) suggests that this is what we should be looking for. Paragraph 6 reads: 'The White Paper emphasises the importance which the Government attaches to the school's role in pupils' moral and spiritual development. Both RE and collective worship have a major contribution to make to this as part of a school's work and the Government is keen to ensure that the developments in RE provided for by the ERA are taken forward more widely'.

RE and collective worship do not provide of themselves, therefore, for the spiritual and moral development of pupils; rather it is implied that without an appropriate curriculum for RE and continuing experience of collective worship, the spiritual and moral development of pupils (and therefore of society) will be inhibited and schools will fail in their overall responsibility to provide for a 'balanced and broadly-based curriculum'.

Practical Problems

The reality conflicts with the intention of the ERA at almost every turn. On the one hand, RE syllabuses are locally devised and approved, largely unexamined and developed without appropriate attention to the purposes and structure of the curriculum in general or the National Curriculum in particular. It is an anomaly that cannot be tolerated further for it isolates the teaching of RE from the rest of the curriculum and fosters the false view that RE alone is responsible for the moral and spiritual education of children.

On the other hand, the lack of status of RE in the context of the whole curriculum and the actual lack of interest in it on the part of most parents and Governors, mean that there are few resources in the average school, whether one thinks of capitation, time on the timetable or management concern. Where parents do complain, they will all too often be seen as a special interest group and certainly a small minority.

Furthermore, there are insufficient teachers, therefore, of an appropriate calibre: many RE classes are taught by well-meaning, dedicated but unqualified amateurs. This is particularly the case in primary schools where the general responsibility of the class teacher will include RE, but this will probably have been only a marginal concern in his or her training.

Collective worship, in particular, requires much careful preparation and attention to intellectual, aesthetic and moral questions in the context of a traditional Christian belief system. The appointment of head teachers cannot simply depend on their capacity to deliver collective worship, yet without it school assemblies will be opportunities for notices, sports results or notification of lost property and matters of discipline. Collective worship, if it is to carry intellectual integrity, moral seriousness and public esteem, requires very much more thought than the average head teacher is able to give it. It also assumes, as well as contributes to the creation of, a common set of values.

Is there a Common Value System?

Increasingly, yes. One could base this claim on four assumptions which in principle begin to command the assent of a large majority in our society and also (a very important matter) of teachers who in a crucial way represent a means by which the values are transmitted.

1 We want an education system which provides the opportunity for each individual eventually to contribute through remunerative employment to the well-being of his or her peers.

2 We want an education system which promotes both the academic and the vocational, since we believe that both are equally essential if the first aim above is to be achieved.

3 We want an educational system which promotes the personal capacities of individuals to make and sustain personal relationships through loyalty, courage, affection and mutual concern.

4 We want an educational system which encourages the establishing and sustaining of open, creative, ambitious, critical but supportive communities (international, national and local in their many forms), both responsive and responsible, which enable human beings to flourish in society.

There are many ways in which these values could be developed, but if one is serious, they require each person, to the extent that she or he is able, to have a knowledge of the physical world, a sense of place and time through history and geography, an opportunity to explore personal identity through literary and artistic study, family relationships, religious enquiry and an ambition to add to the common history and future progress of the human race through imaginative activity and the development of skills.

In fact, what is needed is the development of an understanding of the whole curriculum which takes full account of these common values and the place of RE within it. In my experience, these values are shared by the teaching profession. Indeed, much present frustration is because the profession is being asked to perform technical tasks in the delivery of a National Curriculum whose content and values it has not been asked to discuss. The frustration is all the more intense because at the same time it is asked to accept responsibility for the transmission, even re-development, of values which are recognised not to be part of the National Curriculum and which have to be catered for through RE as part of the Basic Curriculum.

No education system can be said to be complete, let alone effective, which does not attend to each of the four values listed above and does not seek to transmit them through the way in which schools are organised, the curriculum developed, delivered and assessed, the profession trained, supported and developed, and the students taught, assessed and encouraged. The talk of spiritual and moral education outside these general assumptions is pointless.

The Framework for Religious Education

The 1988 Act, and all subsequent Government comment on it, affirms that collective worship 'shall be wholly or mainly of a broadly Christian character' (Paragraph 7 (1)), 'without being distinctive of any particular Christian denomination' (Paragraph 7 (2)). A school or a group within a school may, because of the family background of pupils or their ages and aptitudes, be opted out on the application of the head teacher after consultation with the Governors, by the local Standing Advisory Council on Religious Education; but in principle it is required that collective worship be Christian in character.

Furthermore, it is provided (Paragraph 8 (3)) that all revisions of agreed syllabuses for RE 'shall reflect the fact that the religious traditions in Great Britain are in the main Christian while taking account of the teaching and practices of the other principal religions represented in Great Britain.' The Education Bill 1992, consistent with the White Paper 'Choice and Diversity' and the consultation document on RE and collective worship, requires all agreed syllabuses to be revised within one year of the new legislation coming into force. In this way all agreed syllabuses will in the very near future reflect the fact that 'the religious traditions in Great Britain are in the main Christian'.

The identification of the Christian religious tradition as in some way having priority seems wrong to many and to pose the major problem for the development of a morally justifiable curriculum which includes attention to the spiritual and moral. It conflicts with everyday experience, at least in the mind of the average pupil, who finds that to all intents and purposes the Christian religion is regarded as irrelevant and ignored. There are very few citizens who attend church (perhaps 10%), or who draw attention through their everyday lives to the centrality of the Christian faith or Christian moral practice in them. It seems to be at best humbug and at worst downright deceitful. How could a moral education be based upon such an assumption? If a minority want such an education it is suggested that it should provide it through its own Christian religious communities, through its own schools or through its own places of worship in its own time.

But there are three confusions here. First, the fundamental assumption of the total curriculum must be that all dimensions of the development of the child are provided for, including the moral and spiritual. For this to be apparent to all concerned, no dimension of the school is excluded from consideration. There will need to be a personal and effective administrative system and management structure; there will be integration of the National Curriculum and the wider curriculum; and the pedagogy, including methods of assessment, and the justice (perceived) of any punishments that are imposed, will need to be humane and constructive. And religion is central to this totality because it makes possible the teaching of a belief system in which a community has celebrated its understanding of life and asked questions most profoundly about meaning and sense in the light of experience. RE does not answer all the questions any more than does the practice of religion; it provides a vehicle (a linguistic structure and conceptual framework) within and through which these issues may be expressed, discussed and addressed. It provides a context and a medium, therefore, for the discussion of the purposes of education and the success of any education system.

Secondly, we tend to assume without evidence in this post-modern period, that all that is true and worthwhile can be demonstrated to be so via a logical structure which has a close affinity with what are believed to be the clear and unambiguous methods of the sciences or even mathematics. Where this is not the case, it is argued, then we must simply assume that not only is there no answer known to human kind, but in fact no ultimate answer at all. In the light of these perspectives it is wrong to teach only one view, or even one view as if it was the main view. But this is a mistake. It is, on the contrary, all the more important to take into account one main view in order to provide a consistency of teaching and reflection for the understanding of what at the very least must be regarded as questions which are central to our understanding of human nature. It matters which one, of course – not just any one will do; and it matters, moreover, that one is taught consistently throughout society, or it will fail to provide the coherence of language and assumption (*not* necessarily belief) through which issues may be discussed and decisions taken. On this level it is common sense enquiry and empirical evidence, not prejudice, which will lead one to understand that our schools should base their RE and collective worship on the Christian traditions which in our society have been the basis of its politics, law, social conventions, literature, art and, some would say, science and technology, over very many centuries.

One is not, by this, saying that Christianity is the only truth, merely but very positively, that attention to the Christian traditions found in Great Britain is most likely to enlighten the minds and hearts of the average British child to what characterises us as British human beings and facilitates discussion of human questions of values, life and death in our society.

Thirdly, other religious traditions matter; not only should they not be ignored, they should be celebrated. But this is apparently a problem. We seem to find it so difficult to be interested in what is of profound importance to others that we prefer to exclude it rather than to pay attention to it. Yet it ought to be possible to find a curriculum for religious studies and a diet of collective worship which affirms and explores what is central to the Christian religious traditions of Great Britain but which at the same time recognises that there are communities of Jews, Muslims, Sikhs, Hindus, as well as atheists, who both need to know what is involved in being Christian and who have full freedom within the law to practise their faith.

A Curriculum for Religious Education

It is possible, though it would require much work, to create a curriculum which would enable pupils of all ages to be brought to think creatively about matters moral and spiritual: RE will be a necessary and substantial element of this. Matters moral and spiritual are necessarily of concern to the whole curriculum and to every educator; they are not confined to the teacher of RE or those periods on the timetable so named. Indeed, it is important to recognise that in just the same way as RE offers a focus to the whole curriculum looked at from one set of total perspectives, so also other sets of subjects provide foci from other points of view, whether that point of view be, for example, mathematical, historical, biological or literary.

However, a curriculum for RE, if it is to be consistent with the provisions of the ERA, in addition to being both informative and morally sensitive, will therefore provide knowledge of

a   a religious text, in the first instance the Bible, both Old and New Testaments,

b   religious history, which would include the history of religious ideas of different faiths as well as reference to church history,

c   questions on human nature and the possible meaning of human existence.

If it is to do this well it will have to draw on other areas and perspectives of the curriculum, both in content and methodology, in order to contribute to the possible coherence of knowledge and experience which it is intended the whole educational process should enable each child to construct, discover and consider. Such a stretching of the mind, imagination and moral sympathy is appropriately part of the education of every child of whatever ability.

It provides the opportunity for each child to find his or her identity, to choose the work with others in which he or she will contribute to the common good and, in the light of the best knowledge available, to make appropriate choices about the values which will inform the basis of his or her commitments.

This may be a grand perspective, but to intend to offer less, is to betray our human heritage.

Religious Education should be within the National Curriculum

On the basis of the above argument, I submit that RE is too important to be omitted from the National Curriculum. Its centrality is recognised by the 1988 Act when it adds RE alongside the National Curriculum. The point would be much better made by placing RE within the National Curriculum itself. The curriculum for RE would then need to be nationally planned and assessed as appropriate.

Indeed, it would also follow that there should be provided a separate focus for moral education, for however important RE is and however much it may overlap with it, it is not the same as moral education. Furthermore, some of the difficulties of basing RE for the UK on a diet which is 'wholly or mainly of a broadly Christian character' might be eased if the teaching about religion was separated, at any rate as regards its focus, from moral education. After all, moral conclusions may not simply be deduced from theological statements.

If such a separation could be achieved, then RE, alongside science, history, literature and other subjects, would be but one of the contributors to moral education and would not be assumed to be a substitute for it.

For such a development to be successful, it is clear that there would need to be both additional teachers and additional resources, and both society and government must decide upon how great a priority to give to such a need.

September 1993

20 The Classroom of 2015

Professor David Wood
Director, ESRC Centre for Research in Development,
Instruction and Training, Nottingham University

Summary

1 This Briefing speculates about the impact of developments in educational technology on learners, teachers and classrooms by the year 2015. It is not possible to anticipate the technological developments that will have been made by then, but if the technology already available were to be exploited in education the impact on practices of teaching, learning and cultural transmission would be dramatic.

2 Reliance on books, pens and paper could decrease as a consequence of developments in lap-top computing, communications technology and large-scale, remotely accessible, multi-media databases.

3 More individually based learning could be achieved by the exploitation of interactive, computer-based learning. More significant effects could be achieved through changes in the teacher-learner relationship brought about by the impact that information technology would have on teachers' knowledge of how individual children learn.

4 Aspects of curriculum presentation, instruction and automated assessment could be delivered by technology, leaving teachers with more time to provide tutorial support for individuals.

5 The teaching role could be augmented through communications technology as teachers exploit electronic networking to support increased professional collaboration.

6 If such developments take place, schools will change but not disappear. The recognised importance of social interaction as a basis for learning and conceptual development, coupled with an increased reliance on collaborative learning, will underwrite the continuance of group-based educational provision.

7   The traditional boundaries between education and train-
    ing, classrooms and work environments, will become
    less clear cut as schools become integrated into elec-
    tronic 'Wide Area Networks'. Similarly, divisions
    between different sectors of education (primary, sec-
    ondary and tertiary) will become increasingly blurred.

8   Obstacles to any such developments in education will
    not come from scientific or technological constraints.
    Rather, they will arise from political, economic and ideo-
    logical considerations coupled with a paucity of requi-
    site professional knowledge and skills.

A Day in School: 2015 A.D.

What, I wonder, will command the attention and excite comment by those schooled in the classrooms of the 1980s when they enter a classroom in 2015?

The learning environment

One of the first things that might strike them is the lower number of pupils around. Students spend less time in the school than used to be the case; field-work has become a more central part of the educational process. The integration of project-based learning into the curriculum has been achieved with the innovative use of information technology (IT). For example, our visitor learns that four groups of pupils are currently out with teachers on a research project. The local university is testing a model of the relationships between variations in soil acidity and the height of the water-table in different localities. The pupils have been recruited to gather data from designated sites. They are logging data from four areas and these are being transmitted by radio to the 'home team's' computer. The task of the home team is to aggregate data for eventual test against the model. The project is being directed by a team of teachers from the geography, chemistry and mathematics departments.

Books, papers, pens and pencils are, like pupils, less in evidence in classrooms than used to be the case. The lap-top computer has become the pupil's major means of both personal and mass communication. The 2015 lap-top is, of course, faster, more powerful, smaller and lighter, than its twentieth century ancestors. More significantly, it is not limited to the keyboard, mouse-driven or other mechanical communication channels that constrained interactions with earlier devices. Silicon paper, an experimental medium in the 1990s, has largely replaced its organic analogue. Pupils can hand-write directly on to their machines. Limited vocal communication is possible, each lap-top being trained to accept and respond to simple verbal commands from its owner. The waist-mounted satchel used to carry the machine has a number of compartments designed to accommodate a range of data probes. These enable pupils to record directly into their databases measures of phenomena such as temperature, velocity, acceleration, sound frequency, pressure levels, soil acidity and the like.

Lap-tops have not replaced their larger-screened cousins. Work stations are present in all classrooms and workspaces. Pupils regularly connect their personal machines into the school network both to upload their data, notes, completed assignments and written work and to download new assignments, electronic texts, assessments, electronic mail and timetables. Information that used to be carried around in books and on paper is now stored and accessed electronically on lap-tops.

A network of school machines, Local Area Networks (LANs), has been established in most schools giving access to a wide variety of computational tools. Some of these take much of the drudgery and error out of activities such as calculating, graphic data and solving equations. They can also check and, if necessary, correct spelling, grammar and style. Pupils spend less time than previous generations did in factual recall, calculation, and information reproduction, concentrating more on project-based activities such as authoring multi-media publications, building, testing and refining computer-based models and designs.

Ways of learning
Whilst the value of active, constructive approaches to

learning has long been recognised, vociferous debates about the importance of learning more traditional skills had raged over the past two decades. Should pupils be expected to learn how to do standard arithmetic and algebra, know how to manipulate and solve equations in subjects like physics, and be able to do statistical analyses by hand when such skills are executable by machines? Similar arguments had centred around the need to commit facts to memory when these could be retrieved from a database. One school of thought argued that since these activities could be automated, educational time was best spent on learning how to exploit these tools in problem-solving and 'higher level' activities closer to 'real' work. Opposed to this was the argument that intelligent and safe use of such technology was only possible if pupils and students knew how to perform, and hence to evaluate, such activities for themselves.

This debate had settled down as the development of computer-based problem-solving tools had converged with educational technology. Happily, those aspects of human knowledge that were so well-structured that they could be formalised and programmed (like solving equations etc.) were also those abilities which were amenable to computer-based instruction. Intelligent tutoring systems had been developed which were more efficient in teaching children how to solve such problems than conventional classroom teaching or unassisted learning. These systems were designed to teach problem-solving procedures (in mathematics, for example) and their applications (to engineering problems, for instance) at one and the same time.

The way in which such computer systems respond to the user is contingent upon that user's knowledge and skill. Thus, when pupils are first introduced to a computer agent, their performance is monitored and evaluated by an 'embedded' tutoring system which, if necessary, is able to teach the procedures which the computer agent is able to perform. As pupils master these procedures, tutorial interventions fade and the learner is left free to pursue wider objectives. Using such technology, all pupils can participate in similar project work, but the amount and type of help they receive from the system varies according to aptitude.

Tutoring systems
Another debate which had punctuated the history of developments in educational technology centred on the role of tutoring systems in teaching. Beginning in the 1960s, with Skinner's invention of teaching machines, some had claimed that these systems (and their more versatile offspring) would become central to teaching and learning. Others had later argued that such systems were educationally limited and even counter-productive[1]. It was argued that they encouraged mere reproduction of empty procedures without developing understanding. Instead of systems programming pupils to learn, they argued, we should develop systems which help children to discover how to learn by programming systems! This school of thought encouraged the creation of programming languages such as BASIC and LOGO and underwrote the development of computer-based learning environments and simulations designed to promote learning through discovery and the self-construction of knowledge.

Neither view prevailed, though neither was entirely defeated. The skills involved in procedural learning and in learning certain strategic skills, such as those involved in conducting experiments or in designing extensive written texts, could be learned through tutoring systems. However, a whole range of skills could not be developed efficiently by such means. For example, learning how to collaborate, communicate and to work as part of a team required inter-personal contact and experience in group work. Learning in groups had also proved to be an effective means of helping learners to reconceptualise or to adopt new perspectives on a problem or issue. Where tutoring systems were good at helping to teach procedural skills, peer collaboration proved effective in fostering conceptualisation and evaluation.

For example, research in the 1990s had demonstrated that children's understanding of the physical world could be developed by encouraging them to work in small groups if members of the group brought the right 'mix' of ideas and predictions to collaborative problem-solving situations[2]. Imagine a situation in which none of a group of children understands the forces that govern motion under gravity. One child might believe that air resistance is important but is not aware of the importance of gravitational force. Another might ignore air resistance but realise that gravity must enter into any explanation. Provided that the children find themselves making different predictions about what will happen in a relevant problem situation, there is a good chance that they will each elaborate their own 'model' of the situation to take account of more of the relevant factors. Collaboration can promote conceptual change and stimulate new discoveries.

Advocates of the early generations of computer-based learning environments appeared to think that simply getting children to explore and experiment with them would ensure learning. However, it soon became apparent that without expert help, either from a teacher or more knowledgeable peer, achievement was limited. Thus, fears that new technology might displace teachers had proved unfounded. What technology had done was to change or augment the teacher's role and, as a consequence, it had modified the teacher-learner relationship. Crudely, teachers found themselves spending less time imparting information and testing its reception and more on providing frameworks for project work and on attending to aspects of an individual pupil's learning processes[3].

Keeping track of progress

The arrival of LANs into schools made possible the construction of shared databases in which information about children's achievements, and instances of their work in different subjects, was stored. In small ways at first, this common resource led to more interactions between teachers. Thus, a child's written work in science, say, could be retrieved from the database for work in English. Different genres of writing could be discussed in relation to the child's own work in various subject areas. Information about the child's achievements in mathematics could be exploited in physics lessons; the relations between what the pupil learned in one subject and its use, extension or application in another could be exploited.

Since children's achievements could be monitored automatically as they performed computer-based work, the need to set aside specific times for tests, assessments and examinations declined. Thus, some of the drudgery associated with assessment passed from teacher to machine. Furthermore, the system could provide the teacher with information not only about learning outcomes but also about the learning process by identifying, for example, areas of the curriculum in which a child learned with relatively little tutorial help and others in which they experienced difficulty or in which they outstripped the capacity of the tutoring system to help them. This increased 'visibility' of the learning process provided teachers with new sources of insights into their pupils' learning styles and preferences, enabling them to focus their help and to give support for individualised work[3]. Because many of the 'core' measures of performance could be gathered, analysed and disseminated automatically, teachers and pupils were left with more time to develop individual and group 'portfolios', enabling them to augment core assessments with individual achievement indicators that they could select and create for themselves.

Electronic records of pupil achievement could also be exploited by other computer facilities designed to support teachers. For example, the computer could be programmed to examine pupil assessments to identify groupings which would ensure an appropriate 'mix' of children for collaborative learning. The system could also identify problems which might lead the group to make conflicting predictions and, hence, to motivate conceptual development.

Developing the curriculum
The teachers also had available a much greater range of authoring tools to help them to plan, deliver and assess aspects of the curriculum. Such authoring tools had, of course, been available well before 2015. However, they had become far more friendly, flexible and usable over years of development. Computer-linked multi-media environments also enabled the teacher to make dynamic use of video, audio and textual information to support learning. Thanks to electronic networks, they could access such aids from libraries, museums, industrial training contexts and other resource centres.

Each teacher was left free to decide how to sequence and integrate such information sources and to dictate how and when decisions might be made to allocate children's time between browsing through information, tackling assignments and testing their understanding. Given that computing power has ceased to be a problem, teachers are also able to make use of computationally expensive tools to help them assess the effectiveness of their own curricula. For example, any uncertainty the teacher might have about the most effective way of sequencing material and learning activities could be explored by using machine learning facilities. These could be programmed to try out different sequences and monitor their effects on rates of pupil progress, any unforeseen difficulties they encountered and so forth. The same facility could be used to monitor any effects of differences in pupils' learning styles on preferred learning sequences.

Suppose, for instance, that a teacher suspects that some children would prefer a long period spent browsing or exploring a learning domain before trying to learn how to solve specific problems. Others might prefer to adopt a more 'bottom up' strategy; learning specific solutions before trying to investigate the broader context. This hypothesis could be subjected to test by programming the system to examine interactions between different task sequences and pupil learning style. Since such experimental pedagogy requires evaluations involving relatively large numbers of learners, teachers had begun to use Wide Area Networks (WANs) to contact and recruit colleagues from other schools who were interested in joining in such experimental investigations. Such networks, which enable teachers to share information, curricular materials and ideas, had helped to create special interest groups concerned with a vast range of professional issues.

Fact v Fiction?

The technology There is no science fiction in the imaginary visit just outlined. The technology referred to either exists or represents a modest extrapolation from systems under development:

- Silicon paper, voice-operated machines and data probes are here.
- Intelligent tutoring systems for teaching aspects of mathematics[4], economics[5] and computer programming[6] have been constructed, tested and shown to compare well with conventional teaching.
- Computer-based micro-worlds, which enable children to test and to change the laws of physics, have been used in classrooms[7].
- LANs and WANs to support local, national and interna-

tional electronic communication have been extensively used for years, and new 'wide bandwidth' signal technology (which supports, for instance, real-time video-communication) is being installed in many parts of the world.

- Several machine-learning systems exist and some have already passed from experimental to practical implementations.
- Computers are becoming ever faster, and memory cheaper; it is quite realistic to suppose that the computational power needed for the kinds of applications envisaged will be with us well before 2015.

In speculating about applications I have also been careful to use examples derived from real educational projects. So, the illustrated use of lap-tops for field-work, for example, comes from a recent study in the USA[8]. Indeed, the systems and their potential uses that I have envisaged are, if anything, based on conservative speculation.

Obstacles to change The fiction in the narrative stems from its lack of attention to social and political concerns. Will we find the political will needed to encourage change? Will the considerable economic resources needed be made available? Is it realistic to expect to receive the degree of acceptance and the level of enthusiasm needed on the part of parents and educationalists to support change? How will we ensure that the knowledge and skills we would need in schools to make use of the technology is available? Will our educational institutions permit the dramatic organisational changes that will be required to achieve any such vision?

If the recent past can be taken as a reliable guide to the near future, then one can have little confidence that (even if considered desirable) the kinds of developments in education that have been described will come about. There are several grounds for this pessimism.

Despite the fact that the ratio of computers to pupils in schools has improved dramatically in recent years (e.g. from a ratio of one micro-computer to 60 secondary school pupils in 1984 to one to 13 pupils in 1991[9]), surveys of their use in school, coupled with observational studies, indicate that they have had relatively little overall impact on educational practice. For example, whilst the reported use of computers to support learning in computer studies and business studies is relatively high in UK secondary schools, their use in teaching science subjects is minimal[9]. This, in turn, probably reflects another problem: limitations in the extent and quality of software available. The software most widely used in education is in the form of 'hand-me-down' packages from industrial and commercial applications (e.g. word processing, spreadsheets and databases).

There is no problem with this in principle since, at the very least, pupils need experience in using the kinds of software packages they are likely to encounter when they begin work (though rates of technological change raise serious questions about the future relevance of such experiences). Furthermore, some innovative educational uses have been made with such software. These have been shown to confer some benefits on learning over and above the acquisition of specific skills in using the actual packages themselves[10].

But such software is limited in its educational potential. What we urgently need are well-designed, friendly and flexible software tools to support learning across the curriculum. Usability (or a lack thereof) is widely acknowledged as a major obstacle to the effective exploitation of IT in general. The development of IT tools without a proper concern for 'human factors' is still a major obstacle to technological exploitation. But usability is not simply an issue of system design.

Failure to make innovative and flexible use of technology also depends on the attitudes, skills and knowledge of the intended user population. What evidence we have suggests that many teachers lack both the motivation and skills to make use of even the technology currently available. For example, a recent study of new teachers' knowledge of basic facilities such as spreadsheets suggests that less than 2 in 10 express confidence in their use[11].

The ongoing revolution in communications technology is beginning to make some impact on education, but there are no statistics on the incidence of facilities like LAN and WAN technology, satellite communications or even CD ROM use in schools in the UK. Recent data from the USA indicate that about one-third of all school districts now use satellite dishes and 14% of schools are tied into local and national networks (estimated to involve around three-quarters of a million pupils). The use of CD ROM applications and video discs is also found in around 13–14% of schools[12].

The indications are, then, that the move away from using computers mainly to support single-user applications towards using communications technology for more group-based work is already underway across the Atlantic. Less affluent countries such as Chile, Costa Rica and Cuba have also mounted projects of varying magnitude to explore the use of networking and associated technology in education[13].

Ways Forward?

There are clear signs, then, that the next phase of the IT 'revolution' is already gathering momentum. But will the introduction of yet more technology provoke any more of a 'revolution' in education than was achieved with the introduction of computers?

In terms of time likely to be needed to bring about major changes in a well-established set of cultural practices (i.e. education), 20 years or so is not long. The next generation of teachers to be teaching in 2015 are now, or soon will be, at school. Assuming that most Heads of schools achieve their positions at around age 45, most of those who will manage the schools of 2015 are already teaching. All the evidence suggests that current usage of IT in schools is unlikely to be pervasive or profound enough to develop, within a generation, teachers with markedly different attitudes towards, or knowledge of, new technology (I doubt that experience with computer games will be enough to promote the necessary skills). So, even if education moves towards greater reliance on new technology, the knowledge and skills required to make effective use of it are likely to be thin on the ground.

The speculations offered in this Briefing are presented neither as predictions about what is likely to happen between now and 2015 nor as objectives to be pursued. They are designed to stimulate debate. Education is still, to a large extent, attempting to teach knowledge and skills for jobs that either no longer exist or will not exist for much longer. IT is already a fact of most people's working lives and the information revolution in the workplace is unlikely to slow down. What knowledge and skills will be needed for the work of tomorrow? How much of the current national curriculum is likely to be relevant to the next generation's needs? How do we start to close the gap in knowledge and skill needed to make effective use of technology in education? How might teachers be involved in the design and development of new technology for use in the classroom?

In my view, the best way forward is through local innovation. I do not believe that anyone is in a position to predict or shape the future of education. What we need are illustrations and examples of what schools can do with and through technology. People with knowledge of new technology and its applications need to get into their local schools to see what they might have to offer. Educationalists should seek such people out and recruit their help. Employers in 'high tech' businesses need to ask what they might have to offer to their local schools by way of advice, equipment, software and expert help. Initiatives along these lines ae already being publicised in the USA[14] and the 'real life' projects involved provide glimpses of some of the future uses that we might want to make of technology in education.

October 1993

References

[1] Papert, S. (1981) *Mindstorms: children, computers and powerful ideas.* Brighton, Harvester Press.

[2] Howe, C., Tolmie, A. & MacKenzie, M. (in press) *Computer support for the collaborative learning of physics concepts.* In C.E. O'Malley (Ed), Computer supported collaborative learning. Heidelberg, Springer-Verlag.

[3] Schofield, J. (1989) *Computers and classroom social processes.* In the *Conference on Intelligent Computer-Assisted Instruction.* Orlando, Florida.

[4] Anderson, J.R. (1992) *Intelligent tutoring and high school mathematics.* In C. Frasson, G. Gauthier, & G.I. McCalla (Eds) *Intelligent tutoring systems: Second international conference.* Berlin: Springer-Verlag.

[5] Shute, V.J. & Glaser, R. (1990) *A large-scale evaluation of an intelligent discovery world.* Smithtown. Interactive Learning Environments, 1, 51–77.

[6] Anderson, J. (1987) *Production systems, learning and tutoring.* In D. Klahr, P. Langley & R. Neches (Eds) Production system models of learning and development, Cambridge, Mass., MIT Press.

[7] O'Malley, C. (1992) *Designing computer systems to support peer learning.* European Journal of Psychology of Education, Vol VII, No 4, 339–352.

[8] Grant, W.C. (1993) *Wireless coyote: A computer-supported field trip.* Communications of the ACM, Vol 36, No 5, 57–59.

[9] Department for Education (1993) *Survey of Information Technology in schools.* Statistical Bulletin, 6/93.

[10] Underwood, J. (1986) *The role of the computer in developing children's classificatory abilities.* Computers in Education, 10, 175–180.

11 Bennett, N. & Carre, C. (1993) *Learning to Teach.* London, Routledge.

12 Newstrack (1993) Communications of the ACM. Vol 36, No 5, 11.

13 Press, L. (1993) *Technetronic Education: Answers on the cultural horizon.* Communications of the ACM, Vol 36, No 5, 17–22.

14 Soloway, E. (Ed) (1993) *Technology in Education.* Communications of the ACM, Special Issue, May 1993.